P9-DHK-429

BLESSINGS
IN
DISGUISE

HOW DREAMS COME TRUE

BY
CAROLYN M. BALL, M.A.

CELESTIAL ARTS
Berkeley, California

Copyright © 1996 by Carolyn M. Ball. All rights reserved.
No part of this book may be reproduced in any form, except for
brief review, without the express permission of the publisher.
For further information, you may write to:

Celestial Arts Publishing
P.O. Box 7123
Berkeley, California 94707

Cover and interior design: Shelley Firth

Printed in the United States

Library of Congress Cataloging-in-Publication Data
Ball, Carolyn M.
    Blessings in Disguise / Carolyn M. Ball.
        p. cm.
    ISBN 0-89087-799-8
    1. Ball, Carolyn M. 2. Spiritual biography—United States.
    3. Problem solving. 4. Insight. 5. Vision Quests.
    6. Spiritual life. I. Title.
    BL73.B36A3   1996
    291.4'092—dc20   96-13874
                                                                CIP

First Printing, 1996

1 2 3 4 / 99 98 97 96

TABLE OF CONTENTS

ACKNOWLEDGMENTS

I am very grateful to those who have been a part of the creation of this book—those who have walked through the pages of my life with me, and those who have been a part of the editing process of this book. In particular, I want to thank Mary Thunder, my parents William and Dorothy Matthias, Jeffery White Horse Hubbell, Christine Collins, Wade Batterton, Kim McSherry, Augusta Ogden, Caroll Weaver, Bill Walz, Martin Rastall, Sandy Collins, Patti Terranella, Marilyn Sylvester, David Corrado, Jonathan Goure, Lisa Timpson, Michael Herring, Bill Penczak, Norm Stewart, Rick Essman, Barbara Morales, Diana Goure, Janie Westmoreland, Birdsong, and Suzanne Day for their excellent feedback on this book, as well as David Hinds, Leana Alba, and Kathryn Bear of Celestial Arts for their enthusiasm, feedback, and encouragement along the way.

Special thanks to Chuck Peters for creating the stained glass art on the cover. I would also like to thank others who participated in different ways—the Elders and teachers in my life, all of my Sun Dance sisters and brothers, Peggy and Lou Millin, Christine Collins, Shellie Newell, Martin Rastall, Butch Hennigan, Sparky Shooting Star, Bill Perry, Barry Oser, Neil Rand, Jimmy Schulman, Alfredo Czerwinski, Tony Coburn, and Marisabel Olivares.

I have shared this book with my Elders of the Native American path in order to receive their permission to publish my experiences of some of the learnings and sacred ceremonies, and to assure that I would in no way hurt, misrepresent, or inappropriately refer to a ceremony or tradition. My intention is not to represent myself as particularly knowledgeable about these ways, but only to share with gratitude how they have been a part of my growth.

▲

The names of most of the people in this book have been changed to respect their privacy and to honor the fact that they may see things in a different way than I do. Because I wish to acknowledge and honor their work, I have not changed the names of Mary Thunder, her family, the Elders I have met in my years with her, or my friends who have shared with me in the Sacred Sun Dance.

DEDICATION

This book is dedicated to

The Great Mystery,
The Thread That Weaves Together All Existence,
That Which Has Infinite Names And Forms,
known as Creator, Spirit, Yahweh, Allah, Brahma, the Tao,
the Source, the Force, and God as we understand God to be...

to

Mary Elizabeth Thunder,
whose name means "Truth"—my teacher, my friend, my sister,
Peace Elder, Sundancer, Mother of the Sun Dance, author of
Thunder's Grace, and "Iyeska" or Spirit Interpreter...

and to

William Park Matthias, my father,
who taught me the value of honesty and who showed me
how to stand in my truth with courage.

PREFACE

Our deepest fear is not that we are inadequate.
Our deepest fear is that we are powerful beyond measure.
It is our light, not our darkness that most frightens us.
We ask ourselves, who am I to be
brilliant, gorgeous, talented, and fabulous?
Actually, who are you not to be?
You are a child of God.
Your playing small doesn't serve the world.
There's nothing enlightened about shrinking so that other people
won't feel insecure around you.
We were born to make manifest the glory of God that is within us.
It's not just in some of us; it's in everyone.
And as we let our own light shine, we unconsciously
give others permission to do the same.
As we are liberated from our own fear,
our presence automatically liberates others.

—Nelson Mandela
Inaugural Speech, 1994

Humankind is undergoing a radical shift in consciousness at this time. Never before in human history has so much been changing so rapidly. What lies before us is a long-dreamed-of, long-hoped-for era, a time of peace, of acceptance, of radiance. It is a time which many of us have touched and tasted—in dreams, in moments of meditation and reverie, in unsuspecting relaxations of control—when the mind soars to discover new realms. Since the mid-sixties, a concentrated worldwide search has been on for a way to create a permanent change in consciousness that would reflect and draw us into these new times.

Experimenting with drugs didn't do it, nor did returning to the land. Making a bundle wasn't the answer; neither was focusing on the "me" generation or getting divorced a few times. Even meditation and psychology did not resolve the search. All of these have had a role in leading us toward this shift, but what is the missing piece?

We are moving towards a new way of thinking, relating, and living that, until now, has existed only in our dreams. What is evolving is our actual world view—our paradigms for existence—our basic beliefs about what makes our lives and our world function.

This transformation is very exciting. It is also inherently extremely stressful. You might say that we are in the middle of an Armageddon—that aspect of change that involves breaking down the old in order to make way for the new. However, the destruction of the old, in this case, is occurring less in our physical world than we might have imagined. It is taking place, rather, primarily in our hearts and minds. Life has a way of continuously increasing the magnitude of the messages we are offered regarding the areas in which we need to grow and change, and these challenges are only reflected externally when we do not face them internally.

This "armageddon process," as I have come to think of it, is not a negative process, but rather a much needed cleansing of the antiquated structures and imbedded patterns that we all carry. It ultimately leads us to the higher awareness to which we all consciously or unconsciously aspire. This process is like the death of winter which leads to the rebirth that is spring. It is the seemingly repulsive manure that gives sustenance to new life. To the Hindus, it is the Dance of Shiva; to the Chinese, it is the fire of purification from which arises the Phoenix in each of us.

When I embarked upon the vessel that this book has become, I had no idea what would unfold. Unaware of its ultimate purpose, I was still in the midst of my own transformation process that was slowly being revealed to me. I'd had many spiritual experiences, but at the time I did not comprehend the nature of their impact on my day-to-day life. My original intention in writing was simply to give acknowledgement to those gifts of Spirit which I had received. I had no idea the magnitude of the message that would evolve in the writing. It is only as I have sat at my computer, open and willing, that Spirit has woven from the fabric of my past experiences a clear picture of where we are going on this planet. And it is only in retrospect, as I have read and reread this manuscript, editing according to inspiration of the moment, that I have become aware that the finished book actually contains a map to the next step in humankind's evolution. Each time I reworked the manuscript, I was forced to face the issues it presented and, each time, my understanding of its concepts deepened. This book has truly been written by Spirit in that the information and the blessings I have received from it, and that I now pass on to you, were so completely disguised that, even though I was the author, I did not comprehend their significance until the manuscript reached completion.

What has been revealed is a pathway through the "armageddon process." We tend to think of destruction as a negative or unpleasant experience, something to be feared and avoided. *Yet, perhaps if we perceive it differently, it is the Blessing in Disguise!* The armageddon experience might be the very process that hones our skills so that we can live by the more refined awarenesses of the spiritual or higher realms. Difficult times are often the purifying fires that force us to reevaluate current perspectives and release those very beliefs which limit us in this physical realm. The challenges actually help us to stretch into the evolution that is our destiny. Thus, they become the blessings in disguise which often lead us to the fulfillment of our greatest dreams and aspirations!

Long ago, I, like many of us, had a dream, a deep longing for a planet where there would be peace on earth and good will among men and women. This dream remained unformed as a small, painful, yearning knot in my heart that would not go away as I wandered through my sometimes chaotic, sometimes rigidly controlled, 1990s American world.

Then one day I received a vision for the first time of how that next level of consciousness actually functions. It was suddenly made apparent, in practical detail, exactly what shifts in perception and belief structure were going to be unfolding on the part of humankind in order to step into that next level—that of peace and harmony on earth.

The principles by which humans live, at this next level of evolution, are very simple: Completely conscious of how we powerfully create our own reality with our thoughts, we take full responsibility for that creation. We also exist with a greater awareness of the interactive process between our lives and that of a world we cannot see or fathom—the world of Spirit. This new consciousness also involves a balance of the yang and yin, or masculine and feminine aspects of creation and receptivity. By discovering and creating this balance in a responsible manner, it follows automatically that we enjoy relationships with others which are empowering and respectful; peace and happiness are the inevitable results.

It looked so simple in the vision!

But the gift of a vision is followed by the work that must be done in order to bring it to fruition. Evolution such as this is much like the birthing of a baby: There is labor involved. This book is about the labor towards our next level of evolution.

This work involves becoming the embodiment and the model of our own dreams. It involves the personal work of cutting away the old that keeps us from our dreams, and having the courage to walk forward into the unknown wherein lies fulfillment. As such, this book is also about how to face the fire and burst forth from the flames, to soar high in flight towards the dreams that lie waiting to be birthed within each of our hearts. It is about how to recognize a disguised blessing without judgement by surrendering to the principle that what God has given us is what we will handle right now. In this way, we unveil the blessings, and put them to immediate use rather than struggle against them when they appear to be burdens or obstacles. This book is also about self-empowerment, about our true connection to our Source within. It is about applying our own personal growth as a metaphor and as a tool for global transformation.

We can no longer afford to resist this inevitable change. *The price of denial at this point is too high. As a species, we no longer have the luxury of digging our heels in when it comes to our own evolution. Our planet is in too delicate a balance.* The issues that face us in our world are such that existing, commonly held beliefs and concepts for organizing our world do not hold the solutions! We cannot solve the ecological, economic, and social problems that face us today in the ways that we once did. There isn't the time and there isn't the technology. The existing systems are too antiquated and inflexible to offer support for the social, economic, and ecological shifts that are necessary.

If we care about the lives of our children and our grand-children, it is time to recognize how our thoughts and actions today create our tomorrows. It is also time to live the reality of our Spiritual Connectedness to all life on our planet and beyond. We must actively participate in our own growth and transformation, rather than allow it to happen in the haphazard way that human evolution normally occurs. It is time that we consciously embrace the changes that must occur for the human race to move on to its next level. We each have the power to make this choice.

In writing this book, I have been extremely candid about

my own process—about the thoughts, the mindtalk, the emotions, the habits, and the experiences that shredded the core of my old belief structures and forced me into a greater personal and world view. A friend who proofread this manuscript suggested, "You've exposed yourself so much. Why don't you write this in the third person and allow yourself to step back and be the wise sage." But, you see, I'm not a wise sage, and that's one of the main points of this book. We are nothing more and nothing less than who we are. If I claim the sage within me, I must also claim my fool. We are all both divine and human. What freedom exists for us when we fully realize and live by this simple truth!

If I cannot take the responsibility for my creation before you, the reader, then how could I ask you to do the same? If I cannot bare myself to you, give up my secrets, and stand fully exposed before you, then how can I sit here and tell you to be open with your friends, your family, your fellow workers, the people who have been difficult for you—and with yourself! In some places in the book I have been embarrassingly honest about what I've walked through. But soon we will no longer feel embarrassment, because honesty, openness and vulnerability are the qualities of the coming times. They are the keys to love, communication, intimacy, health, community, and ultimately, a planet that operates optimally.

Today I experience on a daily basis, sometimes even hourly, what we call "miracles." I used to think that only very special people, like Jesus or other extremely graced individuals, could bring about sudden changes in the physical state of things by the power of their word. But Christ said that we, too, would do all these things and more. I am beginning to understand what He meant.

I have been trained in many psychological and spiritual paths, but the person who has taught me the most about how we are shifting into the coming consciousness is Mary Thunder. She is a Peace Elder, a Sun Dancer, and an *Iyeshka*, or "Spirit Interpreter." Her wisdom and teachings are the twine that ties these pages together. The catalyst for most of the events in this book, Thunder has taught me about our current evolution in three ways: First, she lives the truth of who she is to the fullest, her strengths and her weaknesses exposed with no apologies; second, she is unwavering in her faith in the workings of Spirit; third, she tells stories that touch the heart, move the mind, and tickle the funnybone—you might forget psychology and philosophy, but you won't ever forget a good story. Her Native American way of teaching is to bypass the conscious, logical mind, and to address the heart directly through experience, example, and stories.

It was Thunder who got me to write. She kept after me for my written versions of the different experiences we shared. In time I came to see what she probably always knew: As I wrote about the phenomenal events that took place around her and at her instigation, they would come to life, they would take on meaning, they would process through my system and become teachings—not only for me, but for the others with whom I shared these stories. They moved from being "interesting" experiences relegated to the back of my consciousness to becoming amazing, transformative events. She has always been a catalyst in this way for the people who know her—like an artist pushing the clay a little in this direction, molding it with a finger here, a finger there, transforming what might be a meaningless mass into a work of art, and life fulfilled.

This is the story of my journey. It is all true—both the struggles and the miracles. I have written it as an allegory for your journey, in hopes that it will inspire you along your own path to the next level of our evolution. May it also offer you support as you walk through your limitations to the fulfillment of your dreams and expand your connection to both the Spirit within and the greater direction of humankind.

▲ ▲ ▲ ▲

DREAMS AND VISIONS

WE ALL HAVE THE SEEDS
OF MAGNIFICENCE

Each and every one of us holds the seeds of magnificence. Every person has an incredible gift to contribute to this planet. For these seeds to sprout, to grow, to bloom—for these gifts to be manifest—they need to be recognized and nurtured.

Each person has a natural bent, a natural gift, something that stirs within which needs to be focused upon and acknowledged. These seeds of magnificence are a kind of blueprint of our purpose in life, of our greatest potential. Our gift may be great, or it may be modest, but that matters not. For some, it may be singing, or teaching, or making something beautiful. For others it might be helping someone to smile, or getting the columns to add up every time, or making really good doughnuts. What is important is that it is our own unique expression.

This blueprint, which exists within us since birth, is the path to our inner and outer fulfillment. This gift is usually not hidden, yet often it is ignored. Society, family, our experiences in life, *but especially our own minds*, often permit us to put our greatest talent—and love—aside. However, we all have the ability to bring out this unique expression of ourselves, to enjoy it, and allow others to enjoy it as well.

If we don't keep these seeds of magnificence alive from childhood, then Life—the Spirit within—will gradually lead us back to them. We will run into lessons, tests, and events that appear at first to block us from where we think we want to go. But if we consciously undertake the challenges these events offer, if we seek out the gift or blessing in these annoying or painful experiences, *we will always find that they are leading us back to the Source—our original purpose, the original blueprint of our own greatest self.*

Each of us is the hero in our own story. In most mythology and in most fiction, the hero is nothing more and nothing less than the archetype of ourselves as we journey through perils and trials to get to the golden fleece, the promised land, the holy grail. The hero within us never ceases to aspire towards our own greatest potential. This true self never stops trying to make life better, never gives up the vision of our own completeness and fulfillment.

Thus, within each of us, there is an innate wisdom that inevitably carries us through our growth to realign us with the seeds of our magnificence. If we are paying attention, we discover that when we keep our dreams in our hearts, even errors and apparent set-backs will ultimately lead us to the dream. In every hero's story, there is always what appears at first to be failure, the temptation to give up, the seemingly hopeless blocks and impediments to the goal. Yet those obstacles are the very catalysts that bring out the hero in every man and woman.

To fully manifest the seeds of magnificence buried or bursting forth from within us, we must take the courage to be in touch with our dreams, and to undertake the hero's journey through the jungles of our own hearts and minds. We must cut away the thick undergrowth of mental and emotional beliefs in our limitations, and open a path to the fulfillment of those dreams. To move on to the next level of evolution, we must be willing not only to dream our dreams, but to stand by them, and to realize them. *If dreams were easy to fulfill, they wouldn't be dreams!* It would not take effort to make them real, to bring them from the other-dimensional realm of our psyche into physical manifestation. We must create clear pictures of our dreams—in our art, in our writing, in our conversations— and allow ourselves to keep those images of our dreams at the

forefront of our minds. As we SEE them, OWN them, NUR-
TURE them, SPEAK them, SHARE them, BUILD them, they
will come to pass.

The seeds of the dreams that lie buried within us—the very
blueprint for our purpose in life—are held in our Higher Self,
waiting for us to attend to them. They are our personal connection to our own evolution. As each of us brings forth our
own dreams and manifests our personal visions, we enter col-
lectively into a new way of living in our world. One at a time,
each hero's journey ultimately leads us together as a species
into the kingdom of light that is both the foundation and the
result of every individual's dream.

▲ ▲ ▲ ▲

It was about ten years ago, and my own dream was just
beginning to surface into my conscious mind. It was a restless
time, and I was chafing at the bit. Things weren't going badly;
they were actually fine. But there was a void. I felt that the
major part of each day was without any measurable contribution to my world. I wanted to help people to be happier with
themselves and each other; I wanted to help the process of healing on this planet.

The problem was that I didn't know how. I wasn't trained,
and I had no confidence in myself or in what I might have to
offer. I felt that in some ways my dream was big, but I had no
concept of how I could possibly get to it with my current abilities and perceptions of myself. And besides, the dream was so
fuzzy, I wasn't even sure of what it was. I just knew it pulled
strongly on my heart, and seemed to keep calling me, calling
me...

*I would refer to it as "The New Place"— a persistent inner vision
or imagination of a community of people, living and working together
with excitement, joy, caring for each other, and a deep commitment to
the creation of healing on this planet. I saw woods, trees, mountains,*

fresh running streams, clean sweet air, and people interfacing with each other and the earth in a conscious, respectful way. I saw love — love between the people, love for the land, and love for Spiritual Binding Essence—so much love that it created a huge column of light between the heavens and the earth.

The column was like a doorway, or opening, between this third dimension and the realm of the angels, archangels, and all those unseen workers for the Light who exist beyond our physical reality. Because of the intention and love of the people in this community, they were able to draw through this column, this doorway, an infinite abundance of light. Using meditation, these loving earth people were able to ground, or transform, this light into usable energy which helped to uplift and heal all the people of this planet and the Earth itself.

18

It was early in the summer of 1984, and the dream had been tapping relentlessly at the recesses of my consciousness. I was sitting with my friend, Tom, and telling him about this idea, this dream of The New Place, and how very distant it seemed from my reality at that moment. He pondered my words for a bit, then suddenly leapt up, grabbed a pencil, and ripped a sheet off a pad of paper. "Here," he said, handing them both to me. He settled in next to me as if we were about to embark on something that would take a long, long time.

"What are we going to do?" I asked. I always want to know what I'm getting myself into, with all the details delineated.

"We're going to do something with symbols," he began. "Just go with the process. Don't try to think it out ahead, but let it just unfold from inside as I take you through the steps. Put your logic aside and let your intuition work. Now, draw ten boxes about the same size, at least an inch or two square."

I made a row of five squares on the top row, five on the bottom, cognizant that the whole time my mind was making up one scenario after another of what we might do with these boxes. *Put the conscious mind aside,* I reminded myself.

Tom continued, "The *first* box represents where you are today. Draw a symbol that represents your life at this time—how you see yourself at this point in your journey."

"You mean like a stick figure? You mean, a picture of where I work at my job? Do you mean how I feel?" He wouldn't answer. I had no recourse but to allow my intuition to kick in. I drew a stick figure bent over, laboring to walk up a flight of stairs. It felt as if life were an uphill climb, with no clear ideas as to what might lie at the top of the stairs.

"How's that?" I asked, aware that I wanted his approval.

No answer.

"Now, write today's date under the box," he finally said.

I printed carefully: *June 10, 1984.*

"The *tenth* box is your goal, or dream, or vision. Draw a symbol for that."

I wanted to ask him to elaborate a little more, but I knew it was futile. Again, I had to turn to my own inner resources. I emptied my mind for a moment, then found myself drawing three concentric circles, which represented my dream of The New Place. I turned to Tom, a big smile on my face. "OK!" I was starting to get excited. The process was working. Then he asked me to tell him about the circles. As I spoke, it felt as if I were peering through time into a bright but gentle landscape.

The three concentric circles represent both a building and a concept. As a building, the innermost circle is the central core, the holy of holies, the altar, the place where the elders and dedicated ones of the community gather to pray and to call in the Light. As a concept, it is the Source, the spiritual focus of the community, the doorway between the third dimension and beyond.

The middle circle is like the amphitheater, the place where all the people gather around the altar, the seating for those who have come to learn and to add their energies to the purpose. It also symbolizes the community and the commitment of the people, those who practice and strive in their daily lives to live in the world, but

19

also to bring the essence of heaven—truth, harmony, and love—into manifestation on the Earth.

The outer circle of the building contains many healing rooms where various disciplines are practiced in aiding individuals and groups to achieve balance and alignment on the mental, emotional, physical, and spiritual levels. There is the acknowledgement of the Spiritual as the Source, and all healing is practiced within that context. On a symbolic level, the outer circle represents the communities/land/state/nation/world surrounding and served by the two inner circles.

When I finished speaking, it was as if I'd been in a dream. It took me a moment to come back. I could tell that Tom had somehow been there too. He took a deep breath.

"Great! Now put the date below the tenth box," he instructed.

I thought for a moment, forgetting the intuitive and guessing a logical amount of time it might take to create the vision. '1987,' I wrote.

"Are you sure?" he asked patiently. Somehow Tom had picked up that I had shifted mental gears again. I nodded, wanting it to be so. "Now, stay with the intuitive. What is your role in this place?"

This time I remembered to empty my mind, and the first word I heard was "director," but it wasn't quite right. Even though I saw myself as responsible for the facility, I functioned more as a spiritual mentor and facilitator of communications. I saw myself near the entrance of the outer circle, acting as coordinator, as a greeter to new people, and as a counselor in one of the healing rooms. As such, I worked at all levels of the three circles. Then, another piece of the dream came to me:

The New Place was actually created by the cooperative efforts of myself and many people with the same vision, each of whom had pieces of the puzzle to make it all come together.

My thoughts were pulled back to the squares before me as Tom continued, "Now, go back to the second box and draw a symbol for the very next thing you need to do after today in order to get to your goal."

Instantly my mind started swimming with all the things I'd have to do to get to The New Place. First, I'd have to be a really different person than I now was—more confident, more relaxed, and definitely wiser. I'd have to find the land, and buy the land, and build a meeting place. And I had no idea who the people were who might share in this community. In an instant I was overwhelmed.

Oh, yes, I reminded myself, quiet the mind and allow the intuition to work. In a moment, I saw myself employed full-time by the training and counseling organization where I presently did volunteer work. In the second box, I drew an office door with my name plate just outside the office to represent getting the job.

"OK, now in the third box, draw a symbol for the next step," Tom directed.

I emptied my mind and immediately saw myself in graduate school, earning the degree which would allow me to become more involved in the world of transformation. I drew a little stick figure at a desk.

We continued, step by step, never thinking of the whole picture, but rather allowing the next box, and then the next, to be filled one at a time, always staying present in the moment. Finishing graduate school, getting work as a therapist, teaching workshops, opening a center for teaching, locating the New Place, moving to the New Place...step after step fell into place. When I got to box number nine, it seemed to take a long, long time for the picture to come. I sat for about ten minutes, fidgeting, sighing, and trying to get another picture.

"I can't get anything!" I fussed. It seemed as if I had all the steps.

"You'll get it," Tom encouraged. "Just stay with it."

21

I sat a few moments longer. "Oh!" It hit me in an instant. "It's a man, a life partner, someone who shares this dream and who is part of creating it! Of course!" I was really excited. Naturally, I thought, a cooperative community would be created by cooperative efforts! The whole thing suddenly fit together. I was amazed at how clear and obvious it was. It was as if the whole plan had been divinely created. As I had allowed my conscious mind to step out of the way of the creation process, and let the intuitive mind take over, the pieces had just fallen into place.

I never specifically tried to follow that plan, but as the years passed, I would look back and notice that another piece of the puzzle had been integrated into my life. Sometimes the steps in the boxes would overlap, but the sequence stayed the same. The dream would come and go from my awareness, but periodically I would think of those ten boxes and realize that I had just accomplished another step in the plan.

I didn't recognize it at the time, but what I had drawn was not so much a series of things to do as a series of initiations, or lessons. I had outlined rites of passage or transformations which required me to surrender and, at the same time, to push through my limitations. Each initiation brought about a gradual change of consciousness that would ultimately bring about the dream. I kept watching as the puzzle continued to take form. Today, the end is clearly in sight. Or is it the beginning?

Years later, in the fall of 1992, I had completed about seven of the boxes in my vision. At that time, a vision occurred which gave me a clearer picture of the change in consciousness that is soon to come. This time, the picture did not come from the yearning in my imagination. It was a gift from Spirit. It deepened my awareness of what my dream had been about, and helped me to understand the evolution of humankind. It demonstrated to me how my dream, like the dreams of so many other people, was a part of the changes to come.

I heard on the news about a young Hispanic girl who saw two angels as she was praying in her backyard in the east side of Houston. As she looked up to the heavens, they appeared to her on the roof above the neighbor's garage. In the days that followed, they returned again and were soon joined by two other angels. Then, Mother Mary appeared. Mary spoke almost daily with the girl, giving the same message she has so many times before, asking people to pray for peace in this world.

Although I was not raised Roman Catholic, I still feel a special affinity for Mother Mary. I had read extensively about the various Marian apparitions—in Lourdes, Fatima, Garabandahl, Medjugorjie, and other places where devotion was strong and the people were humble. I visited the Houston site of the appearances of Mother Mary and the Angels fairly often during that autumn. The little chapel, built by the father and friends in his backyard where the appearances were occurring, was filled with thousands of flowers, pictures, rosaries, and that energy of devotion that is so special to the Hispanic people.

I didn't know for sure whether Mary was there—I personally couldn't see her—but I experienced something special whenever I went there to pray. I had recently suffered a deep loss, and I would go to the little chapel feeling burdened and sad. Within ten or fifteen minutes at the altar, I would be filled with peace and an understanding of the greater picture of what was going on in my life. My loss would become less significant and my thoughts would then turn very naturally to prayers for peace on a global level. Surely something very holy was happening in this place.

One day, I returned home from the chapel by a different route. Much to my own surprise, I simply took the wrong exit, even though I had been living in that area for years. Instead of driving directly to my house by way of the crowded city streets, I ended up threading back along the beautiful residential streets by the university. Undisturbed by the detour, I felt incredibly relaxed and peaceful, admiring all that I saw, and

23

enjoying the beautifully kept homes and the sunlight sprinkling through the green canopy of trees above me.

As I turned the corner, my eye was caught by an elderly man jogging across the street. He had white hair and appeared astonishingly healthy. He didn't seem to strain or push himself; instead, he appeared energetically present in his body. He wore a T-shirt with a drawing of the world, encircled by the words, *Take care of our mother, love the earth, save the world.* There was something about the image of this man that impacted me strongly: He was a person who appeared to be immersed in the world of wealth, success, and tradition yet still chose to project an image of deep concern for the direction in which we are going on this planet.

All of a sudden it seemed as if the color of the sunlight changed. It appeared to become more pink, and somehow iridescent. In fact, the neighborhood sharpened in focus, becoming much more vivid. I was still driving down the same boulevard, but I suddenly seemed to be existing in an alternative time, or perhaps a different dimension. The houses were still familiar — beautiful, elegant homes of doctors and professors, gardens exquisitely landscaped, and all in bloom. A woman strolled with a baby carriage and yard men mowed the lawns. Placards for the upcoming elections were posted on several of the lawns.

It was clearly the boulevard I knew, just a few blocks from my home. Yet this luminous pink light seemed to radiate from everything. I perceived that I was somehow in a world of love and respect where all people took complete responsibility for themselves; each person knew fully that personal choices made were the means by which the experience of life was created. In this dimension, everyone understood that our thoughts are the creative force, and that those thoughts are visible to everyone by their physical results. Hence each person was very careful to think consciously, and to fully embrace the results of those thoughts.

My attention was first drawn to the yard men. Somehow I knew that they were very aware that they wanted to be yard men. They had chosen this work and they enjoyed it. They were happy despite low salaries, because of the pleasure gained from the special connection with nature afforded them in their work. There was no resentment towards the wealthy homeowners but rather, an understanding of the symbiotic nature of the relationship. In other words, they took full responsibility for their choice of work.

The wealthy homeowners in this luminescent dimension also took full responsibility for their choices. They completely understood the symbiotic nature of this mutual support system, feeling grateful and respectful of those with whom they worked. There was no sense of superiority. They recognized that their choice to focus on creating abundance also gave them responsibility to share. Since their money was gained in part from the labors and the pocketbooks of others, they recognized the responsibility of returning part of their wealth back to the public, and they all did this in their own creative ways, supporting culture and the arts for the benefit of all.

Each person was completely aware of how his or her own thoughts immediately manifested into physical reality. There was no judgment about another's choices, nor was there discontent about one's own choices, since it was generally understood that one could change anything simply by changing the thoughts about it. Because of this, on a cultural level, the habit of blaming others was virtually nonexistent, leaving people free to feel and express abundant gratitude.

The mother with her baby was fully committed to her choice of motherhood. The culture of this different world held the perspective that we choose our parents before birth, so children assumed a much greater sense of responsibility for themselves than is expected in our current way of life.

The election placards on the lawns also seemed to have a different kind of meaning from normal, three-dimensional consciousness. Elections were viewed more like a friendly sport with a higher purpose. Each candidate recognized that the results of the election were a message from the public endorsing a combination of each politician's thoughts and ideas. Rather than exchanging insults, as is often

25
〰〰

the case today, now experience, each candidate offered an honest and heart-held vision to share with the people. There was no disappointment in loss or triumph in winning because of the community's basic faith and knowing that a Greater Consciousness held the results appropriately in its Hand. The winner inevitably incorporated the other candidate's visions in proportion to the choices of the people.

My total understanding of this realm of awareness took place in the time it took to drive about five blocks. Yet it felt as if I'd been there much longer; every perception in my sparkling, glistening surroundings seemed to be clear in minute detail. And, while my senses were being filled by external impressions, I felt expanded from within by an exquisite, overflowing sensation of peace, unconditional love, and quiet acceptance. I knew that this was how it felt to exist in this dimension.

My vision continued until I got to the end of the residential part of the boulevard. The final image in this altered state of consciousness was the last placard on the last lawn as I slowed at the intersection. It was that of a politician I had just met half an hour before while visiting the chapel of Mother Mary. Somehow this placard had the effect of both grounding the vision and at the same time returning me to normal consciousness.

I drove the three remaining blocks to my home in awe.

The experience of entering into this other realm of consciousness was repeated several times in the next few weeks—on another visit to the Mother Mary chapel, at several Native American ceremonies I attended with Mary Thunder, during a regression, and also during a massage session. Each time I experienced a world of joyous people fully satisfied with themselves and their lives, because they knew they were creating their lives with their conscious choice of thoughts. In each instance, I experienced a luminous pink or peach light as a part of the atmosphere. Often I saw other iridescent colors, especially blues and greens and purples as part of the clothing—or were they actually simply the fabric of existence in that dimension?

26

I can't say for sure that I was experiencing another dimension, but this is what I believed happened. It seemed that I was being shown the next level of our evolution for Planet Earth. We are currently moving towards a level of consciousness in our human community where we are beginning to truly understand the creative force that lies within our own hearts and minds. We are beginning to comprehend how even the physical aspects of our lives are a manifestation of our thoughts.

The density of the third dimension—living on the earth—slows materialization of thoughts, so it is difficult to see the relationships between what we think and how it manifests externally. Yet when we look with an eye to see, the evidence of this truth becomes quite apparent. For people who involve themselves extensively in spiritual practices such as prayer or fasting, it soon becomes evident that there *is* another fairly accessible reality where the connection between thoughts and manifestation is more easily perceived.

I kept pondering the implications of my experiences. What if the transformations, or "earth changes," unfolding in these times of transition were into an entirely different level of existence for our species? What if we were *all* to move into the next vibrational level of existence on this planet, one that is more responsible. What if we all realized that we have the ability to create what we want to create? What if our cultural perspective in this dimension no longer included the "win-lose" paradigm of competitive thought, but, rather, embraced the "win-win" paradigm as truth—that all people can benefit and that none have to lose? What if each of us bypassed countless wasted hours and resources in intellectual and theoretical solutions and, instead, expressed our creativity by being highly attuned to our intuitions? These questions also presented some very interesting thoughts about how some of the economic and environmental problems of our world today might be solved with a cultural embracing of the knowledge that thoughts do, indeed, create whatever reality we choose!

We have long thought of, prayed to, believed in, and known of other dimensions of consciousness, other levels of evolution. We have pondered life in the beyond—in the future, in "life after death," in the fourth or fifth dimension, or in seventh heaven. Every religious tradition speaks of angels, of devas, of guides, or of beings who exist in a realm other than our third dimension of physical form. Crossovers to and from the "spirit world" have been documented on countless occasions as far back as history has been recorded. What if the veil were to become thinner, so that crossovers weren't that unusual? What if we were all to ascend a few increments in our ability to hold our thoughts and our emotions in a place of love and clarity of intention in our creation? Was it that far out of the realm of possibility?

I began to ponder these ideas in relation to the "hundredth monkey principle," popularized by Ken Keyes, which says that there is a point in the collective consciousness when a concept reaches a certain level of acceptance, and then suddenly becomes generalized to the entire population. This "principle" was named after some experiments with monkeys which took place on several islands in Japan. A certain group of monkeys on one of the islands had learned to wash their sweet potatoes at the shore. This ability rapidly spread among the monkeys in that area, but then almost overnight, monkeys on several of the other islands began washing their sweet potatoes as well— without any connection or communication having transpired!

What this demonstrated was that there is a point of critical mass in awareness when a "quantum leap" occurs in the consciousness of the culture as a whole. Once it reaches a certain level of acceptance, a concept no longer needs to be passed on from one person to another. It seems to be instantaneously and telepathically transmitted and received throughout the species. It suddenly becomes an idea whose time has come, a new field of knowledge available to all, a new component of the consciousness of the culture as a whole.

I reflected on this for some time. Could this be the way we

would bring balance to our planet as well? If solutions to our global, social, economic, and ecological problems—and our spiritual disconnection—could not be facilitated quickly enough by linear, logical thinking, then surely there was another way. Imagine each person, one at a time, bringing forth the hero within, facing the challenges of personal growth and nurturing the dormant seeds of magnificence in ourselves and in others. How quickly we would come into alignment with our deepest dreams and most inspired visions!

Perhaps if enough of us begin to live intuitively, to learn to be aware of our thoughts, and to create them consciously, then humankind could make that quantum leap together to a higher level of evolution. Archaeologists have told us that such evolutionary leaps have happened before. All the signs, the predictions, and the predicaments of life at this time seemed to be pointing in that direction. Was it possible that all we needed to do was to be willing to face our dark side and pop through to the light—into a glittering realm of conscious living and conscious loving?

I knew I wasn't thinking about something easy here; it was about nothing less than the birthing of a new way of thinking and of living on Earth. Like the birthing of a child, it needed a period of gestation, some intense labor, and some big pushes— efforts by those who held the vision of a planet in balance and at peace. But, then, people had been working on this for years; people had been preparing for it for a long time. The last decade, in particular, had already brought about a radical change in people's thinking. What many of us had been teaching and talking about to small groups of people in the early seventies, was now material for corporate seminars: Environmental awareness; health care that involves the body, mind, and spirit; psychology that incorporates spirituality, and spirituality that incorporates mental health; team building, a win-win perspective, cooperation, communication, and global awareness—these are now much more a part of common consciousness.

29

"Perhaps," I thought to myself, "the baby is already in the birth canal!"

How do we start in the direction of the new consciousness? What can one person do? When each of us brings ourselves into relationship with our dreams and visions, we can start giving life to the seeds of magnificence within ourselves. The most important piece of this planet for which we are each responsible is that which is contained within the flesh of our own bodies. Get your vision clear in your mind; make drawings of it, write about it—do something to keep the dream before your awareness daily. Share it with others whose dreams are similar and stimulate each other with your excitement. Visualize both your personal and your global dreams and see how they might fit together. Then go for it. When things don't go right, keep honing the picture. Don't give up. Here are some questions for your journal which will help get you started:

1. What do you love? What do you enjoy? What have you always wanted to do, be, or create?

2. What were your childhood fantasies and imaginings? Pretend you are a child again, and write about them with childlike awe, enthusiasm and your ability to fantasize without regarding the "rules" of "reality."

3. Recall any visions you may have received, or perhaps daydreams or night dreams about a future fulfilled.

4. What is your dream? Draw a symbol for where you see yourself today in the first box. Write down today's date. Now, clear your mind and open up to your dream; enter into a daydream state of mind. Then draw that symbol in box number ten. Listen for the date. Next, starting with box number two, without planning, empty your mind and allow the steps to come forth one at a time, drawing a symbol for each as they surface in your consciousness.

date _____

| | |
|1|2|

| | | |
|3|4|5|

| | | |
|6|7|8|

| | |
|9|10|

date _____

5. If you would really like to expand with the concepts you've just read about, don't just put it aside when you are finished reading. Hang out with the book; re-read it and repeat the exercises until they are fully integrated into your daily awareness.

RUDE AWAKENINGS

DISCOVERING THE BLESSINGS
IN DISGUISE

A major personal loss in family, relationships, career, finances, health, or other areas of life always brings us back to face who we are and how we fit into our world. Our sense of reality is ripped apart, and we have no idea where solid ground lies. Whether on a personal or global level, the forces of loss and destruction tear apart the very core of our being. Like it or not, difficult times often force us to reckon with what does not work in our lives, and this can be the beginning of a course correction that leads us to a higher level of evolution.

Yet, so often it seems as if life just happens to us. Countless events, situations, and people support this sense of victimization, and we would change *them* if we could. Other people do things to us—they leave us, hate us, insult us, injure us, go to war with us, steal from us, get sick on us, die on us....

How can we keep our dreams when "they" scoff at us and tell us it will never work? How can we keep the vision alive when there are kids to feed and bills to pay? How can we create that magnificent, wonderful, new life when the credit cards are "maxed out" and we can't leave our jobs without losing retirement? How can we consciously create anything if, at the end of the day, we have only enough energy to flop in front of the tube and be a couch potato for one more evening? Who can even think about dreams, what with the state of the economy, the lure of drugs, the rise in violence, the increase of pollution, and all the other challenges of life?

"Why me, Lord?" we implore.

But do we have the courage to discover the answer to "why?" Are we willing to look deeply for the greater purpose of those things which cause us pain?

Within the mind, we have choices. We can succumb and give up, either blaming ourselves, others, the world, or God. We can tell ourselves, "I'm no good; things never go right for me; this is just my lot in life; I can't handle this; I shouldn't have these feelings; my life is ruined," or even, "This didn't happen."

Or, we can use the upheavals to our benefit. We can shift the focus in the rude awakenings in our life from the "rude," which implies we are blaming the source of the feedback, to "awakenings," which leads us to use the experience for our inner expansion. We can make the choice to take the spiritual and responsible approach—to examine the situation and discover what purpose it serves in our growth as a human being. Instead of lamenting, "Why me?" and looking no further, we can seek out the honest answer to that question. In *searching* for the underlying blessings in an event, we can use any experience as an opportunity to see the reflection of how we manifest our reality. In other words, we can learn to look to the internal rather than the external implications in anything that occurs in our world in order to see where our expansion lies.

What benefits do apparently destructive and hurtful events provide for us? So often we look back years later and say to ourselves, "I didn't realize it at the time, but it was actually beneficial for me to go through that." What if we look *through* the pain instead of attempting to avoid it when something undesirable happens? What if we probe the pain we experience *in the moment* and seek to understand its purpose in our lives? In fact, what if we take *every* adverse situation, large and small, and examine it for its deeper purpose, for its gifts?

This is not an easy thing to do. Personal responsibility is difficult to grasp when facing a natural disaster, or a car accident where the other guy crossed the median. If we get fired, or a loved one leaves us, our responsibility is more apparent—perhaps. Even then, our first impulse is to blame someone or something external to us, and to believe that we have been victimized. Often, we never get beyond this perspective.

How we unconsciously disempower ourselves when we do this! There is a place inside each of us that intuitively knows the reason and purpose for everything we suffer *as well as* how and why we participate in setting up those situations. In order to bring this knowledge to the surface, we need to make a habit of looking for our responsibility in each and every situation in our lives. This *does not* mean to blame ourselves and beat ourselves up. It *does* mean to seek out how we have participated in choosing and setting up each situation. It *does not* mean to hide from our hurt or to pretend difficult situations aren't painful. It *does* mean that we need to seek to understand the greater purpose and benefit of how we create our lives.

It is possible, even when we are steeped in the deepest of tragedy or emotion, to allow a part of us to step back from the drama. We can do this by cultivating a part of us which is deeply curious rather than reactive about the "bad" things that happen to us. It is *not* about pretending we don't have reactions. In fact, allowing ourselves to fully experience them is a necessary part of the process. At the same time, we have the ability to observe ourselves while in the reaction, and to redirect our energies toward discovering our responsibility in the situation. In doing so, we also discover the gift that comes from the blessing in disguise, the benefit of an apparently non-beneficial circumstance.

As we become more and more willing to discover the seen and unseen ways that we create our own reality, we are softened by our willingness to be vulnerable, and humbled in the face of our own humanity. In this process, we begin to see how the Spirit works in our lives. The Native American people sometimes call God the "Great Mystery," reflecting the truth that we humans, limited in our earthliness, can never really know the workings of the Infinite. But if we have faith, if we are open and curious, if we seek to discover how we have created our experiences, if we are willing to accept that the Creator works in and through us and others for our greatest good, then even those things that seem to come from an external source—other people, governments, nature, accidents—can be seen as part of the Greater Plan in our lives.

If we are looking, we can recognize, discover, and appreciate the blessings in disguise as they come to us in the present, rather than in retrospect. If we constantly strive to step back from our myopic view of life and seek the greater picture, then we are more apt to discover the gifts that the Creator gives us. Then we can also see our own involvement in the Divine Plan for the fulfillment of our blueprint, of our dreams—the becoming of all that we are meant to be.

35

▲ ▲ ▲ ▲

I was first made aware of the concept of "blessings in disguise" during a rude awakening that actually set me free to follow the dream in my heart. However, I certainly did not see it that way at the time.

In the two or three years that followed the diagramming of my Dream of the New Place, I found myself fulfilling each of the steps within the first few boxes pretty much in the order that I had seen them unfold. I worked with a foundation that specialized in personal growth trainings, and then dove into graduate school. Next, I counseled part time in a weight reduction program and started seeing clients privately.

At the time, I was meditating regularly with a group I'll call the "Peace People," and I imagined that the New Place was something that was going to be created with them. I had been with them for twelve years, and I loved them dearly. Together we had studied and taught yoga and meditation, created a conscious community in the city, and shared dreams of creating a

retreat together. But I became more and more aware of a phenomenon I have since realized is quite common to spiritual
communities: In the attempt to be "good," "spiritual," and
"peaceful," members would sometimes be less than completely
honest with each other. They would close themselves off to
feedback and differing opinions. It seemed that in the interest
of maintaining a calm and unemotional appearance, suppres-
sion and repression became acceptable alternatives to genuine
and clear communication.

This way of relating just didn't work for me. It wasn't real. It
did not acknowledge our humanity as part of our divinity. I
began to realize that our personal growth had to include psychological as well as spiritual work. We cannot ignore our emotions; they are an integral part of us. If we cut off a part of who
we are, we not only isolate ourselves from our world, but more
importantly, from our passion and our purpose in life!

As I was reaching out into my world, returning to graduate
school, and teaching and sharing what I was learning about
personal growth, the Peace People were becoming more ex-
clsive, creating more rules for membership, and ultimately
requiring people to swear unconditional allegiance to them. It
was ironic: Seven years before, we had all left a yoga organization because the leader had required that we swear total allegiance to him or leave. We were together because we had felt
that his demand was inappropriate. Now they were doing the
same thing! Nonetheless, I stayed a part of the Peace People
for some time with the idea that we would find the New Place
together and create the unfolding of the Dream.

But one day I attended a very confusing and directionless
meeting. Some members wanted to talk about elusive sub-
jects that, as far as I could tell, did not relate to the purpose of
the meeting. Others kept repeating that we weren't being "in
integrity." The meeting ended with nothing accomplished.

Afterwards, I walked out to the car with my friend, Rob, who,
like myself, had been very involved in creating a new form of

36

balanced and democratic government for the Peace People. It was the day before Easter, and I had plans to drive out to the country to spend the holiday at a friend's retreat. I felt I had really wasted my time staying around for this meeting.

"What the heck was that all about?" I asked.

Rob coughed and cleared his throat. He was visibly uncomfortable. My question had been rhetorical, but I could see that his answer would have a little more substance than I had expected.

"Well," he said, looking for appropriate words, "they had a closed corporate meeting last night and changed the rules for the group that met today."

I looked at him, dumbfounded. "What? "

"They had a secret closed corporate meeting last night." He repeated. "They only told certain people about it."

I was flabbergasted, speechless. Rob and I had worked for six months pulling together endless legal paperwork to get non-profit status for the Peace People in order to create a legal structure for the dreams we shared. The group had spent years forming an organization that was built on cooperative efforts and a democratic process—a balanced community. Nothing allowed for secret or closed meetings. Now it appeared that certain people were misusing the legal structure I had worked so hard to create in order to build a power base for themselves. Suddenly the comments by some members during the meeting about "getting into integrity" made sense. But clearly as a group, they had decided not to do so.

I was shaking all over. This group of people had been my friends and family for twelve years. There were a number of us who over the years had always helped to maintain a balance of power, and assure that each person was accepted and respected. But there had always been a group that wanted the power, that wanted control over the direction of the Peace People. It seemed that they finally had manipulated the situation so that they could have it. Keeping a political balance had

37

always felt like trying to shore up a crumbling dam; now it seemed that the dam had been washed away.

"How can you, in all conscience, abide by that?" I asked Rob, not just angry, but genuinely wondering. "How could you be a part of such a gross lack of integrity?"

"Well," he said, "sometimes you don't agree with things, but if you're committed, you go with what the majority wants. I'm committed to the purpose of the Peace People."

It was an explanation I could understand, but I couldn't align with it personally. Perhaps their purpose wasn't what I thought it was. To me, the end did not justify the means. Peace at all costs only meant peace for some people. Secret meetings were not an option in my vision of community. In that moment I realized that my relationship with that group was over. Our values were very different, and I couldn't ignore it any longer. They had been an important part of my life for over a decade, but now we were going in different directions. I hated to face it, but it was time to let them go.

I drove out to my friend's farm in a stupor. The hurt was so intense that at times I was dizzy. It felt as if I'd been shot through the chest with a cannon, and that there was a giant empty chasm where once there had been a heart.

The loss I felt was not only for those who had been my friends for twelve years; it was also the loss of the Dream. How much we had shared over that time; how much we had grown together. We had weathered times with no money and no resources, times in which only faith had kept us going, times in which that faith had clearly demonstrated to us the presence of God in our lives. We had struggled together to form a new kind of government; we had looked together for land to build a shared community; we had sat together for many hours, joined together in sacred silence, meditating for the dream of a new way of life on Earth.

These people had been my life. I could not comprehend what had happened or the direction events had taken. I tossed and turned all night. Easter dinner was a fog. I cooked and smiled at jokes, but I wasn't even in my body. The pain was so acute that I had gone numb. I was in deep, deep shock.

As I drove back to Houston that Easter evening, I stopped in a meadow full of wildflowers—bluebonnets, scarlet Indian paintbrush, daisies, purples, yellows, pinks. It was unusual to see them all clustered together in one field. Some were in bunches by color, others stood by themselves. As I sat in their midst, I allowed the beauty of the spring day to work on me, to settle into my soul. Maybe we don't all have to be alike, I thought. Maybe some of us are supposed to be different. Maybe, like the wildflowers, we just stand where we stand— some together, some apart. We each have our own unique beauty, and there is no right or wrong—only being what we are where we are.

39

I continued my journey home, a little comforted but still a bit dazed. I found myself in the left-hand lane, cruising behind a green van which was identical to the one owned by my closest friend in the Peace People. The back of the van in front of me became a movie screen on which memories replayed from my years with the Peace People. Lost in thought, I was now oblivious to normal safety standards. "I'm not with them any more. All that work we did to bring light to the planet will be no more for me. Did I not come here to this planet to do this work? Have I somehow failed my purpose? Do I have any reason to live any more?"

As these questions raced through my mind, I failed to notice that the green van had pulled over to the right. I also did not see the pick-up and boat trailer without tail lights that had stopped in front of me, preparing to make a left-hand turn.

Then, in an instant, I came to awareness. There was no time to see if there was anyone next to me. I yanked the wheel to the right, missing the boat by inches, and tore through the right lane and onto the red dirt shoulder of the road. Grabbing the wheel with both hands to steady the vehicle, I glanced in the rear view mirror and saw that the other cars had seen the danger and had moved safely out of the way, and were now engulfed in clouds of red dust.

I eased back onto the highway, shaking, but fully present for the first time in two days. Well, I thought, perhaps my question has just been answered. I guess I must have a reason to live, because I am alive. I could be dead right now, but on some level I just made the choice to live. Perhaps there is a purpose for me. I wonder what it is?

I thought about the symbolism of blindly following behind the green van, which had almost led me to my death. Could it be that I had also blindly followed the Peace People even after it was apparent we had grown in different directions? Had I compromised my own standards in order to do the powerful meditation work that we had all trained ourselves to do? Would losing sight of my own values in order to be a part of that group have ultimately led to my own inner death?

I thought further of the symbolism of my near-collision with the boat. Boats relate to water, which sometimes represents emotion. The group which had taken control of the Peace People had always hidden their feelings, and feared the expression of emotions in themselves and in others. Openness, honesty, and vulnerability cannot co-exist with repressed feelings. The secret meetings were but a byproduct of the fear of emotions.

I realized that spiritual communities have a way of magnifying and mirroring our own dark sides, as well as our light. The very intention to live with others in the light exposes that which is not of the light. I realized that I, too, had been afraid of my emotions. In fact, in order to be accepted within the group, I had been as concerned about repressing my feelings as anyone. The stopped boat could also be seen at the vessel of my own soul that had been stuck in the waters of stuffed emotions. Now I was free to sail in new directions.

Suddenly I had a new perspective on life. It was time to

redirect my focus according to the callings of my own heart. Although I missed my friends and the meditation work of the Peace People for quite a while, in time, the gift of that loss became clear. Integrating that clarity involved allowing myself to grieve, to feel my emotions and let the sadness wash itself away.

Then, as I sought out the purpose of the loss, and the purpose for my new life, I gradually came to see that I had attempted to keep my dream alive within a group of people who did not hold the same dream. Their intent was to become more sequestered in order to focus on their work; perhaps, in order to achieve their dream, they needed to do that. I had tried to change them into what I wanted, too afraid to go out alone and find other people with whom I was more aligned. I didn't have to see their choices as wrong, only as different.

My choice, however, was to reach out to others and share what I'd learned *as well as* to meditate for world peace. At first I felt like the fledgling being pushed out of the nest by its mother. But I started to teach meditation again, and to gather like-minded people around me who shared my desire to work for global healing and to create community in an open and honest way. Within two years I opened a center where others could also teach and share from their experience and training, where all aspects of the self were honored and accepted.

As time passed, I realized that I had needed to go in my own direction in order to fulfill my own destiny. In a sense, that Easter brought not my death, but my resurrection. I had experienced it at first as a rude awakening, but it opened me to the blessing—the gift—of a life more aligned with my own nature, interests, and purpose.

▲ ▲ ▲ ▲ ▲ ▲ ▲

When we first start to be aware of the existence of blessings in disguise, we need to practice looking at everything we don't like with an eye towards the gift. It involves two steps. The first is to allow ourselves to *fully immerse in the emotions of the "negative" experience.* This can take as little as five minutes or it can take months. But in allowing ourselves to *feel*—doing nothing but feeling, and breathing through it—we allow the message of the discomfort find its way to the surface. Without expectations, and with full willingness to experience the pain, we thus honor fully that which is within us. Then, once the emotion has been totally experienced, we can *ask* ourselves what the benefit or blessing of that event might be.

The following questions will help you process some of your disguised blessings. You may wish to make them a regular part of how you process anything you don't like from day to day.

42

1. What have been some of the rude awakenings or unpleasant situations that have actually helped to move you forward in your life?

2. List ten to twenty of the "negative" experiences that you can think of in your life. Then go back and write at least one, or perhaps more, benefit(s) you gained from each experience.

3. Consider how others—individuals, communities, but especially spiritual communities—can have the effect of magnifying and bringing to light our own "dark side," helping to bring it to the surface so it can be healed. When have you found yourself rejecting another person or group, only to discover that the quality you are wanting to avoid in them is actually a reflection of something you would rather not see in yourself?

4. What is the most important blessing in disguise you recall in your life? Note your initial thoughts and feelings when the event first occurred, and how they changed over time.

FACING THE DARK, FACING THE LIGHT

EXITING OLD PERSONAL PARADIGMS

As we embark upon our personal hero's journey, the recognition that rude awakenings can be blessings is a small, but critical, aspect of our path. The greater challenge lies in integrating, practicing, and utilizing that principle, which means unraveling a world of old perspectives, paradigms, and belief systems—the ways in which we mentally organize our perceptions of life. We cannot seriously think about global transformation without first recognizing our personal responsibility to transform our own thought processes. It is, in fact, through our willingness to face the challenges of both the darkness and the light within ourselves on an individual level, that we begin to perceive and comprehend global solutions. The microcosm that we each are is but a reflection of the macrocosm that we all are.

We all grow up with a certain world view, each person's being slightly different from another's. For the most part, we reproduce the same perceptions, thoughts, beliefs, and actions that we learned as children. We tend to repeat many of the economic, religious, career, educational, relationship, recreational, environmental, emotional, thought, and language patterns of our parents and their parents.

Our predisposition to interpret things in a habitual manner affects our whole experience of reality. When we have decided we "know" how something is, or think that things "should" be different from how they actually are, we have pre-judged, or prejudiced, the outcome. For example, based on our past experience or on what we heard our parents say, we might think we "know" how men or women are, what rich or poor people are like, what is "good," "right," and "spiritual" and what is not, and who should be the next president. Unwittingly, we often make choices and decisions according to preconceived notions of what life is like, without genuinely assessing the situation in the moment. We shortchange our options and our experience of life.

Ultimately, this "prejudiced" perspective also affects our self-image, for we judge ourselves most harshly by the rules we set in stone. If we think we are good, that is our experience of ourselves. If we judge ourselves as bad, or inadequate, or incomplete, then this is so, as far as our personal reality is concerned. If we think we are happy, we are. If we think we are sad, we are. If we think we deserve to live in abundance—or in a lack thereof—we do. If we think we have to be in control, we will surround ourselves with situations and people we try to control, at the same time seeing others as trying to control us.

Most of us want to be "good." We want to do the right thing, make the right choices, be comfortable, be liked, and avoid mistakes at all costs. The thing is, no two people interpret "good" and "bad," or "right" and "wrong" in the same way. These values are all a function of our personal experiences and learned perceptions. Thus, these old mental programs directly affect how much we allow ourselves to enjoy ourselves and our life, for they limit us by referencing all that we experience to the past.

As we go through life with the familial and cultural filters of what is right and good, we are often unable to see the blessings before us, for we have already decided what we shall see. Christ said, "Except that you become as little children, you shall not enter the Kingdom of Heaven." How, then, can we learn to see with "new" eyes, without the filters of our previous conditioning? How can we learn to let go of the old paradigms that say we "know" what is good and what is not, and discover a new way of perceiving our universe that is filled with the wonder, curiosity and awe of a young child?

What we do, according to what we learned to believe, is to consciously or unconsciously set our world up to conform to our expectations. More often than not, we set things up unconsciously by our unexamined habitual thoughts.

Whatever beliefs we have about how life will be is exactly what we end up experiencing. Except, we don't "end up" with it by chance, but rather by the focus of our thoughts, and therefore by our own creation. The more we put our focus or attention on something, whether it is positive or negative, the more we magnify it in our own minds, and thus the more important it becomes in our reality. In addition, we seek out confirmations of our perceptions, and in this way, further draw to us that reality.

For example, if we believe "most people are very kind," we focus on the kindness around us, and respond to it according to that perception. If we think, "Most people are greedy," we will tend to be suspicious, to interpret very neutral or even generous acts as greedy or having an ulterior motive, and respond by being very protective, even greedy, about our own possessions. We tend to miss the fact that it is our own mind which is creating the experience, and not the outside world.

It seems so often that life just happens to us. As we interact and interface with loved ones, families, friends, enemies, job situations, society, the system, and the government, it certainly doesn't *appear* that we are writing our own story. But on closer inspection, if we are willing to look—*if we are willing to look*—without judgement, we may find that we are both the author and all of the characters in our own drama. We are both the hero and the villain as we gallantly strive towards our higher purpose while slyly hiding our self-sabotage from our own awareness. In order to recognize how we create our own reality, how we set up the journey, and how much we are willing to walk towards our goals, we must become willing to look at ourselves with the same childlike curiosity and interest as we might examine a butterfly. Our dark side, as well as our light side, is often difficult to see unless our desire for the Truth is very, very strong.

45

If, in fact, we are the creators of our own reality, then it would follow that those experiences we *thought* we didn't like, are actually, on some level, of our own choosing. It means that, *on some level, we set them up for the purpose of fulfilling our dreams.* It means that even making mistakes and going backwards actually leads us forward: They show us what directions don't work, and offer us course corrections to better reach our goal. In a sense, we create our own obstacle course so that we can strengthen and grow, so we can gain the tools and skills we need to move along our path.

There is a kind of deeper internal wisdom within each of us, of which we are often unaware, that helps us through life's obstacle courses. Our strengths and our weaknesses, our "good" side and "bad," all work together so we can become that worthy warrior, the hero who ultimately slays the dragon, heals the sick, saves the damsel, captures the holy grail. Ultimately, if we look in an unprejudiced manner, we can begin to see and appreciate the wholeness of who we are, and how our light and dark sides both play a part in our evolution. At the same time, in releasing old perceptions about obstacles, losses, unkindnesses, violations, and seeming bad luck, we can open to new possibilities about how they may be *actually* helping us to achieve our dreams. In that sense, they are truly blessings— blessings in disguise—the sand that polishes the stone.

▲ ▲ ▲ ▲

The challenge of shedding some of my own outdated personal paradigms—facing both my dark and light sides—was brought home to me after I left the Peace People and first met Mary Thunder.

I was leading a double life at the time: I played the conventional psychotherapist by day and taught meditation and spiritual healing by night. I liked the changes that I had created in my life, yet there remained that gnawing need, buried deep in my soul, to have a community of spiritually dedicated people as part of my life. At the same time, I was very clear that I would not be a part of any cult-like activity. What I had experienced with the Peace People reinforced my own commitment to honesty, to truth, and to expressing feelings openly. Being able to control the mind was not enough, although I still valued that kind of discipline and focus. Practicing love as well as mental and emotional truthfulness had to be a new part of my own path and that of my community.

Then one weekend I sponsored a guest speaker to present a program in Houston. When the seminar was over, I was approached by a woman named Barbara on behalf of someone called Mary Thunder. I'd never heard of either one of them. Barbara asked if I would donate some tapes from the seminar to Thunder. I thought her request a bit much from a stranger, but I suggested that we barter. Did this Mary Thunder do anything? How about a psychic reading?

Barbara hesitated for a moment. "Well, that's not exactly her focus. Thunder's a Native American who counsels and teaches universal truth. She has a deep interest in all forms of spiritual truth and all spiritual teachers."

I didn't know much about American Indians, and it probably showed in my blank expression.

Barbara quickly added, "But I think you might say that she does readings, in a way. She certainly has the ability. She'll be in town next week. I'll set you up with an appointment."

I liked Mary Thunder right away. She had bright, clear eyes and the warmest smile I'd ever seen. She was short and chubby, but she seemed to have an infinite amount of energy. She was like a grandmother. As I sat with her, I felt very comfortable and safe—yet challenged—to come into a greater part of myself.

Thunder was drinking a big Pepsi and smoking cigarettes most of the time while we talked. "Boy," I thought to myself, "my old spiritual friends would write her off in a second if they could see that." Not that I enjoyed being around smoke that much—I was actually allergic to it—but there was something very real and honest and human about this woman. No hidden feelings or dishonesty here, of this I was already certain.

Her name, Thunder, she told me, meant "Truth." Now, I liked that too. I was also impressed by Horse, her "half-side." Half-side—I liked that expression much better than "significant other." It sounded more loving, connected, and committed. Horse had an easy, kind smile and an unassuming, deep wisdom. I was sure we had met somewhere before; he seemed so familiar. I must have asked him a half a dozen times if he was sure we didn't already know each other.

I sat with Thunder for well over an hour and a half. As we neared the end of the session, I asked if there was going to be the spiritual partner in my life that I was seeking. With a twinkle in her eye, she answered, "In about two months something will happen. Let's see now, that should be about May 15."

"What do you mean 'something'? I want a high-level, very special kind of relationship." She just twinkled and didn't say any more.

On May 15, "something" did indeed happen. I met a man whom I dated for several months. It was "something," but that was about it! As I look back, it wasn't the relationship that was important, but rather the fact that Thunder had demonstrated her level of connection to Spirit. Predicting the future is not that unusual, but pinpointing a date accurately is extremely rare. Thunder tends to keep this ability very private. But she (or Spirit) made an exception here, and it was enough to pique my interest and bring me back for more.

Six months later I found myself doing a Vision Quest with Thunder. At the time, I didn't really understand what a Vision Quest was; Thunder tended to allow the experience to be the teacher and so she did not explain it to me ahead of time. I soon discovered that this Vision Quest was the beginning of the kind of change within myself that I had prayed for most of my adult life. It was only much later that I began to comprehend the magnitude of this ancient Native American ceremony, and how powerfully one could connect with Spirit through its process.

Since it was my first year to go out "crying for a vision," I was committed to only one night out on my blanket. It was a time to pray for direction in my life. I was alone—alone with nature and alone with myself. I sat for the better part of that first afternoon, doing my best to stay prayerful. Yet, when I looked up, I discovered I was facing a tree whose bare limbs looked like devil's horns rising above the trees around it. It was eerie. Each time I looked up at the "horns," I felt a chilling fear gnaw at my insides. Recently, my man and I had been fighting. I was angry at him and disappointed in myself. When would I learn to create a relationship that was not just "something," but was dynamic, loving, and radiant instead? I thought of the ninth box in the diagram of my dream, the partner who would share that dream. I was nowhere near that part of my goal! I kept staring up at the horns above the trees as dusk slowly turned the day to darkness. "It's a sign," I thought to myself, slumping in my seat. "I'm really a devil." With nothing to keep me busy, my mind was running rampant. "I'm a horrible person. I'm totally unlovable. I can never get it right." I buried my head and cried and cried until I dozed off, losing my sorrow in the unconsciousness of a night's sleep.

When I awoke in the morning, it was already a glorious day. The sunlight backlit the field of grasses nearby as dragonflies, butterflies, and bees busied themselves in a celebration of life. I breathed deeply of the spring-like autumn of the Texas hill country. Across the field was another gnarled live-oak tree that had added to my jitters the evening before. In the morning light it looked very different, much more friendly. In fact, as I admired its majesty, I noticed that the way the shadow now fell, it appeared that there was a woman sitting at its base, playing a guitar. Fascinated that there could appear to be such detail from one tree trunk, I gazed at it for a long time. "I need to get back to my music," I thought. "It's time to break out the old

49
〰〰

guitar and start playing again." Music had always been a touchstone to my Self. Playing the guitar, I would always feel complete, whole, in alignment with myself.

The Vision Quest experience was amazing. It seemed that nature had a way of acting as a communication device for God, if we were open to it. Or, maybe it was that the Creator had a way of using nature to speak to us. Or, perhaps this was a dimension where there was no separation of the physical from the spiritual. As I prayed for a vision which would give purpose and direction for my life, I realized that the answer to my prayers might not come in the form of a full-blown, dream-like, movie-type vision. No, it seemed that answers were coming to me through the interaction of the Spirit with the physical plane.

Then, with a jolt, I remembered the horns above the trees. I glanced up quickly, hoping the symbol of my "badness" had disappeared, or that the light had altered them as it had the tree trunk in the field. But no, the horns looked just as ominously negative as they had the night before. My heart sank. I wanted to return from my Vision Quest miraculously renewed, but my own dark side still loomed heavily over me.

It seemed as if I was much more fragile than I realized, and I wanted to cry again. Not knowing what else to do, I returned my thoughts to my prayers, reminding myself that they were my purpose here. I looked up periodically at the horns, then back to the guitar tree, then out to the fields teeming with sunny life. I shifted my focus from one to the other, and began to notice that, as I changed where I put my awareness, my thoughts and emotions would follow. Each time I focused on the horns, depression set in. When I looked at the guitar tree, I was filled with a sense of self-nurturing. When I gazed out toward the field, I felt attuned to the greater world picture, and peace started settling into my heart.

Finally, I decided I'd had enough of focusing on the horns. I'd spent a good part of the previous evening beating myself up and thinking about all the mistakes I'd made recently. Sure, there

50

was a dark side of me, but right now I was getting tired of look-ing at it. I was now facing north; I stood up and stretched, turned a hundred and eighty degrees, and settled myself facing south.

There, above the tree tops on the opposite side, was another set of protruding bare branches. These, however, did not feel or look ominous; instead they appeared friendly and inviting. I gazed at the form created by the tree and the light; it appeared to be an angel swooping forward from the leaves, like a maiden mounted on the bow of a ship! "Ah, that is me, too," I thought.

I considered all those people whose lives I had touched: The satisfied clients, the many people who had attended my work-shops, my friends, and my family. Most of my days were filled with happy service. As I reviewed the time since I began walk-ing through the steps to my dream, I realized I was much fur-ther along in my desire to make my days purposeful, to make a difference on my planet.

No, I wasn't just the devil, and I also wasn't just the angel. I was both. There were parts of me that were irritable and that played the victim. There were also parts which I still could not see, and that created unworkable situations in my life. And, too, there were parts of me that expressed my magnificence, my power, my higher self. I was all of these. Interestingly enough, there were times when I didn't want to face either of those parts of me—the horns or the wings—for they both brought with them the challenge of self-examination and of taking responsi-bility for my creations.

Yet, I realized I could focus where I chose. I could look at the horns or look at the angel wings. For much of my life I had wrestled with self-esteem issues. No matter how much acclaim I received for my accomplishments, it never felt as if I were really "measuring up." Now I saw how I habitually focused on the horns—my mistakes and weaknesses—until I made myself thoroughly depressed and angry with myself, thus creating a personal reality fraught with pain and anxiety. I rarely congrat-ulated myself, appreciated myself, or identified with my wings.

51

There were much greater heights to which I was capable of rising if I so chose!

I sat there blanketed by the warm, sunny, yellow autumn, and I began to see with new eyes. I realized that I had not been exercising my ability to choose where to focus my mind. It was time to give the wings the attention they deserved. Not that we should never look at our horns: If we are unwilling to see our dark side, we cannot grow. But I needed to see my light side as well. I needed to perceive myself more as a divine being—the spirit that I am—housed in a body. From the horns, I could learn how to grow, and from the wings I could draw my strength as well as acknowledge my progress.

Good and bad, right and wrong—I had been so busy judging myself that I wasn't enjoying the beauty before me. "We can focus wherever we choose," I thought to myself, "and therefore we have the power to change how we perceive things at any moment!"

Thunder explained to me.

*Feelings of insecurity that come from being humiliated by parents, teachers, or other students in early life; that come from abuse, trouble with the law, credit, family matters, business failures, not meeting other people's expectations, guilt from family or church, unrequited love, difficulties in overeating, divorce, or anything that nags from the past can be changed so that it no longer negatively affects you **if you take responsibility for your part in the actions and reactions in a positive way.** Seeing it through new eyes, think for a moment: What is eating you? What from your past lingers to discredit the present and will no doubt snake into the future.*

Everything that has happened in your life is stored somewhere in your mind. But most people consciously remember just a small part of what actually took place. This is because the brain deletes, distorts, and generalizes your experiences at phenomenal speeds. Your brain assigns positive and negative emotions to all memories. You can be limited if your brain assigns negative emotions such as guilt, remorse, anger, fear, or resentment. Yet, when you embrace the strengths within, you will move toward a bright future!

When a person undertakes a Vision Quest, or participates in the Sun Dance, the following year becomes the working out and manifestation of the prayers offered in that ceremony. In the months that followed, it seemed that self-esteem issues kept coming to the surface at every turn, and learning to embrace those strengths became my focus. By the next fall, I was launched into writing about how to know and love yourself in my first book, *Claiming Your Self-Esteem.* At Vision Quest, I'd heard Thunder tell the story of how her elders had sent her on the road to "teach what you most need to learn." Clearly, this approach had now become a part of my path as well.

53

Part of facing our dark and light sides includes recognizing that any transformation is not an overnight process. The same issues challenge us again and again and gradually, over time, we chip away at the rough edges.

Not long after my first Vision Quest, I was once again given the opportunity to re-evaluate my old beliefs and constructs about myself and my spirituality, and to discover more clearly how we create our reality through our choice of focus. It was my first time supporting at a Vision Quest, which meant helping Thunder and her crew with the behind-the-scenes activities that assist the Visioners in their journey into the realm of Spirit. It meant cooking, cleaning, tending the fire, and being in prayerful service to those who were questing. "It's a chance to get out of yourself and into service to others," Thunder would say, and I was soon to discover what she meant.

The Vision Quest was being held north of Dallas, and I had driven up with my friends Melody and Susie, and Susie's daughter, Lucy Morningstar. It had been a great day, and we were all filled with light and love—until the clouds rolled in. It started raining shortly after dark and, since there was really no shelter, I had hunkered into my tent to stay dry. Melody, Susie, and Lucy were all nestled into their tents as well. I wasn't used to camping, and roughing it wasn't all that appealing. In the middle of the night, water started seeping through from the thin mat beneath me into my sleeping bag. I shifted around in the dark, half awake, trying to find a dry spot. Each time I turned, the dryness would last ten minutes or so, until I was barely dozing off, and then I'd feel the cold wetness creep in again. Finally I roused myself, groped about for my flashlight, and surveyed the inside of my tent, issuing forth a loud groan at what I saw. Apparently I had settled into a shallow gully. My tent, mat, and sleeping bag, blocking the flow of run-off waters, had become a small dam, absorbing gallons of water from the "riverbed" beneath me.

54

Wearily, I abandoned the whole soggy mess and climbed into the car, covering myself as best as I could with a small blanket that had been left there. But it wasn't enough to keep me warm, and I shivered, tossed, and turned in my cramped quarters for another hour or so. Then I'd had it. I was out of here.

I climbed out of the car and looked for signs of life from my friends. I was going home, and it seemed best to let them know. Then I noticed that there were people over by the Sweat Lodge fire, huddled together, drenched—and singing! How weird. Suddenly, Thunder's husband, Horse, walked by and I caught him on the run. He paused, fully present with me.

"Hey, I'm soaked." I was a little annoyed.

His voice was kind and his face was cheerful, showing not a bit of strain from the wear of weather and the late hours. He was still dressed in yesterday's clothes, which were quite wet.

"Yeah, we really got a drenching."

"I'm going to head home," I told him. "I've had enough."

Horse didn't try to talk me out of it; he just said he was sorry it had been difficult, but if I felt I had to leave, that was up to me. Then he added, "Well, I've got to keep moving; we've got Questers out on their blankets, and we've got to see how they're doing." He thanked me for being there, gave me a hug, then hurried along.

Oh. I had forgotten about the people out on their Vision Quest. *They* didn't even have tents! Somehow, I'd thought they would have all come in out of the rain. Of course not. They were out there to pray, to receive a vision for their lives. What was a little rain?

I stood there in the cool night air. The rain had just stopped and I could hear the soft strains of song from the supporters sitting around the fire, praying for those who were "out on their blankets." I wasn't sure what to do. A bedraggled supporter limped by, wet from head to toe and mud splashed up to his knees—and with a warm, loving smile on his face. "Guess it's time to put on some dry clothes," he said.

"How did you get so muddy?" I asked.

"Oh, I've been tending the fire all night," he answered. He smiled and hurried along into the darkness.

I looked at my watch. It was four in the morning!

Still riveted to the spot where Horse had left me, I began to wonder about Thunder. What had she done, what had she said, that could so inspire this large group of people to be in such happy and contented service, to forget about their own discomfort? Not a single person seemed to share my distaste for being cold and wet. They were there to pray. How was it that the people around Thunder were happy when they should have been miserable? They knew how to convert something negative into something positive by putting into practice that principle of facing the dark and facing the light which I had first perceived in my own Vision Quest. This was a different kind of spirituality, one that dealt with life instead of ignoring it; one that created life from a completely different paradigm than my own.

"I don't really understand this yet," I said to myself, "but I want to learn from this woman."

I went over by the circle of singers and sat down. I leaned forward and warmed my hands over the crackling fire. Someone had a guitar and was singing Lisa Thiel's song, "Oh, holy mother, mother of all things..." I joined in. I was wide

55

awake, energized, at peace, and in prayer. Whatever Thunder did, it was obviously based on choosing a different view of reality, and it certainly seemed to be working.

Just then Thunder appeared out of the darkness, with Horse at her side. She had just come back from checking on the Questers. Her hair was wet and she was splattered with mud. But she had that wonderful smile on her face. She stood by the fire for a few minutes, told a couple of jokes, and asked how each of us was doing. Then she looked over at me. "Carolyn," she said, "you sing like an angel. I could hear you all the way up on the hill. It made the Questers very happy."

She waved as she turned and disappeared back into the darkness. I sat gazing at the fire, feeling warm and content and very much a part of my new spiritual family. I had moved into an attitude of service, and everything had changed. Now, I felt happy, too.

▲ ▲ ▲ ▲ ▲ ▲ ▲

As we gradually shift our old, limiting paradigms and allow ourselves to enter relationship with the wholeness of who we are, it becomes more and more evident that the "armageddon process" is not an external process at all, or only symbolically so. In the past, the concepts of our three-dimensional physical earth world were only comprehensible in terms of externals. Our history books are written in terms of "what's out there," not "what's inside of us."

Yet "what's inside of us" is where the real work of any change occurs. We cannot ask our world to change unless we have been willing to undertake our own personal changes. By being observant of the thoughts by which we create our reality, we can begin to make shifts—moment by moment, thought by thought.

We *do* have the ability to radically shift our own paradigms—our thought creations, our personal interpretations of our lives and our world. We have the ability to shift from seeing ourselves as insufficient and powerless to magnificent and wise despite our weaknesses! We have the ability to begin to under-stand the magnitude of the creative force of our own thoughts, and to start consciously creating a reality that is workable, lov-ing, supportive, caring, and profound.

By answering the questions below, and by continuing to ask yourself these kinds of questions, you can raise your awareness of the old paradigms that have created your life. In time, as you master knowing the light and dark aspects of yourself, you will be able to better empower yourself to create your reality in a more conscious manner.

1. Make a list of those values and behaviors you have believed were good or bad, right or wrong. Then, using this list, make note of real life situations which turned out to be the oppo-site of how you had judged them.

2. For one week, at every opportunity, practice noticing any judgments or falsehoods (positive or negative) you have about yourself and replace them with loving, accepting, truthful statements.

3. Make a list of ten to twenty characteristics of your "dark side." Then go back and note how each aspect has helped or benefitted you at some time in your life.

4. What are some aspects of your "light side" that you don't tend to claim to yourself or others, either out of habit or "modesty." Write them down in terms such as "I'm proud of..." or "I enjoy my..." or "I'm very good at..." To further stretch this ability, practice telling other people about these qualities of yours.

5. If this self-esteem aspect of growth is one that you would like to pursue further, you may want to read my first book, *Claiming Your Self-Esteem.*

THE ELDERS AND THE FIREFLIES

A SPIRITUAL CARROT

When we set a spiritual course in our lives, Spirit responds in some way and lets us know that our prayers and intentions have been heard and are being supported. While the external forms of various spiritual practices may differ, this principle is held as true in all religions.

There is an interactive aspect of Spirit in our lives that, because it is usually unseen, we are sometimes tempted to label as luck or coincidence. *We are always and completely* immersed in relationship with the spiritual world, yet it is often only at unique times that this relationship comes into our awareness enough to recognize it as part of our reality. No matter how spiritual or religious we may be, it is not unusual to go through our average work day without particular awareness of the non-physical realm. Yet every religious tradition tells us that God is always within us!

It is not my intention here to define God or Spirit for you; each person reading this book will have different experiences and definitions of the Divine. Twelve-Step programs have done us a great service in referring to *God as you understand God to be,* thus allowing people to share their spirituality without having to get involved in the divisiveness of trying to make belief systems match.

Our increasing awareness of our spirituality and our relationship with God is an essential aspect of the change in consciousness we are now experiencing. Yet, since our beliefs aren't all exactly the same, I have chosen to refer to the Divine

THE ELDERS AND THE FIREFLIES

in this book primarily as Spirit, using other names for God as
they fit the context of the story, such as Spiritual Binding Force,
or Creator, or The God Within.

One of the names for God that I learned from Mary Thunder
is "The Great Mystery." I like to use this name, because it keeps
me aware of how all-encompassing, yet totally fathomless, God
is in our lives. It helps me to remember that for all the work I
do to shift my personal paradigms and take responsibility for
my creations in life, there will always be an aspect that is
Unknowable that works for my growth in ways I cannot know
or comprehend. As such, it is often in retrospect, once I see a
better outcome than one I could have planned, that I know the
Great Mystery has touched my life.

If we start living our lives with an awareness of the constant
presence of the Great Mystery, we can begin to understand that
there are times for creating our reality, and times for surrendering, and we may not really know which is which. Out of this
"not knowing" comes true humility. As we become sensitive to
the balance between our creating and our receiving, suddenly
miracles begin to happen in our lives.

In this time of transition, we as a species are starting to comprehend what spiritual teachers have been trying to tell us all
along: The Newtonian "laws" of the physical world only apply
to us here on earth when we do *not* apply higher spiritual laws.
The three-dimensional consciousness in which we now exist
operates under a certain set of assumptions and beliefs regarding the laws of life in the physical world. Higher levels of consciousness, on the other hand—that which we on Earth think of
as the "spiritual realms"—operate under more refined assumptions and beliefs. As we make this evolutionary shift, we are
gradually comprehending and putting into practice these
higher laws, and are thus taking on an entirely new perspective
as to how our world functions.

Many of the blessings we receive from Spirit—answers to
our prayers—are often well-disguised. At times they can only

be ascertained in retrospect. Other blessings, however, are easier to identify. Either way, they are gifts. It is not unusual for Spirit to grant us such a gift—one that is clearly from beyond the physical plane—that demonstrates to us the nature of true reality.

We often refer to these gifts as "miracles," or events that do not seem possible according to our normal, three-dimensional rules of awareness and the "laws" of nature. As they impact our awareness, they strongly impress upon us that there is so much more to reality than what we perceive from our five physical senses. In this way, miracles keep us strong in our faith and moving forward on our spiritual path.

Yet, the mind, accustomed to old ways of perceiving our world, has a hard time fitting miracles into everyday life. It is not easy to make sense of something that does not come from the world of logic and the five physical senses. And so, rather than allowing these gifts to make a radical change in our perspective on life, we will often simply relegate them to the realm of "very interesting coincidences," filing them away for when we need a good story to tell someone who's not too judgmental.

And perhaps there is a reason for this. We do not tend to allow for too many sudden changes in our personal paradigms. It takes time for us to acclimate to perceiving the physical world as one created primarily from thought—our own thoughts within the physical plane as well as the "thoughts" or visions from the world of the Great Mystery.

The concept that we create our reality with our thoughts is not new, yet culturally it is only now beginning to find a firm foothold in the core beliefs of humankind. As we allow ourselves to practice awareness of the concept that we are the creators of our lives, then the miracles that were once unexplainable cease to be so extraordinary. We become more comfortable with the physical results of the invisible projections of our thoughts. At the same time, we recognize the interactive nature of our own selves with the realm of Spirit, and we naturally accept, with increasing gratitude and a little less awe, gifts from the realm of that unseen world. It is often these gifts that propel us along our own path towards our magnificence.

To place our awareness and focus on something is to magnify it. This was my original intention in writing this book: To magnify—or have a greater appreciation of—God's miracles in my life. As we give our attention to the miracles and other good things in our lives, thinking of them with gratitude, contemplating their purpose in our lives, and sharing our wonder and enjoyment of them—their frequency increases, and we thus open the doors to a communicative interaction with the Great Mystery.

▲ ▲ ▲ ▲

I'd been involved with the community of people around Mary Thunder off and on for about two years. At that time, I did not yet know her well, as she was still "traveling on the road, following the Pipe, and teaching what she most needed to learn," according to the instructions of her elder, Grandma Grace Spotted Eagle. I was working on some of the boxes from the diagram of my Dream that addressed learning to function in a corporate world, and learning how to create prosperity. So, for a while I had put aside my goal of looking for the New Place. In the past, I had already scoured Arkansas, peeked around Oregon and Northern California, and had looked closely at Georgia and Florida. None quite had the qualities I was seeking. It needed to be a place that really called to me, a place I *knew* was home. It had to *feel* like a place of healing and peace. And I was certain that when I found it, there would be no doubt.

Now it was time to explore the mountains of North Carolina, not only for a much needed and long deserved vacation, but also in hopes of recognizing the spiritual home I had long sensed existed, but had not yet discovered.

Before leaving Houston, I called Thunder and asked if she

had any suggestions or instructions. Were there any people she thought I should look up? She mentioned a few friends in the area, then said to be sure to take some tobacco to the elders.

"What elders?" I asked.

She didn't answer. This wasn't unusual. You either caught what she said or you didn't. Time tended to prove the wisdom of paying attention. I wondered if she was referring to someone specific. I was going to the original home of the Cherokee. Perhaps she somehow knew I'd meet some elders, I thought.

I was traveling once again with my friend Susie, her daughter Lucy Morningstar, and Bart, another friend I had met through Thunder. We rendezvoused in Greensboro, picked up a rental car, and headed up to the northwestern end of North Carolina, then turned southwest on the Blue Ridge Parkway. We seemed to enter a land of enchantment as we wound our way along this old highway that traced now invisible Cherokee trails. The Blue Ridge is a road built during the New Deal days by hands grateful for work when conservation was important and 45 miles per hour was about as fast as anyone would ever think of driving.

At one bend in the road, there was a forest of rhododendron in a riot of pinks and fuchsias intermingled with shocking orange and magenta wild azaleas scattered here and there. At the next, we were suddenly ten feet from a thunderous waterfall tumbling down sheer cliffs so close to the road that all you needed to do was lean out the window to catch a little mist on your face. Every few miles, an overlook displayed a view of piles and piles of pristine green mountains, which appeared almost completely untouched by man, and stretched so far into the distance that they surely seemed to reach to the end of the world. The air was rich with scents of honeysuckle and wild roses and dank, dark, rich earth that probably contained as much life in it as any place on earth. Each breath was an intense, sensual delight. These were among the oldest mountains on this planet, one hundred and twenty-five million years older than the Rockies! How could this magical place have stayed so free of human contamination? God must have had a hand in it.

After a brief overnight stop on the outskirts of Asheville, we headed west towards the town of Cherokee, the tribal center of the Eastern band of Cherokee Indians. Since Thunder had instructed us to take tobacco to any elders we met, I thought perhaps we would make some important connections there. We picked up several packs of Bull Durham, a natural form of tobacco tied into little cotton bags. It was a preferred traditional gift for honoring those medicine people and elders who brought their wisdom and spiritual abilities to the people.

As we were driving towards Cherokee, we could see Mount Pisgah, named after the mountain on which Moses stood when he first saw the Promised Land. This Mount Pisgah was so named by an early explorer and preacher as he stood at its peak and surveyed the magnificent view of what is now Asheville, Hendersonville, and the Pisgah National Forest. I wondered if this would be my promised land as well.

63

As we threaded through the mountains, it seemed as if the ancient ways of the native people still somehow lived in every rock, every tree, and each waterfall. The town of Cherokee is one of the two remaining enclaves of the people who once called this area home. The Cherokee had been one of the tribes most adaptable and receptive to the settling of the Europeans, but in the process had compromised many of their own traditions. Ultimately, their friendly ways were met with betrayal. In 1838 the infamous Trail of Tears relocated most of the Cherokee to Oklahoma. Thousands died on this horrible, forced journey. The government's roundup of Cherokee for the relocation had sent those who escaped into hiding high in the Smokey Mountains along the border between North Carolina and Tennessee. One community remains basically secluded in the far western part of the North Carolina mountains. The other community in Cherokee and the surrounding Qualla Boundary has, to a great extent, adapted to western Carolina's booming tourist trade; at the same time, they have put great effort into resurrecting the ancient ways of their ancestors.

We pulled off the interstate and started the winding journey into Cherokee. I began to feel this incredible sense of *déjà vu*. It seemed as if I knew these hills, these trees, this path—no, road—down into the town. I couldn't shake the feeling of familiarity mixed with awe and a touch of sadness. Had I lived here in a past life? Were there some unknown relatives from these parts whose blood still ran in my veins? Many of the different Native American spiritual traditions encompass a belief that our ancestors continue to play important roles in our lives, helping us from the Spirit realm and passing on a consciousness and connection from generation to generation. I wasn't sure what the pull was that I was feeling, but it seemed as if the Spirit world was somehow closer to Earth in these hills. The merging of the spiritual into the physical that is inherent to most Native American traditions had always attracted me. It was very, very tangible here.

We were all feeling a heightened sense of awareness as we pulled into the town. Everything was a strange mix of old and new. Western-type boardwalks and old stores stood next to fast food hamburger joints. Vacationing families in matching T-shirts wandered by licking ice-cream cones as ancient wrinkled Indian men slowly, silently whittled and carved, bringing life and form to pieces of old driftwood from nearby streams. We parked the car and strolled around. Above one store, and extending to the peak of the mountainside behind it, was a sightseers' chair lift. Wanting to get an overview, we all hopped on board. The ride was a floating dance through wildflowers and butterflies as we swung up the mountainside. The journey down provided a spectacular view of the town, with the bustle of the tourists directly below. We could see a lively town event or fair off in the distance, and lush, green hills and streams merging to the edges of town in every direction.

I sensed a separation between the public, tourist-oriented part of town and the private, Indian part. It wasn't something I could see; it was more felt. The Cherokee people I met were entirely cordial, yet reserved. I wondered if their behavior reflected an on-going struggle to maintain their culture in the face of more than two centuries of relentless squeeze by the white culture and government, or perhaps it had to do simply with maintaining dignity while creating a living as a tourist attraction. I stretched my mind, trying to imagine what that would be like, and couldn't. It felt too invasive. Sadness and respect mingled with the awe and joy I already felt from these few days spent in the mountains.

We strolled the streets, poking our heads into one little store after another. At one end of the town we found the tribal museum. It wasn't very crowded, and we wandered in. The space was filled with very old craft work: Pipe bags beaded with intricate designs, quilled leather shirts, rattles and drums, blankets and pottery, all made with incredible precision, skill, and love. It felt as if we had walked through a time warp. There was no doubt that each of these items was sacred, each carrying the energy of many, many ancient ceremonies. We looked in silence, feeling as if we were walking on holy ground. It seemed as if we were in a portal to some other time.

Later we wandered over to another part of town, and suddenly found ourselves in the middle of a pow wow. It was the event we'd seen from the chairlift high above the town earlier that day. We watched the fancy dancers, decked out in magnificent costumes, with bright colors and ribbons and feathers and fringes, flying in all directions, bouncing to the beat of the drums. Then the eagle dancers began; no longer human beings, they perched on mountain peaks, surveyed the land below, strutted back and forth along the craggy ledges, then soared into the sky, the highest flying of all the winged ones.

Before we knew it, it was late afternoon, and the next morning we would be returning to Texas. Texas...it seemed so far

65

away. Susie wanted to get Lucy in bed early, so Bart and I decided to spend our last evening there taking a walk in the Smokey Mountain National Park. There was an entrance at the edge of the next town over, Bryson City.

It was early evening and still daylight as we pulled into the park. There weren't many people there on this beautiful, warm spring evening. It was surprising, but then it was nice to have the park to ourselves. We hiked up the trail to a stunning water-fall that tumbled down the mountain alongside the trail. I stared, amazed at the rock formations and the gnarled tree trunks; there were so many that resembled bears: Bear faces, bears standing, even bears climbing up the rocks in the water-fall. Each looked as if it had been intentionally carved. I turned to Bart next to me.

"Do you see what I see?"

He nodded. "Sure looks like bear country!"

And it was true. The Smokies are famous for being bear ter-ritory. Lapsing into silence, I pondered the interweaving of the spiritual and physical worlds which seemed so apparent here—somehow closer together. Could it be that the predomi-nance of bears in this area was actually reflected in the trees and the rocks? I thought of my Vision Quest, and how Nature seemed to have spoken to me very directly. How did the Great Mystery work, anyhow? Perhaps the spirit world, that unseen life-force beyond the third dimension, was much more respon-sive to interaction with the physical world than I had imagined.

We sat by the stream in silence for a while, taking in the full-ness that surrounded us. Then, in the gathering darkness, we headed back down the trail, musing aloud about how Thunder had asked us to take tobacco to the elders we had never met. Suddenly we saw what appeared to be a spotlight shining through the trees. Moving back and forth until we could see the light source, we were surprised to see that it was the full moon, which had just peeked over the ridge.

"I know," I said, feeling compelled to make completion on

66

Thunder's suggestion, "if we can't honor an elder in the physical, we can offer tobacco to Grandmother Moon!" Bart liked
the idea, noting that, in fact, we were surrounded by the
ancient ones in Spirit. They were in the rocks, the trees, everywhere. He felt moved to bring Thunder's greeting to them, and
pulled out the tobacco that he had been carrying in his pocket
for the last three days.

"Let's sing 'Nisa nisa'," I suggested, thinking we might make
a little more of a ceremony of the offering if we were to sing
the old Indian song that honors the moon. Bart laughed. He
was famous for a three note repertoire, and "Nisa" was usually
sung in a round. Usually, people did not ask him to sing. But
once in a while he sang pretty well, especially if he was singing
ceremonial songs. "OK," he took a deep breath. "I'll try."

Facing the moon, we offered some prayers with the tobacco,
thanking the Creator for our wonderful journey and all the
blessings we had received along the way. Then, sprinkling the
tobacco in front of us in the brush, we launched into the old
song honoring the moon.

As the sky was getting darker, the moon's brightness seemed
to intensify as it rose higher in the sky. We got the round going
quite nicely, and I was very impressed with how well Bart was
holding the tune, not to mention managing the round. As we
let go of our focus on the technique, we merged into the harmony of honoring and gratitude.

All of a sudden we noticed five or six fireflies coming from
the right along the edge of the path, just over the bushes closest to the trail. They were moving towards us, more or less in a
row, and what was remarkable was that they weren't flashing
on and off periodically as fireflies usually do, but rather, *were
keeping their lights on!* I'd never seen anything like it! They
slowed when they got a few feet away, just in front of us,
between where we were standing and the moon. There, they
seemed to "dance" in mid-air as we continued to sing! We
stopped singing in amazement.

67

"Look at that!" I exclaimed. But as soon as we stopped singing, their lights went out.

Right away we started singing again, and immediately they lit up again, dancing in front of us like little Disney cartoon characters! Then from the left, three or four more came, then a group appeared from deep in the woods directly in front of us and moved slowly towards us until they were barely two feet away!

As long as we sang, our little "fire-friends" continued to hover and dance in a bouncing little line before us. Periodically, a few more would join the party, as if they had just heard about it, or had a longer way to come, until there were about twenty-five or thirty fireflies dancing in the moonlight!

68

A couple of times we sang off key and once I felt irritated because I thought Bart wasn't doing his best to sing. Each of those times the fireflies' lights would go out, one by one. But when we cleared our minds and sang from our hearts, they were still right there, bobbing up and down to the music, their tiny lights staying on as long as we sang.

Immersed in the magic of what we were experiencing, we continued singing for about half an hour. Then, since it was getting late, and although our little friends were still dancing before us, we offered some more tobacco and, overwhelmed with gratitude, we started back down the path.

Our rent-a-car was the last vehicle left in the huge parking lot. Still in awe, we silently walked back to the vehicle and climbed in. Then, incredibly, as we pulled out of our parking space and headed for the exit, the whole parking area appeared to light up with a million sparklers. Thousands of fireflies flashed and sparkled and glittered as we stopped the car and stared! There was no way to make any sense of what we were beholding. We just watched. It didn't stop until we left.

Outside the gates of the park all was normal. Occasional fireflies dotted the drive back to town. I tried to bring logic into what had just occurred, but I could not. Finally, my mind gave up the effort and settled into receiving the gift. We drove in wonder out into the night. Later, I told the story to Thunder, and asked if she could give some kind of explanation for this incredible event. Her answer was simple:

"It's the Great Mystery. Don't think; just be grateful."

▲ ▲ ▲ ▲ ▲ ▲ ▲

The object of our attention becomes magnified in our reality. Think of the meaning of the words of Mother Mary when she said, upon first learning that she was to carry the child of God: "My soul doth magnify the Lord."

If we focus upon and feel grateful for the "good stuff" in our lives, soon our thoughts begin to create that good stuff as reality. Any action we take to "magnify" that which we like (or enjoy, or is beneficial) will only increase that focus in our experience, thus it becomes grounded into our reality. Here are some ways to do that:

1. List all of the miracles, large and small, that have happened in your life.

2. Think of the times in your life when you have received outright gifts from Spirit, or "carrots," that have encouraged you along your path in life. Spend some time thinking with pleasure about those gifts, and how those experiences have affected you in your life. To further magnify those experiences, write about them in detail.

3. What are the new directions in your life that are a result of the gifts you have received? Gifts of Spirit may not always be dancing fireflies; they may also manifest as the kindness of another person, something that turned out unexpectedly well, or some other kind of blessing.

69

THE REALM OF THE GREAT MYSTERY

DISCOVERING THE SOURCE AND
THE TEACHER IN DAILY LIFE

If we ask for growth, for understanding, and for awareness, they will be given to us. However, these changes do not all come in the form of visions in pink light and miracles of dancing fireflies—the little carrots held before us to inspire and lead us into our evolution. Rather, most transformative gifts of the Spirit come in the form of everyday challenges and tests. Opportunities to expand our consciousness appear constantly in the course of ordinary life, which offer all the opportunities for learning necessary for our evolution.

Yet daily life also tends to lull us into falsely believing that we know how things are. We create our lives into systems and patterns that become familiar, even comfortable, no matter how dysfunctional they may be. We form a primarily logical, left-brain view of life based on old, good/bad, right/wrong belief systems called "how it's always been." Once we have settled on a particular pattern and perspective in life, we tend to think we "know how it is." Although we don't realize it, we usually put a great deal of effort into controlling our environment so that it matches our old pictures.

Yet when we ask for growth, we are inherently requesting that old habits and ways of seeing things be broken. Any transformation at all implies a disruption of what is "known," and what is comfortable. It inevitably entails releasing the need to maintain old systems and old creations within our control. It requires giving up judgements and prejudices. Ultimately, this transformation sets us free into an untethered, "go with the flow" attitude.

Small children perceive the world this way. We can see it in their eyes—total, non-judgmental absorption of whatever comes into their field of vision. But slowly, slowly, as family and cultural issues and rules impress themselves upon the young mind, there is a natural attempt to start mentally and emotionally organizing reality accordingly. Even before a child is verbal, the concepts of "what life is like" begin to solidify.

For example, the tiny, new mind begins to notice that "This kind of cry brings Mama, but this other cry gets ignored." Or, "I can expect to get fed, but I can't get any help when I need to burp." Or, "These mushy diapers won't get changed until late in the morning, so I'd better learn to hold it all in." Before there are words to express them, the laws of living on Earth start forming in the mind. As we get older, we find similar situations and, seeing them through past perspectives, we create for ourselves realities such as, "I'll only be heard if I speak in this tone of voice" or, "Life will provide my basic needs, but I'm not going to get any nurturing" and, "What I want is not important, so I'd better keep things to myself."

Thus, it is no wonder that seeing with the eyes of a child tends to cease as time passes. Often, that degree of openness, vulnerability, and receptivity is not very comfortable. It involves letting go of some of the very "rules" and beliefs that have helped us to survive and function in the world. It is usually easier to discover these implicit family and cultural rules, and then try to live by them.

However, when we learn to cease our efforts to mold our environment into the prejudiced perspective of our unconscious mind, we return to the realm of wonder, of awe, of the Great Mystery. We take things as they come, without the filters of our learned beliefs. We allow Life to become the teacher, so that *each new experience offers new information* instead of being perceived and mentally catalogued according to past experiences. As we practice this release of control, we also allow Spirit to be active in our lives, for we do not pre-classify the messages and miracles we receive as something mundane. Gradually, we open to the concept that all things are of Spirit, and therefore every event and each person is an aspect and gift of Spirit.

If we are serious about our growth, we will go beyond overcoming our resistance to Life's lessons; we will seek out ways to expand, ways to see with new eyes. To help open ourselves in this way, we may find a teacher who can support our work. If we are wise and intuitive in choosing our teachers, we will find those who see the magnificence within us, as well as our resistance to our own evolution, those who have walked their own growth, and are skilled in guiding us through the unseen recesses of our psyche. Such teachers show us not what to see, but *how* to see for ourselves with new eyes.

The new direction in consciousness brings back into balanced use the appropriate application of right-brain, emotional, and intuitive processes. It involves entering the realm of the Great Mystery—that which is out of our control and beyond our understanding—and allowing virtually every experience in life to be seen as an action or aspect of Spirit. When we conceptualize God, or the Creator, or the Universe as "The Great Mystery," we automatically allow the unknown, the mystery, the miracles, the wonder to exist in our lives. We let go of prejudice, pigeonholing and control, and we are better able to receive new directions, experiences, and growth. No matter what religion serves as our base, this new awareness always entails letting go of all that we think we know, accepting both the limitations and the limitlessness of our humanity, and becoming "as little children," so that we might genuinely "enter into the kingdom of heaven."

▲ ▲ ▲ ▲

After the firefly experience, I began spending more and more time with Mary Thunder. The group of people close to her became my new spiritual family. I perceived within Thunder a great wisdom, and asked if she would be my teacher. Bless her heart, I wonder if she knew what she was taking on! She became my introduction to the Great Mystery, and my honing stone for sharpening my awareness and skills in allowing the Mystery to weave Its miracles into my life. Thunder is called by her elders an "Iyeska"—a Spirit Speaker or Spirit Interpreter. She sees many things about people, such as their original "blueprint" or purpose and direction in life. While she does not reveal this, she said to me one day when I had asked about it, "Every day we are healing closer to the blueprint of the stars!" Like many things she said, it left me pondering a greater perspective for my life. The more time I spent with her the more I saw how inexorably her life was merged with the world of Spirit.

Through Thunder, I gradually began to grasp how to experience daily life as my teacher and spiritual Source, to see that God is not a separate or distant entity, but an integral aspect of normal human existence. For a long time I tried to define exactly what Thunder did that was so different, and so effective, but I simply couldn't put my finger on it. As much as I tried to identify, classify, or otherwise explain to myself how she worked, I could not fit what she did into any category with which I was familiar. I kept trying to break down what she did into techniques or processes that I could dissect and duplicate, but it was quite some time before I began to let go of my own old pictures enough to see. As far as I could tell, hers just looked like everyday life, with ceremonies offered from time to time.

Yet around Thunder, people changed and grew. They became stronger, more gentle, and more loving. I was profoundly touched by the integrity, the honesty, and the willingness of the people close to her to work on themselves and their issues. I was inspired by the depth of their commitment to their spiritual work. I saw healings occur often, on the physical, mental,

73

emotional, and spiritual levels. It wasn't uncommon; it was part of Thunder's way of life.

While Thunder herself had received teachings from many different spiritual traditions, her natural, Native American, intuitive, "go with the flow" approach remained illusive to me for a long time. It wasn't the disciplined structure I knew from my Christian upbringing and Eastern meditation training, but my mind still kept struggling to fit it into a structure. There seemed to be no rules, no specific steps to enlightenment, and no commandments, as such.

Intuition seemed to be the basis for most choices and decisions made by the people who had been around Thunder for a while. For example, they lived on what they called "Indian Time," which meant that things were done when it "felt right." Most plans were preceded by a "maybe," which allowed for any changes that might be wrought by Spirit. I would show up at an appointed time for some event, and everyone else seemed to somehow know to show up one or perhaps two hours later, which would turn out to be exactly the right time. This certainly wasn't a place to bring your Daytimer!

My training in psychology didn't fit here either. In fact, I was told in no uncertain terms to leave that at home. At first I was insulted, but gradually I realized that Thunder was helping me to let go of my preconceived ideas. Over and over again, thinking I had an understanding of a person or a situation, I would discover that some apparently casual comment made earlier by Thunder (which I had considered to be completely mistaken) turned out to be exactly correct. Slowly I became aware of her uncanny ability to read people and her ability to predict their behavior. In many ways, Thunder seemed to be as much of a great mystery as the Creator who led her life. As a teacher, she explained almost nothing. In time I came to recognize that she *lives* her truth, demonstrating constantly the interaction between Spirit and human, between the Mystery and perceived reality.

Awareness seemed to be the key word in this community of new friends. When I told Thunder that I meditated, she explained to me that "walking meditation" was her practice, which simply meant keeping clarity of mind in the midst of the activities of service. This was not the kind of sitting meditation that involved shutting out the world that I had practiced years before. Rather, it was about becoming so quiet inside that one was able to perceive an infinite amount of information coming from the world around—from nature, from animals, from individuals, from groups, from Spirit. It meant letting go of those preconceived ideas and being open, being discerning, being able to see.

Thunder once said, "Little things are the stuff of our lives, moment to moment. It's not a question of importance; it's a question of paying attention, of being aware. Why? Because each moment in life is absolute in itself. That's all there is." I was amazed at how present Thunder always seemed to be. "Always be in the *now*, Carolyn," she would often say. Sometimes I would watch her watching others; even in the most intense situation she would appear relaxed, her mind quiet, and every sense alert and in complete attendance to what was happening before her.

The people closest to Thunder were called her "Warriors." With my non-violent yoga background, I found this to be a strange concept. Yet I came to understand that a warrior was not necessarily someone with good fighting skills, but rather someone who had mastered the art of awareness. "Peace Keeper" is what Thunder had been called by one of her elders, and I saw her teaching this to her warriors. Instead of fighting, they protected and kept the peace through wise and appropriate action, and by wisely "disarming" negativity often through the use of humor.

Oh, the humor. How they would laugh and laugh and laugh! I had never thought of laughter as a spiritual practice, but here it clearly was. Thunder wrote to me one time when I asked her to describe herself, "I am an event led by Spirit. I wake people

75

up, take them on an adventure, illuminate people, enchant them, share with tremendous happiness major truths and good laughs. I am getting closer and closer every day to myself—and to having fun with responsibility!"

And it was true. Mistakes were not analyzed, punished, or judged. Seeing with the unprejudiced eyes of a child, Thunder would discover and delight in whatever might be humorous about a person's errors. She would turn these lessons into the funniest stories I've ever heard. The stories were then told and retold, getting funnier and funnier each time, until the person who had made the mistake lost all shame in the error, as well as any desire to ever repeat it again. This was a path of humanness, acceptance, and love. Slowly, slowly, my logical way of seeing the world began to give way to the path of intuition and of "going with the flow." As time passed, I began to learn to allow and accept that which came into my reality, rather than to judge, plan, resist, and otherwise control.

It was only with time, as I put aside assessing Thunder's work in psychological terms, that I began to see what a genuine and close working relationship she has with the Creator. Over and over again I would ask her, "How did you do that?" or, "How did you know?" Countless times, with the patience of a saint, she would say, "It wasn't me, it was Spirit." Slowly, I began to see that Thunder really did turn to Spirit in all matters in life. Gradually, she brought it to my awareness that the healings and changes that occurred around her were not at all a matter of human interaction, but rather the interaction between human and Spirit.

Thunder's own mind, emotions, heart, soul, and being are so completely connected to Spirit, that even her personal, human side is a gift to others if they allow themselves to see her that way. In fact, there are times when she shares about her own weaknesses, addictions, and negative emotions as lessons in her teaching. Unlike most spiritual teachers I have met, who tend to either hide their weaknesses or be in denial about them,

Thunder is incredibly vulnerable. She sometimes uses herself as a mirror for others to heal themselves, openly sharing her personal feelings with immaculate timing. Thunder's sharing is not one of "dumping" but of offering personal experience in just the moment that will benefit and be heard by the ones who have ears to hear. When she is excited, she bubbles over with childlike joy. When she is hurt, she cries, no matter who is watching. When she is angry, she says so. When she makes a mistake, she apologizes. As a spiritual teacher, she does not pretend that her human side doesn't exist, but instead shares and embraces it.

Thunder also brings out the Divine in those around her. So often, when people think they are absolutely at their limit and can't possibly go one step further, do one more dish, stay awake for another second, or love for one more moment, she has a way of demonstrating to them the absolute illusion of their limitations. Her faith in the Great Mystery clearly carries her—and others as well—through one situation after another.

For instance, when Thunder was considering the purchase of the Thunder-Horse Ranch—when she first walked on the land—she had thirty-eight cents to her name! With absolutely no financial backing, and with Spirit as her only Resource, she decided to buy the property anyway. She, too, had a dream of a "New Place." She had been on the road for nine years at the behest of her elders—teaching and sharing, offering sacred ceremonies, and following the Pipe. Her vision was to create a Spiritual University, "a place for her elders and for teachers of all colors to come to share, a place where people of all cultures could come take a drink of spirituality, and perhaps take it home and put it to good use in their own lives." She saw it as a healing place, a ceremonial place, and foremost, "a home for the Spirit."

I resonated with her dream, and while Thunder was making plans to buy the land that is now the Ranch, I wanted to help. I took the day off and went out to see the proposed new property.

Now, I like to think that I have excellent intuition on real estate. As I pulled onto the land, I didn't like the feel of it at all! It was barren and dry, the wind whipping dirt devils around the parched property like ominous little tornadoes. The property was surrounded by areas that had been drilled for oil and natural gas, and the land looked as if it had been raped. The owner had a few cows grazing on the land, but for all the forty-three acres, you could see that he brought hay in to supplement their diet. That's how sparse the greenery was. The only trees were gnarled, half-bare cedars and some very dead-looking live oaks. Fire ants clearly ruled the territory. There were three partially completed houses on the land; whatever had been planned for this property had been abandoned mid-stream, like a small ghost town. *I did not like the looks of it one bit!* In fact, it was spooky.

"What do you think?" Thunder asked me later.

"DON'T buy it!" was my emphatic answer. In fact, I argued with her, and did my very best to get her to keep looking elsewhere. Finally, one day, when it seemed apparent that she was not following my expert real estate advice—and I did have a pretty good track record—I turned to her and asked:

"Did Spirit tell you to buy this land?" (I was starting to get the drift of how she works.)

She smiled that cherubic smile of hers, and nodded.

Oh. What could I say to that? Nothing. She was probably right, because she usually was, although I surely couldn't see it yet. I just shook my head.

That was in 1989, and she is still there today. Miraculously, the land is lush and green, filled with wildflowers well into the summer, with ponds and gardens here and there, a gentle Quan Yin garden of statues and flowers near the house, a Sweat Lodge tucked away over in the cedar forest, a medicine wheel and a beautiful women's lodge down by the big lake. There are dogs, cats, ducks, horses, peacocks, and even three buffalo, the symbol for nourishment for the people.

The Thunder-Horse Ranch became a working model for my own dream. I did everything I could to help the Ranch prosper and grow. Each time I went to visit, I would hand Thunder a hundred dollar bill, even when I didn't have a hundred dollars to spare! Some part of me was beginning to have faith, to trust that the stretching of my own limitations was bringing benefit to myself and to others. The more I gave towards this spiritual work, the greater was my own return. It seemed mysterious at first, but I became accustomed to this basic principle of abundance. The Ranch became my model for community, for people learning to live together harmoniously, for families healing their dysfunction, for trusting the Creator. Through my service to Thunder's Spirit vision, my own dream was being refined and honed.

Sometimes, being around Thunder was difficult; the experience stretched the edges of my reality to their limits. Other times it were outrageously funny or profoundly inspiring. But spending time with her was always an unfolding of the incredible mystery of how Spirit works in our lives.

I discovered Thunder to be universal and ecumenical in her spirituality, although her Indian heritage has remained the core of her ceremonial practice. Generally, the Native American spiritual way is not separate from the culture. Unlike the separation of church and state that is the basis for American culture, there can be no such division of the secular and the spiritual for Indian people. Thunder constantly demonstrated to me that life is life of the Spirit, life connected to the Earth, life as a part of the people, all the people. As I got to know her, I saw that she taught by her example the meaning of *Mitakuye Oyacin*, or "all my relations." It is the "Amen" that acknowledges the interconnectedness and oneness of all life, all people, all animals and plants, and even the rocks, the sky, the wind—the Consciousness that runs through all things.

In the path Thunder walks, those honored as the ones with knowledge, the ones to emulate, are not those who have had the time and money to attend four or six or eight years at college, but rather, they are the Elders—those whose wisdom come from their own years of personal work and their own connection to Spirit. The Elders and the children are considered to be the wise ones for they, in the end and beginning of life, are the closest to the Great Spirit. Far from being hidden away in old age homes and day care centers, they are more likely to be cared for in the home by the extended family, whether related by blood or not. The elders and the children are both respected and regarded as very worthy, contributing members of the community.

As I spent more and more time around Thunder, I became aware that she is greatly respected by her elders—Leonard Crow Dog, Rolling Thunder, The Chipps Family, Grandpa Wallace, Grandma Grace Spotted Eagle, and Grandma Twylah Nitsch—for her integrity and her honor of the Sacred Pipe. She was once the assistant to the mayor of Indianapolis, but left that world to be a drug and alcohol counselor for the Inter-Tribal Council of Dallas. She participated in The Long Walk and many other events in which Indian people sought to join together to bring awareness to the abuses that were—and still are—going on.

Years before I met her, Thunder experienced her first Sweat Lodge with Grandpa Fools Crow, who heated the entire lodge with one cold stone. He told her not to weep because she had been abandoned as an infant by her mother, but rather to give thanks to her real mother—Mother Earth. Thunder has shared ceremony and been friends with legendary people who took a stand at the Second Battle of Wounded Knee in 1973, some who spent years in prison for speaking the truth, and many who have overcome unfathomable obstacles and indignities in order to protect the culture and traditions of their people. She tells of many of these experiences in her book, *Thunder's Grace* (Station Hill Press, 1995).

One time I asked Thunder if her walk on the spiritual path had given the answers to her problems. She seemed pensive for a moment, then looked me in the eye with great clarity and said, "What it has given me is character." Part Mohawk, part Cheyenne, part Irish, and adopted Lakota, she has sometimes been criticized for not being full-blood, for being a woman, and for teaching universal principles as she does. Yet she has never wavered from her path. She has danced in over twenty-five Sun Dances, one of the most difficult and transformative of ceremonies. Her name, "Thunder," means "truth," and she seems always to be able to express it in a way that it can be best understood by those she is with in the moment.

I once heard Leonard Crow Dog, her Sun Dance Chief and adopted uncle, call Thunder "a Teacher of the Teachers and a Healer of the Healers." She is gentle, but she can also be tough. I have watched her breathe deeply and let go of some of the most hurtful and disrespectful treatment imaginable the moment it happens. Yet she will not shy away from confrontation if it will be of benefit to someone.

Thunder always teaches people to be respectful of the old ways. Because of this, many elders have come to visit the Thunder-Horse Ranch to share their wisdom. For many years she danced alone, but in recent years, at her elders' request, she has taken a small group of people to the Sun Dance, people who over time have demonstrated their willingness to put aside their own ideas, and to be quiet, observant, and to honor the ancient traditions. More than anything else, those who enjoy the privilege of being with Thunder are those who have a heartfelt desire to serve.

Service is the means by which Thunder teaches: Make a meal that everyone loves, clean the house to get rid of all the old energy, water the flowers, play with the children—each job is turned into a gift if one is willing to look. I came to see that Thunder has an amazing way of turning everyday situations of life into growth experiences. If you hate to cook, you may find yourself in the kitchen, delighting in the creation of some gourmet experience. If you don't like children, you may suddenly find yourself in the middle of a game of tag or hide-n-seek, giggling and acting silly with the youngest of the bunch. If you hate to file, there will be a mile high pile of file folders waiting for you somewhere. This last task was mine; the Ranch staff laughed at my "fear of filing" until I actually found it pleasurable to create order in Thunder's endless stacks of interesting stuff.

I learned that if I prayed to heal a certain issue, somehow I would find myself in an experience of service which brought that issue to the surface for healing. Whatever I didn't like or feared was exactly what I got to do—until I surrendered and my aversion to it disappeared, at which time it would miraculously become someone else's job! "Action in service is the answer," Thunder would say, "and service must come from the core of your heart!" Thunder is not called a "Spirit Speaker" for nothing! If you are near her, the Creator is working in your life. If you are near her, you are learning about your *own* connection to the Great Mystery.

When Thunder leads a gathering, "joy and celebration" are the focus. Yet she has little use for "bliss-ninnies" and those whose idea of spirituality includes selfishness, judgement, exclusive beliefs, or a lack of responsibility. Once I heard her say, in response to a couple of people who were sitting around at a gathering doing nothing but criticizing and complaining, "Leave your attitudes at the gate when you enter, for it is only your own attitude that keeps you out of service. There is only one attitude here, and that's mine! I have been trained by the greatest attitudes in the world, so if you came here to 'run' this gathering with your attitude, then know I can out-attitude you." And she can. She can match anyone at their game, yet she always has a way of turning that game into growth and benefit for her "opponent." At her gatherings, people learn, grow, confront their issues and fears, and somehow end up thinking it was all part of the fun.

I have so many memories of gatherings and sacred ceremonies orchestrated by Thunder, in which I thought I was just

going to help out, but my life was changed instead. I remember
Leonard Crow Dog holding hot red coals in his mouth as he
prayed and did healings on the people; Dennis Banks and
Buddy Red-Bow chanting and singing while joining Thunder
and Horse in marriage; William Baker joyfully dancing on his
toes as dawn peeked through the tent windows after an all-
night ceremony; Charles Chipps talking from his "feminine
side" to the women Sun Dancers; Grandma Kitty welcoming
hundreds of guests to the opening of Wolf-Song II Gathering of
Peace Elders; Grandma Twylah Nitsch, always available by
phone when Thunder needed *her* honing stone; Luciano Perez,
the compassionate warrior, averting potential disruption with
split-second timing and peaceful words of patience and kindness; Tsultrim Allione spinning, spinning, spinning the Chud
rattle in the ancient Tibetan ceremony; my happy friends coming out of the Sweat Lodge where they'd had a vision of a dove
and an eagle after Horse's first "Men's Role, Men's Soul"
Workshop; the perfect buffaloes in the clouds and the triple
rainbow over our camp after the opening rounds of the Sun
Dance at Crow Dog's Paradise the year Thunder, by her Elders'
instructions, brought in the first group of white people to serve;
and finally, watching from the corner of my eye as Thunder,
Mother of the Sun Dance, edged up to me from the side in the
Sun Dance Arbor to say with a kind and twinkling smile,
"You've been busted for your glasses," thus leading me into yet
another level of surrender as I faced four days of dancing virtually blind. There are so many other memories, too. And who
was always there, who was running the energy, gathering the
people, making the arrangements, making sure everyone and
everything was OK, who made it happen? It was always Mary
Thunder.

She, however, always gives the credit to Spirit.

Thunder teaches people how to bring their fantasy into reality by learning to control their thoughts and hold clear pictures
of their dreams. She teaches people that their emotions are the

83

worst of all addictions, and helps them to move out of old patterns. "Walk your talk," she says. "Let your actions match your words." She teaches people, by her example, how to love and nurture both themselves and others.

Somehow, in my life, I had missed this concept of self-nurturing. I was told at one point that I might have breast cancer, and I turned to Thunder for help. She was always incredibly patient and kind with me. There was never a time when I looked into her eyes and didn't see immense love. Breasts, Thunder explained to me, represent nurturing, femaleness, gentleness. At some level, I had been trying to kill myself off rather than nurture myself. Thunder did a Sacred Ceremony of Stone People's Lodge—a Sweat Lodge—for my healing.

As part of my preparations for the healing, she told me to go get a cedar branch, and to wrap the stem in red cloth. I picked out a branch, a dried and gnarled one, and knotted a scrap of fabric on the end. When I handed it to her, she looked at me with surprise and said, "This is what you think of yourself; this branch is gnarled, with thorns, and it would bruise you. Now I am going to take pity on you and get another branch that is soft and without thorns, for this is what I will be using to brush out the illness that you have put into yourself." Then she asked Horse to go and find a soft branch. He did this, and he also lovingly braided a red cloth onto the stem. After the Sweat Lodge, she softly brushed my breasts with the cedar branch, and I felt as if something was taken out, and that I was healed.

Then Thunder had me run for a while up to the end of the land and back. For the first time, I felt a connectedness with the ground below me, with the original nurturer of all, Mother Earth. I remember that, as I ran, I looked back at Thunder and saw that sweet smile on her face and little tears running down her cheeks. In my life, she was the one to teach me about nurturing, and I realized how much I loved this woman, and how deeply grateful I was to her.

After the Sweat Lodge, Thunder gave me several exercises to

do to help integrate my healing from cancer: I wrote about my resentments and cleared them. I ran the length of a room and jumped into a pile of pillows while another woman was there to support me. (I kept hurting myself until I simply let go and allowed the pillows to catch me in their fluffy bosoms.) I spent some time cooking in my kitchen—blindfolded. I didn't like that one bit! No control. Yet something started to let go and I began to sense an inner space from which I could start to nurture myself. I thanked Thunder for putting so much energy into helping me learn how to care for myself. Of course, once again, she told me to thank the Great Mystery.

The next year I went through a period of doubting whether I'd actually been healed, because I had never received a medical confirmation. Thunder asked me, "Do you still have thoughts of dying or of breast cancer?" "No," I answered, and I realized that the possibility of still having cancer was not even part of my doubt. "If you have been healed of those thoughts, then you will not have breast cancer."

I pondered that, and realized though I had doubted the miracle of the healing, I had never once since that Sweat Lodge thought that the breast cancer would return. I knew I didn't and wouldn't ever have cancer. It was then that I understood, and I thanked her again. "It's not me," she replied as she often did. "Thank the Spirit." Shortly thereafter, *Woman's World* did a story on Thunder; they quoted me about my healing experience with her, and how the mental and emotional were also part of the physical healing work she did with Spirit.

As I gradually stopped attempting to analyze what made Thunder so effective, I became more aware of the way in which she related to the Great Mystery. I saw how often she stopped to listen inside for what felt right. I noticed that when things weren't going as planned, she seemed to shift gears quickly and pay close attention to how Spirit might be redirecting the course of events. I observed how her intent was always to serve Spirit and the people, and how she constantly utilized daily events to that end. I also saw that when she received guidance from Spirit, she seemed to follow it absolutely and without hesitation, no matter how illogical or inconvenient it might seem at the time.

For example, sometimes Thunder sent a person on a mission of some sort that seemed to be about one thing, but, in the end it was about something completely different. These "missions" sometimes appeared to be a "favor" for Thunder or service to Spirit, but usually turned out to be a blessing to the one in service, and more often than not, were an answer to that person's prayers. Yet, to see this, one has to look. One has to be in awareness. One has to suspend judgement and be open to receive.

In time, I came to see that whatever energy I put out in service around Thunder invariably came back ten-fold. Every single time I sponsored an event for Thunder at my Center in Houston, when publicizing my own work was the last thing in my mind, I would meet someone who would become a new client, or who would want to take one of my workshops. Once, I helped her set up a television appearance, and ended up being interviewed myself as well. In helping to edit her new book, I received countless ideas and inspirations for my own book. It seemed that every time I did something to help Thunder, an unanticipated gift was returned to me from Spirit.

One time Thunder was doing a series of programs in Houston. I was chauffeuring her and Horse around while they were in town. On the day before they were to leave, they had a whole series of errands and stops to make, and we darted from here to there, laughing and talking about all the things that had happened in the past few days.

But I was having trouble with my car; the clutch kept slipping and I was seriously concerned about whether I'd be able to get them back that evening to the house where they were staying. Miraculously, we made it, although the clutch was all the way to the floor by the time I dropped them off and returned home.

The next morning I didn't give the clutch any thought when

I drove over to say goodbye to Thunder. As I stepped out of the car, I noticed a pack of tobacco on the passenger's seat; I brought it in to Thunder, thinking she'd left it there by mistake. She just smiled, saying that she had prayed with the tobacco and left it in my car on purpose. She suggested that I tuck it away in some corner of the vehicle. I thanked her and turned my attention to all the Houston friends gathered together to hear a few more good stories before Thunder and Horse left. But when I got back in my car to head home, I realized that the clutch was back to normal! In fact, I never had trouble with that car as long as I owned it. I thought about it for a long time. Was this a coincidence? I didn't think so! It seemed that my experiences around Thunder always left me pondering the Great Mystery.

▲▲▲▲▲▲▲

Our daily life provides us with a constant interaction with the Great Mystery. This interaction *appears* to be taking place with other human beings. What people and situations in your life have worked beneficial changes in your life?

1. Who are some of the people who have impacted your life, who have been instrumental in key changes along your path?

2. Think of five or six situations where events in your daily life became the catalyst for your personal growth.

3. Write about several times when you have been in the realm of the unknown, when things have felt unstable and uncontrolled, that have been major turning points in your spiritual life.

4. List all of the "good things" that you can think of which have happened in your life. (This may take more than one sitting!) Thank God (Spirit, Creator, Great Mystery, or God as you understand God to be) in your own way for each of those good things.

·6·

A RELUCTANT TRAINEE

MEETING THE RESISTANCE OF OUR
VICTIM-CONSCIOUSNESS

Most of us would like to be perfectly magnanimous and good, but in fact, we are all perfectly human. We are all magnanimous and good sometimes, and at other times we all have fears, make mistakes, and have ways—sometimes hidden even to ourselves—in which we manipulate and try to control others. We each tend to cling blindly to old concepts of how we ought to act in order to be "good," "acceptable," "nice," or "spiritual." The stronger the injunction about what we must do in order to have value, the more we tend to disguise the ways and reasons we have when we cannot or do not live up to those injunctions. Invariably, we shut down our growth when we lock into these old, self-perpetuating systems.

The most limiting of old belief systems is the one that says that we are not responsible for what occurs in our lives. Unaware of the creative power of our unmonitored thoughts, we settle for, "I just can't seem to..." and, "If it weren't for..." and, "I would if only..." Such statements become the final seal on what we allow ourselves to create, and we tend to look no further. We would like to believe we are victims of someone else's inconsistencies and unkindness or, at minimum, to our "lot in life." *In choosing to perceive that other people, circumstances, or God are the reason for things we don't like, we allow ourselves to avoid examining our own actions.*

Sometimes we don't like to think that we are responsible for what occurs in our lives. That thought can be painful! To look at how we have created the unpleasant and negative things in our lives means we have to take responsibility for either changing them or being satisfied with keeping them the way they are. It is much easier to simply close our minds to our participation and assign the fault to someone or something else. This form of denial is so pervasive—and so human—that it is firmly grounded in the belief systems of our culture.

Denial is a powerful emotional mechanism that keeps us seeing ourselves as powerless and thus unable to create a different reality for ourselves. As long as we maintain the perspective that the "other guy did it to us," or that "we can't help it," we can give ourselves permission to avoid deep introspection and effective actions toward growth. Hiding safely in this victim-consciousness, we can effectively resist for years the very changes we say we would like to have in our lives.

Facing how we create that which we *think* we do not want can be scary. Every fiber of our being is set up to resist the mirrors that reflect the need for change. Twenty-year CDs, thirty-year mortgages, forty-year retirement plans, and "til death do us part" vows suggest a core belief that things will not change. Sometimes, we just want to close our eyes and ears and attempt to continue life as it always used to be, even if it wasn't comfortable or satisfying. More often than not, we choose to deal with the crisis when it hits instead of when it is merely knocking at our door. Even then, it is not unusual to still want to assign the responsibility elsewhere. It is very human and normal to resist change, to resist growth, to attempt to bring ourselves back to a state of stasis. Thunder once said to me, "Keep resisting your resistances, and you will find yourself. Life is a drama, and we write the script!"

"What about situations such as a robbery, a rape, or an accident, where you don't even know the other person?" is the question inevitably raised.

"Look closer," I say, "look closer." Listen closely to the thoughts, the mindtalk, the fears running in the background of

89

your consciousness. Not too far under the surface are beliefs and worries that these things will happen. These thoughts, conscious or subconscious, act as a magnet for the events we visualize—positive or negative. We are all much more psychic than we acknowledge in our culture. If we are afraid of anger, we will draw angry people to us. If we are worried about cancer, it could manifest. If we organize our world around avoiding being controlled, we will somehow manage to gather around us intensely controlling people. Unaware of the subconscious way in which we create these things, we then perceive ourselves to be the victim—victim of another person, or victim of circumstances.

Styles of victim-consciousness vary from person to person. However, what tends to remain constant is the belief that we are not responsible for the reality we create. We blame others in our lives for being too dominating, too needy, too manipulative, or too unsupportive, without ever looking at how we not only choose these people to be in our lives, we also encourage those traits in them we most detest. Often we simply create an energy vacuum with our thoughts through the negative picturing of our victim-consciousness. This vacuum actually draws abuse or unwanted behavior out of other people. If the other person doesn't give us what we want—show up on time, tell the truth, listen to what we are saying, have sex when we want it—how often do we blame that person, and how often do we ask ourselves what we might be doing to foster that behavior?

This is *not* to say that we are to blame or are responsible for others, any more than they are for us. It is to say that what we experience as our reality is much more our own creation than we realize. There *is* an answer to "Why does this keep happening to me?"

We all have the ability to overcome the limiting beliefs and victim perspectives that keep us from fully embracing who we are and who we can be. We make a bold step towards owning our personal power when we ask ourselves, *without blame,*

"How did I participate in creating this?" or, "In what ways am I responsible for this situation and in what ways am I not?" On the other side of this challenge is a greater sense of our Self and of the magnificence we can be as individuals, as well as our contribution to a more evolved and effective species.

When we are ready for growth, it is not unusual for us to create a catalyst to help us move away from our old habits and patterns, and towards our vision—walking towards it with conviction, power, and love. A part of us may want change but, invariably, another part desires the comfort of what we have always known, no matter how useless or detrimental that may be.

Therefore, catalysts for change are often blessings in disguise. They will ultimately benefit our lives, but they sure may not seem to at the time. A catalyst for growth is sometimes as simple as a kind person in our lives, or a prayer, but quite often it comes in the form of an argument, a catastrophe, or a loss of some sort that forces us to examine how we are living. At times, the catalyst can be someone we bring into our lives who holds up a mirror so we can see how we have locked ourselves into old ways; how we are actually resisting the growth we want.

The hand of the Creator works with us in the unfolding of our vision, our creation, in fulfilling our greater purpose on Earth. So often we say a little prayer: "Help me with this, Lord," only to have that help come in a way we neither expected nor imagined. Whether we realize it or not, that prayer is indeed a request for help in moving through areas in which we have been resistant. It is a plea for assistance with what we'd rather avoid: Breaking through our own denial, useless habits, and outmoded interpretations of our reality.

▲ ▲ ▲ ▲

My own prayers for growth were answered, in part, through my choice of Mary Thunder as a teacher and a powerful catalyst for change in my life. They were also answered through her compassion and love, in that she was willing to play those roles with me.

Later in the year, after my trip to North Carolina and my experience with the fireflies, I was sitting in my back yard in Houston, ankle-deep in autumn leaves—oranges, yellows, greens, reds, and browns. I liked this big old house, with its shady green yard, in the quiet University part of town. It was my home, my office, and the Center I had finally created—another one of those boxes in the Dream plan achieved. Thunder had been the first one to present a program at the Center the year before, a Pipe Ceremony that was both a blessing for the new Center and a celebration and gathering of her Houston friends and supporters. As usual, her presence energized the Center, and it had been a year of many successes.

This house, and Houston itself, had served me well. But as I scuffed my feet through the crackly leaves that surrounded me, it felt as if the city itself were crowding in to crush me from all sides. Memories of the country, the mountains, the woods, the fresh running streams, and the thick pungent scents of countless growing things all gnawed at my mind and left me feeling discontented. When would I find the New Place? Where was it? North Carolina had been nice, but I was certain I would *know* beyond a shadow of a doubt when I found the right place. And I didn't *know*. The only thing I did know was that the New Place called to me, and I had no idea where it was. I looked at the leaves below me, then out to the skyline of the massive Houston Medical Center to the east, then back to the leaves.

"I don't know where I'm going," I suddenly said to myself, "but I'm going. I'm not putting it off any longer. Maybe I'll go up to Arkansas, or perhaps I'll head for Oregon and check out that locale a little more, along with anything that's between here and there. Maybe explore more of North Carolina. Or maybe just hit the road and see where it takes me." Then it occurred to me, "Ah! Maybe I'll ask Thunder what she thinks."

I headed out to the Thunder-Horse Ranch the next day. It was Saturday, which meant there would be a Sweat Lodge—a good time to purify, pray, and get clarity. Besides, I knew that talking with Thunder would, as usual, provide some insight into what direction I might go. She rarely gives direct answers, but usually says something that is a key in some way—if you're listening closely. Whatever she might say, I was ready. I wanted to be in Nature. I wanted to get started with the Dream. I never expected the answer that she gave.

"Maybe it's time for you to move here to the Ranch," Thunder suggested. I was amazed. I had wanted to serve on staff with her for a long time. Now that I had pretty much given it up, I was being offered the opportunity. Even before she and Horse had bought the Ranch, while they were still living on the road, I had wanted to learn from this woman. I would watch those who traveled with her, and others who had been around her for a long time. They seemed to move in service to others with such joy, such ease. I wanted that.

93

When Thunder presented me with the opportunity to join her staff at the Ranch, all the other options disappeared instantly. I was so excited! Perhaps now I would learn her secrets; perhaps now some of that wisdom would rub off on me. I didn't give it a second thought. We began making plans for my move right away. I would rent out most of the Center in Houston, and maintain a single office so that I could go back and see my clients for a couple of days every two weeks. The idea was very workable, and seemed to meet both my need to move to the country and my desire to continue learning from this unique woman.

As we lay flopped on Thunder's bed, talking about some of the details of my move, it looked as if everything was falling into place with incredible simplicity. Then she made a statement that seemed to be in passing, and I might have missed it had I not been so intent upon garnering every detail. "It's a year commitment," she told me, "but don't think badly of yourself if you don't get to do the whole time." That was an odd statement, I thought.

"Oh, don't worry," I countered, taking it almost as lightly as she had said it. "I won't leave." She just smiled her loving smile, and moved on to discussing the preparations. But her statement kept coming back to haunt me. Why would she have said something like that? I pondered it for a while, but soon forgot about it in the excitement of the pending changes.

I imagined a retreat situation in a little bungalow not far from the main house and office. Perhaps my room would overlook the fields and the wildflowers, and I would awake each morning to the birds singing. Maybe I would have time to meditate on a regular schedule while living here at the edge of beautiful, Texas hill country. I imagined doing ceremonies each day, listening to great stories every night, and opening up to being a perfect channel for the Spirit—becoming, finally, the wise woman I imagined I could be.

But I had forgotten that the process of reaching that goal involved releasing my old patterns. And I was resistant to that.

I once wrote an article about Thunder which said, in part:

" 'Thunder' means 'truth.' Thunder *is* truth. Don't come around unless you want the truth. Don't come around unless you want to have a mirror held up for you to see how you create the reality you've complained about. Don't come around unless you want to stand naked before the Great Mystery, because this is a woman whose connection to Spirit is very, very great. Don't come around unless you want to be a part of the greatest changes that have ever happened on this planet. Don't come around unless you want to laugh and love and be loved and sing and dance and move ever closer to the blueprint of what you always knew you could be. Because when you hang around Thunder, you're in the presence of a Spirit Speaker, a Master, a divinely inspired catalyst disguised as a human being."

And a catalyst she was. We laughed and played and told

jokes and did wonderful things to help people, and had amazing spiritual experiences. I helped her in the office each day, and learned first-hand how to create and manage a spiritual organization and a spiritual retreat. We planted roses everywhere, and painted little statues and designed altars and created beauty in every corner of the Ranch. We played with the animals and videotaped crazy funny things, like the buffalo tossing a Mercedes Benz like a toy (which landed safely, fortunately) and later chasing our friend Frank (who was often arrogant and lazy) around the property.

If it was time to clean, Thunder would make it fun; we'd crank up Aretha Franklin and dance quickly through the chores with a little boogying on the side. We held ceremonies and welcomed honored elders, and witnessed many healings. We sewed dresses for the Sun Dance, and traveled around "on a mission for God" with laughter and joy and celebration. As I look back, it was such a unique opportunity, such an amazing gift.

But when Thunder offered feedback about my old patterns—as I had said I wanted—I would fall back into a victim perspective and avoid hearing what she shared with me about how I was interacting. She would say things such as, "Learn to control your emotions and negative memories. Uncontrolled emotions and negative memories do not need to rule your life. Negative feelings from the past and anxieties about the future can be virtually eliminated! I believe it is time that people stop reliving the past and start to live in the present making wonderful vibrations for the future." And she would point out to me how I was setting myself up to repeat old patterns.

Thunder told me once how her Sun Dance Chief, Leonard Crow Dog, used to say that "ourselves" are the "Great Mysterious," because everyone else can see us, but we can't see ourselves. I did not see how resistant I was to the information she was trying to give me, and I would continue to retrench into my old, familiar emotions. I look back now and marvel at

95

the love she had for me; she allowed me to be in her home and her office while she held the mirror for me to see my own personal version of victim-consciousness.

Abandonment issues, relationship issues, authority and abuse issues, concerns about my self-esteem and about relating to groups—everything that I wanted to heal came to the surface. Thunder supported me in looking at all of them. But I always seemed to think they weren't my fault. I had them fairly well-disguised from myself. I liked to think that I was a hard worker and better at solving problems than anyone else, so I assumed that whatever negative situations might arise at the Ranch were probably someone else's laziness, negativity, or lack of commitment. I did not see the rippling effects on all of the people around me of my self-absorption into my own concerns and issues.

At the time, I really didn't see what I was receiving from Thunder and the others at the Ranch. I was not grateful. In the light of this intensified spiritual environment and Thunder's uncanny ability to perceive the heart of a situation, my own patterns seem to be magnified.

Despite the love and support that surrounded me, I perceived life at the Ranch as hard, hard work. My workaholism immediately found its way to the surface although, at the time, I had no idea how I, myself, was creating the difficulty. I was usually up at 7:00 in the morning, which didn't seem all that early except that I never went to bed before 2:00 or 3:00 the night before. I would clean the house each night after everyone was asleep, priding myself in my service, but not taking responsibility for the exhaustion I was creating for myself!

Most of my time was spent in the office in front of a computer. I almost never took a break or went outdoors, completely forgetting my original reason for leaving Houston. I pushed myself mercilessly, imagining, somehow, that I was keeping up with Thunder. I usually juggled twenty things at once, and began to think that Thunder was holding me accountable for more than I could physically handle. I didn't consider that a great deal of my overload was self-imposed. I did not see how I was creating most of the tension in my life, or how this tension was affecting everyone else. Needing to see myself as better, I neither saw nor appreciated the wonderful ways the others at the Ranch served, nor their attunement to the Spirit flow that Thunder continuously established.

I didn't realize it at the time, but I began to feel a subtle level of resentment—and I aimed it at those who did things better than I, at all the work there was to do, at those who rested when I worked so hard, towards the men because I perceived them to have the easier jobs, and even towards Thunder, because I could not keep up with her. Sometimes, I would think I had a better idea or angle on something than she, and I would feel hurt or frustrated if she didn't use it or show great gratitude for it. In fact, Thunder often *did* make use of my input, and *actually* thanked me almost daily.

97

We would have household meetings, and I would feel hurt, and even sometimes cry, at feedback I was offered. I projected that other people were simply being unkind. Yet, I have to say, in retrospect, that this feedback was *always* given in a very kind and compassionate manner. I thought of myself as a victim, and acted as if I were being mistreated and misunderstood. I was completely unwilling to be held accountable for or to examine my behavior.

Thunder sometimes pointed out how often people choose a brilliant new teacher in their lives, and then immediately try to get that teacher to do it their way. When the chosen teacher doesn't do it their way, they immediately contrive major resentments. "With a resentment like that and a pot of coffee, you could start your own 12-step program," she'd say, and we'd all laugh. Of course, I didn't think her words applied to me. But they did, and I wasn't willing to see that. I was resisting the very teachings I had so long desired.

As I look back now, I know that the teachings I received

while living at the Ranch were the greatest gift of my life. It was a very special and rare opportunity to work day in and day out with a woman who held many of the puzzle pieces for my life that I didn't even know were missing. I had no idea at the time how much was changing inside of me from day to day, how my limits were being stretched, how my understanding of human nature was being honed, how my ability to love was being grounded, how my own old, dysfunctional patterns were being slowly and gradually erased. I was in the midst of transformation, but I could not see it.

I only became aware of the benefits of my work with Thunder during my bi-weekly visits to see my clients in Houston. *They* were growing very quickly. Insights would come from within me that I had no idea I had integrated; I was beginning to counsel more experientially and effectively—working much more intuitively—and it was showing very clearly in my clients' progress.

One day, while Thunder was on the road, I was in her office juggling, as usual, what seemed to be fifty million things, including coordinating preparations for Sun Dance, which was now barely a month away. People would say, "I don't see how you do so much" (which I loved—that kind of praise fed my old pattern). As stressed as I was, I prided myself in thinking I was doing more things at once than anyone else—except Thunder. And, in fact, I *was* able to do more than before; my level of awareness and ability to stay in balance had increased dramatically.

Bart was standing in the office as I walked in. I had just handled one more emergency, and I was perfectly calm and ready for whatever was next. Suddenly I heard myself say aloud, "Well, I might as well Sun Dance." I wasn't really saying it to Bart or to anyone else; it was just something that hit me. If I could juggle all of this and stay fairly balanced, I could probably Sun Dance. I had always doubted my ability but, at the same time, I had been feeling this immense pull to dance. I had first attended the Sun Dance years before, and it always touched my heart deeply. I had almost pledged to dance in the last two years, but the four year commitment had scared me, and I kept changing my mind. But I had Vision-Quested for four years now, so the Sun Dance seemed to be an appropriate next step to undertake if I so chose, and if I was accepted.

At that moment, as I stood in Thunder's office, I felt that the world needed more dancers, more people to pray in this intense way for the changes happening on this planet. I didn't want to put off this service any longer. It meant that for the next four years I would spend four days of each year fasting, dancing, and praying for the people. I suddenly realized I finally wanted to make this commitment.

When Thunder called in from the road, I took a deep breath and asked her what she thought about my decision. All she said was, "Well, the decision to dance is yours, not mine, so if you choose, get ready." I began to make preparations right away.

Choosing to Sun Dance means choosing to get out of your own illusion and be in service to the people. If your illusion is in the way, the energies of the coming Dance will bring those patterns to the surface to be cleared. It seemed that whenever I tried to handle an aspect of the preparations, something would block it or someone would undo it. This happened over and over again. I began to see the wisdom in the tradition of committing to Sun Dance a year before. Once that commitment is made, a Sun Dance pledge gets a year's worth of accelerated lessons. As the Dance gets closer, the challenges to growth appear faster and faster. I realized that by not making the commitment one year before, I had further condensed that intense process. Not only did I have insufficient time to get ready, but there was now an enormous amount of growth that I needed to process in order to be prepared to walk into that Sun Dance Arbor. My fear of commitment had created for me an almost unbearable compression of lessons that began the moment I decided to Dance.

The sense of balance and awareness I thought I had achieved began to melt away very quickly. I kept imagining a runaway freight train careening down a mountain, brakeless and out of control. All the work I was doing, everything in which I was involved, immediately seemed to fall apart; there were loose ends everywhere, and I couldn't do anything about any of them. I had thought that, after all this time at the Ranch, I was finally in control of myself, my work, my life. But now, all around me, everything seemed to crumble.

I could not talk to Thunder about everything that was going on because she was away, and when she arrived home, there was an enormous amount of work for her to do in the few days before she left for South Dakota. In addition, there was an illness in her family, and all kinds of issues to think about in bringing together a group of support people of all colors into a traditional Lakota Sun Dance. Her plate was already very full.

Then, the morning of the day I was to leave for Sun Dance, something occurred that was to radically alter my life. The change did not happen at that moment, but in the months and years to follow as I continued again and again, with Thunder's help, to examine what happened that day and why. Like peeling away the proverbial layers of the onion, Thunder gradually, patiently, helped me to dissolve my own layers of resistance and denial so that ultimately I could see how insidious and injurious this type of behavior is. Even during the two years while I was writing and rewriting this book, she took hours and hours of her valuable time to help me see in myself what is probably the most destructive pattern on our planet, and how the very message of this book could not be clear until I fully faced these issues myself.

Thus, before continuing with the story of the event which became such a catalyst in my growth, I want to share some of the insights I later gained so that you can read with clarity about this pervasive human behavior which, in our ignorance, we often consider to be acceptable or even admirable.

The behavior to which I am referring I have termed *victim-consciousness*. "The world loves a victim," Thunder recently said to me, and I realized how true that was. Every book, every play, every movie or television show has bad guys and good guys, and the good guys are always the victims who somehow prevail. I have never met a human being who did not manifest victim-consciousness in some way, in some aspect of his or her life. To be in the role of the victim is to see ourselves as the good guy. *To be in the role of the victim is to believe we are not responsible for how we set up what unfolds around us.*

There is no doubt that there are times when we may genuinely suffer at the hands of an oppressor, and I am not saying that these kinds of experiences are not real and painful when they occur. Yet, more commonly than not, once we have experienced or become accustomed to being a victim, we discover—often subconsciously—the hidden benefits of that state.

Instead of putting the pain aside when it is done, we can hold onto the victim perspective, perhaps fearing to let go of what is familiar, but also subtly sensing the power of the victim position. We can see ourselves as a martyr, if not actually Christ-like. We can often stand in our righteousness without looking any closer at the situation. We can think we deserve sympathy or help, without any obligation to reciprocate. We can give ourselves all kinds of excuses for doing or demanding almost anything we want because, after all, we are the victims. We can even allow ourselves (and this is very common) to become the perpetrator because, of course, we are the victims.

The more insidious part of victim-consciousness, however, is that in order to continue in the role of the innocent victim, we need to establish someone as our aggressor, our perpetrator, our abuser. Of course, our conscious mind does not see this, nor would we ever consciously do this to someone, especially someone we love. *Yet it is being done all the time—on individual, cultural, and national levels!!!* To maintain the victim perspective and enjoy its benefits, we need an oppressor—someone to play the bad

101

guy so that we can emerge guilt-free, doing what we want and looking good in the process. Worst of all, we may even set up others to harm us by pushing them into the role of abuser. The way we do this is to find their "buttons" and then subtly, persistently, even if unconsciously, push them until we get the desired results—until they "lose it," and we can be satisfied, once again, that we are not to blame. It is sometimes called "passive aggression."

Thus, in seeing ourselves as the victim, we hold an enormous amount of power and control. Righteousness, excuses, power, looking good, getting support or help, doing whatever we want—the benefits of being a victim are multifold!

But what is the cost? In order to stay in the victim stance, we must give up our integrity. We must give up taking responsibility for our lives—and that includes our dreams and our personal fulfillment, as well as our "negative stuff" that we don't want to see! We also give up our self-respect, our spirituality, and our sense of wholeness, for in setting up someone else to be our abuser, we violate the other person as well as our own values in life. It is the most elusive, camouflaged, and frightening aspect of ourselves.

It's a hard pattern to look at, for once we discover the advantage of perceiving ourselves as the victim, every aspect of our personality is then geared to deny our own responsibility for our lives. Yet, in order to grow, we must see it. Thunder sacrificed considerably to help me see this.

That morning, as I was getting ready to leave for Sun Dance, I created a great big upset. Although I wasn't aware of it at the time, I had a habit of creating negative endings to relieve old anxieties about separation and abandonment. I also tended to get into arguments as a way of relieving the stress I created for myself. That morning, I tried to set Thunder up as the bad guy so I could leave that day without feeling those horrible, lonely, and anxious feelings. Instead she turned it into the most important

102
〰〰
〰〰

lesson of my life in that amazing way she has of allowing Spirit to work through her own humanness and vulnerability.

I staggered out of my room at dawn that morning, after only a couple hours of sleep. I had been awakened by what sounded like the slamming of every cabinet cupboard door in the kitchen. Trent, who was Thunder's lead "road warrior" (after Horse), was looking for something. I was barely awake, but I was already angry.

"Geez, Trent, couldn't you make the slightest attempt to be quiet in the morning?" I was exhausted and my irritation was unmasked. There was still so much to do before leaving for the Dance that afternoon. I wanted just a little more sleep, and it was Trent's fault that I wasn't going to get it. I didn't think about the fact that he had been awake for several days himself, helping with a Vision Quest in Arizona, and had arrived late the night before after driving straight through to Texas. I also didn't see how hard Thunder and all of the Ranch staff were working, and how tired they were as well. Now Trent was up early, getting some breakfast for Thunder. At least he could have tried to be quiet, I thought. Indignantly, I slammed the door to my room, not thinking about who else might still be asleep.

Suddenly, two strange black dogs started fighting outside the back door, growling and banging into the metal screen door, breaking it down with frightening violence. I groaned and turned towards the living room.

Hearing all the commotion, Thunder appeared from around the corner. She immediately pointed out how much of my time I spent in dissatisfaction, judgement, and irritation. I was surprised and hurt. I wanted her to tell Trent to be more considerate. She said the dogs were fighting just outside the door because they were picking up on my energy and that their violence was a reflection of what was inside of me.

I couldn't believe it! How insulting, how unreasonable! I gave no thought to what Thunder was saying; I felt like such a

103
〜〜
〜〜

victim! In fact, in *my* judgement, *they* were all being unreasonable. After all, *I* had to get ready to leave. What *I* was doing was important! What the others were going through did not enter my mind.

Thunder kept trying to explain how my irritability affected other people, and how my self-righteousness left others angry and unwilling to work with me. She pointed out to me how, the day before, I had insisted on giving an enormous shopping list to a Sun Dancer in Arizona who had just had an accident, had cleaned up the entire Vision Quest site, and was about to leave for the Dance without even having the time to catch a little sleep before he left. She said I needed to get out of "me, me, me" and start being more aware of others.

Unwilling to hear the feedback that Thunder was offering me, I thought she was attacking me for no reason—after all, I had been working so hard. I found refuge in old, familiar feelings of shock and hurt. At first, I tried to manipulate myself out of the situation by "stuffing my feelings" and just waiting silently until she was done. It didn't work. Then I tried using humor, proud of myself for applying a tool I was just beginning to understand. But it didn't get me what I wanted either, which was for her to correct Trent instead of me. Thunder kept trying to explain what I was creating with my energies, but I heard nothing but unreasonable accusations directed at the wrong person.

Then my buried anger began to surface. "The heck with this," I said to myself, "I'm just going to be honest and say what I feel." At the time, I didn't know the difference between being honest and simply dumping on other people. Forgetting that I had literally begged to be on staff at the Ranch, I told Thunder that I really didn't agree with the way some of the things were done around there. Forgetting her teachings about nurturing and loving service, I stated indignantly that I didn't believe in this business of women having to cook and serve the men, and that I had my own way which I liked better. This was quite an outrageous thing to say to the Mother of the Sun Dance on the day I was leaving for a month on the reservation—at my own request—supposedly to be in service to the people. That's when she got really angry.

"So you think my way and the way of my people is wrong!" she cried.

Now I was really angry, and I felt very righteous about it, unjustly accused.

"Fuck you!" I thought, forgetting that Thunder could not only hear Spirit, but she could also hear the thoughts projected by those around her. I turned on my heels and headed up the stairs, knowing I would regret it if I said it aloud. Somewhere inside me, there was an inkling of memory that Thunder, herself, had been going through a lot recently, and I realized I needed to get away before I made it worse. But she had heard it anyhow.

Thunder was now in tears. "Don't walk away like that!" But I kept walking, giving her no opportunity to reply. I didn't consider that I, who had been so close to her, was turning my back on her. I, who had asked for her help to heal the part in me which made people abandon me, was now abandoning her.

"Come back here," she cried through her tears, following me up the stairs, pulling at my hair, and stopping me. I immediately dropped to my knees and hunkered motionless into a little ball as if she had beaten me. Scenes from long ago, when a man had badly abused me, filled my mind, and replaced the scene before me of Thunder trying very hard to awaken me to the energy I was carrying and to the seriousness and responsibility of the Sun Dance I was about to enter. Many times I had heard Thunder talk about how we try to recreate old patterns of abuse from the past by setting up other people to participate in those patterns but, at the time, it didn't occur to me that this is what I was doing. My projection of her as the abuser and my identification with victim-consciousness were at their peak.

Suddenly I heard Trent, always the peaceful warrior, gently

105
〜〜
〜〜

say, "Let's stop this right here," and he calmly led Thunder back to her room; she was crying. I scurried up the stairs, tears now streaming down my face as well. I collapsed in the furthest part of the house I could find.

Here it was, the morning I was to leave for Sun Dance, and I was up in the far reaches of the house crying, and Thunder was down in her bedroom crying. The situation was awful, awful, awful. Never had I seen Thunder this upset. Some part of me knew that I had driven her to this kind of reaction, but I didn't understand how. I loved Thunder so much, and I would never have wanted to hurt her, yet it seemed as if I had made things horrible, and I was frightened that I did not know exactly how or why. It wasn't until much later that I would finally see the dynamics of what I had created that morning, or how deeply my behavior had hurt Thunder by pulling her into a drama such as this when her whole life was about creating peace. As the tears tumbled down my cheeks, I tried to understand, but my mind seemed to shut down, to go numb. I felt stretched far beyond the outer recesses of my limits, yet I still had all of Sun Dance before me. The stretching had not even begun!

An hour later, Thunder and I were hugging and telling each other we loved each other, yet there was damage done. We agreed to talk some time during the day; however, in the rush to get ready, it never happened. She had asked me not to talk to anyone about it, so I was left, in my time before Sun Dance, to ponder, to review, to pray, and to seek out my own answers.

Later, I looked back and realized that the one thing I didn't do that morning was just surrender and really listen—simply listen to what Thunder was trying to tell me and be willing to be aware of what was outside of my own limited view. In time, I began to see that I had been trying to be in control in ways I had never imagined were in me, and at levels that were so ingrained and pervasive in my life that I was completely blind to them. If I had been genuine, I wouldn't have been trying so hard to be perfect. "Control stuff" can really look like "posing

106

for holy pictures," as one friend used to say. It was a matter of trying to look "good" while covertly judging and manipulating. By setting myself up as the victim, I was actually the perpetrator, drawing others into my own personal, "powerless" drama and hurting them in the process instead of being responsible for keeping a balance in my own life. Not taking responsibility for myself meant that I made others responsible for me, by either blaming them or wanting them to take up the slack for my choices.

Much later, when I was finally ready to hear some feedback from Thunder, she shared with me more about the mechanics of victim-consciousness:

107

"When we are self-absorbed in our own 'stuff', we can't see what others are going through. I try to live my life as when you throw a pebble into a pond and the ripples flow out and hit the banks—I am aware of those energies, how those ripples will affect others. Will all the ripples create harmony going out and coming back in? Most times we are so unwilling to give up our own stuff; the ripples just go out and create more stuff for others. It is as if, when we are in our own pain, we want everyone else to see, feel, be, and have pain also.

"I somehow felt that you were trying to create total abuse for yourself by trying to get people to be angry, abusive, or even to hit you, which is a very normal thing for people to do who have been the victims of child abuse. It was later suggested that I may have actually saved your life by taking on the responsibility of the drama that morning, and thus also taking on the karma of defusing the energy of abuse you were drawing to yourself. It might have come to you in a much worse fashion if you had gone into the magnifying energies of the Sun Dance magnetizing abuse in that way.

"I also knew if you talked about it to others in the group, it would create a great backlash at you. It would have gotten back to the Elders, the Warriors, and the Sun Dancers, who would have taken my position, not yours. You would have been seen as 'trashing' our way of worship, in which, by the way, you were petitioning to dance!"

I knew she was right; these were sobering thoughts, and very clear information about how victim-consciousness works. I shivered to think how accurate she was about what the magnified effects could have been at Sun Dance. The negativity I was creating surely would have resulted in my not being allowed to dance or, even worse, in harming or interfering with someone else's dance.

I look back now and wonder at Thunder's kindness, compassion, love, and mastery as a teacher, and I am deeply, deeply grateful. I have watched her over the years do what it takes to teach each person who comes to her to learn. Perhaps it is the mark of a great teacher to be willing to sacrifice her own ego and comfort in order for the student to master a lesson. I once asked her why she allowed one particular staff member to sleep so much. Implicit in the question was why she seemed harder on me. She told me that each person needs something different for their growth. "Truth needs to be there, and growth must be the end result," one of her warriors once said.

Over the years, Thunder and I have become very close, and I now see the enormity of the gift she gave me that day by entering into my pattern of dramatic negative endings, and sacrificing her balance at that time so I could see the pain I created for others with the selfishness of my victim stance. Because of her love, my life has been changed; that day began the unveiling of the gift and the message of "Blessings in Disguise".

▲ ▲ ▲ ▲ ▲ ▲ ▲

We are already the creators of our reality. But, for most of us, much of that creative process is still unconscious at our current level of awareness. No matter how much psychological and spiritual training we've had to live otherwise, we can still fall into thinking of external events and people as the cause of much of our experience. However, we are not the victims that we often think we are. As we come to know and respect ourselves, we can take back the power we have assigned to others. In that process, we must release the victim within and reclaim our own creative abilities.

In order to empower yourself, look at both the positive and negative creations in your life. Once you can admit to creating something you don't like, it frees you to see the full spectrum of your creative ability. These questions will help you with that process.

1. Make a list of the typical situations and circumstances you tend to blame on others. Then go back and write about how you set up each one.

2. List ten or fifteen scenes from your past in which you experienced yourself as the victim of someone else's behavior. Then look for the repeated scenarios within your list, ie., the patterns to your "style" of playing victim.

3. Think of several times when you have wanted information or understanding for your growth, but then resisted it when you received it. Write a paragraph about each one. Which lessons did you ultimately integrate? Which ones are you still working on?

THE ROAD TO THE DANCE

BOUNDARIES AND BOUNDLESSNESS

When do you "own your power" by asserting yourself and being clear about your boundaries, and when do you surrender? When do you expand your limitations and recognize the infinite potential of humankind (especially yourself), and when do you say, "No, I need to take a little time to rest and nurture myself"? And, when is it all the work of the Creator anyhow, despite what you think might be your own conscious choice or intuition?

It would seem that we are getting two different messages in the "personal growth industry" these days, and they apparently call for opposite actions. From a self-esteem perspective comes the message to set boundaries, take responsibility for ourselves, nurture ourselves, and avoid codependency. By honoring our feelings, we develop our intuition and a sense of self-empowerment which enables us to step forward into the creation of our dreams. Yet, from the perspective that humankind has the potential for limitlessness comes the concept that we can do about anything we choose. This idea of the boundlessness of the human spirit says that the more we stretch our limits and serve others, the more we expand our abilities and awareness into the Union of All. It is a trust in "going with the flow." When we release the confining belief that we are bound by our physical form and our mind, we enter into the infinite world of Spirit. In fact, it is often when we have pushed ourselves beyond a state of exhaustion, when the mind releases its control over our normal functioning, that mystical experiences sometimes occur.

So, which one is correct?

The answer may well be that both are correct. Sometimes, we need to relax and take care of ourselves, check inside to see if we do or don't want to do something, and be willing to stand alone for what feels right and comfortable inside. Sometimes we need to stretch, to expand the outer limits of our minds and bodies, to put aside our personal desires and perspectives, and to discover the world where conscious control dissolves and the Great Mystery supersedes the rules of the physical world.

But when do we do which? How can we know?

111

Perhaps the answer is that we cannot know. It is very humbling to recognize that, even when we have done our very best, the results sometimes seem to come out all wrong. At other times, when it seems that we have screwed up really badly, things turn out miraculously well. Often, it is only in retrospect that we realize the true outcome. Over and over again, what is demonstrated to us is that the Great Mystery runs an incredibly awesome and complex universe absolutely beyond our understanding. As we strive to control and condense this universe to fit our logical minds, we simply limit some of the possibilities available to us.

Thus, as we move through life, choosing sometimes to center into the self, and at other times to expand our limits, we can never truly know exactly what is right at what time. Only our intuition and our connection to Spirit can serve as guides, for our minds cannot fathom the magnitude of the intricacies of the Divine interactions with human lives. From this recognition of the fact that we *do not know* comes a deep sense of humility. In the Hindu text, *The Bhagavad Gita*, God tells his devotees to do their best, but to surrender the fruits of all their actions to Him. All we can really do is strive to keep a balance and offer up to the Creator our best efforts as well as our worst weaknesses at any given time, knowing only that, if we err, we will probably learn something, and if we succeed, it may be due in part to our own efforts, but may well be, to a great extent, because of Grace. As we go toward the dreams in each of our hearts, we cannot possibly understand the Mystery of how our creations can work out for a greater benefit than we could have imagined. It is a perspective of surrender and great peace.

▲ ▲ ▲ ▲

It was with an increasing attitude of surrender that I headed for Sun Dance that year. I couldn't have done anything else. My brain was fried. As I made final arrangements to leave the Ranch, my mind had all but shut down. I could not possibly process all that had gone on that month—not to mention that day in particular—and still pack. I frantically gathered the last of my personal items together, hoping to have a little time to leave the office in good order. But then Buster, my traveling companion, showed up.

Now, Buster is quite a character. His presentation is something like that of a biker; he wears black motorcycle T-shirts, long hair pulled back in a braid, and a little belly hanging over slightly oversized and tattered jeans, not to mention the typical reflecting "shades." However, he's an artist, and much of his life is focused on creating beauty. He'll tell you twenty times an hour that he'll kill you if you don't do this, that, or the other thing, yet the truth is, he'd give his life for you if he cares about you. If he can find your buttons, he'll push them. "I'm just a mirror," he'd say, laughing. But if you need a shoulder to cry on, he'll be there for you. I used to find him pretty difficult, but he's mellowed during the years he's been around Thunder. Now he calls everyone "Sweetie" and the great big heart that used to be hidden lights up a room when he walks in.

But this was a few years back and when Buster showed up

at the Ranch that day, he hadn't yet gotten to the "Sweetie" stage. He had spent two years on the road with Thunder as her warrior, and had been a very effective, albeit bossy, organizer. However, when Thunder told stories about him, he had a way of laughing at himself that somehow demonstrated a level of humility that is seldom reached. Still, I wasn't very comfortable about the idea of traveling together. Stressed as I was, I could not imagine we'd reach Sun Dance without blowing any circuits I might have remaining. (Remember, all the integration necessary in order for me to write the previous chapter had not yet taken place. I was just at the pivotal point in awakening to my "they did it to me" perspective.)

So I was more than a little skittish about traveling with Buster. Over the past six weeks, I had managed most of the preparations for our month camped at the Sun Dance without much help. Buster, to date, had done almost nothing, so I assumed that he would at least pack the truck while I finished my office work.

"Carry that stuff down and load it up," he said, nodding toward the boxes of supplies I had packed and piled on the second floor landing.

I looked at Thunder, amazed. I knew she was aware that he hadn't contributed much, and I was sure she'd correct him.

"He is a Sun Dancer. You are here to serve and help him prepare for his dance. You haven't even danced yet!" she said, nodding towards the door.

WHAT? I couldn't believe it! As my victim-meter hit the top of the scale, my ears were ringing. I looked hard to find a place of surrender inside of me. I had never been very good at that, but I wasn't about to make any more waves, not after the morning's incident. I hauled one huge container after another from the second floor out to the vehicle. And, *of course*, while I did, a heavy downpour suddenly began, drenching me and every box I carried! What else could come along to challenge my sanity? Buster issued one instruction after another. I wanted to

113

drop from mental and emotional exhaustion. I couldn't believe how thoughtless everyone was being. This was *not* my day.

When the truck and trailer were all finally loaded, we discovered a flat tire, and Buster wanted me to go into town with him to get it fixed. Once we were there, he wanted me to help him shop for some things he needed for the trip! I took a deep breath. Why hadn't he done his shopping before? There was work in the office which I at least needed to tell someone about! And Thunder and I hadn't had a chance to talk yet. But when we returned to the Ranch, Thunder, exhausted, had fallen asleep, and it was time for us to leave. It didn't seem right to wake her. So there was one more unresolved issue, one more thing out of control. As I left the house, my heart was heavy. It seemed as if I were leaving behind a trail of loose ends.

I sat in the truck as Buster made a last circle around the vehicle to check everything. As he climbed inside the cab, I suddenly remembered that the blankets had not arrived. The gifting blankets! I'd ordered two Pendleton blankets, the traditional gift for the elders at the Sun Dance. One was for the Sun Dance Chief, Charles Chipps; the other was for Thunder. I certainly didn't want to present myself to Dance without appropriate gifting!

"Perhaps this is a sign," I thought sadly to myself. "Maybe I'm not supposed to Dance."

But as we slalomed through the mud down the long drive and out of the gate, the rain suddenly stopped. The clouds separated and the sun beamed down upon us.

"The very same sun that shines in the Sun Dance Arbor," I thought to myself.

As I jumped out of the truck cab to close the front gate, the UPS truck showed up with a delivery. It was the gifting blankets!

"Maybe I *am* supposed to dance," I thought.

As we headed out into the late afternoon sun, my spirits lifted for the first time that day. The door felt as if it had opened again for me to dance—with another clear message about the results of waiting until the last minute.

The sky was filled with light, fluffy clouds as Buster and I headed onto the highway; the air was fresh and sweet following the afternoon storm, and it felt as if a weight had lifted. We sometimes talked casually, and were sometimes silent, enjoying the drive, although I knew we were both constantly aware that we were now headed for the challenge of Sun Dance. "This is not a vacation," Thunder's voice echoed in my mind, bringing us back to our purpose. But right now, it felt like a vacation. There would be plenty of time ahead to focus on the prayer, sacrifice, and surrender of the Dance.

As we drove north, the view of the sky out our left window turned from baby blue to turquoise to yellow, to orange, to red, then magenta, and then purple, and finally a deep indigo, dotted with bright stars in a now clear sky. Since Thunder had asked me not to talk about what had happened that day, I had no choice but to allow it all to marinate in my mind rather than blow off the energy of it and get sympathy. Clarity came slowly, in pieces, like the transitions in the sky. By the time we reached Dallas, I was feeling very grateful to Thunder for pushing me so hard to see these things, and also regretful that it had taken so much of her energy to do it.

We stayed with a friend in Dallas, laughing and talking late into the night and over a long breakfast the next day. It was noon before we finally got on our way. We had twenty hours of driving to cover that day. Everything seemed fine. The energy felt light. I was finally relaxing now that we were on the road. But I've never known a Sun Dance road trip that wasn't an adventure of some sort...

A little test...

A little push into the Spirit World.

Shortly after we headed into the vast, empty plains of Oklahoma, we started to hear noises from somewhere under the truck—scrapings and clunkings that seemed to come from the

115

back. Then it started to rain again. Fat, heavy drops splattered loudly on the windshield, making it both difficult to see where we were going and to hear what was going on with the vehicle. We stopped a couple of times, trying to find enough cover to check under the truck, but we couldn't figure out what it was, and we opted to stay dry and continue driving.

The noises got worse and worse, horrible metallic scraping sounds, and I started to feel afraid. I'd never heard anything like it. I mentioned my concern to Buster a few times, but that just seemed to irritate him. He told me I was creating the problem with my thoughts. I sat silently, wondering how this situation might be like that at the Ranch the previous morning, and feeling very confused.

I tried to control my thoughts, but it didn't help; the terrible scraping sounds got louder as the tension level inside the truck continued to climb. There was almost zero visibility, and it seemed to me that Buster was having a hard time keeping the truck on the road. We were hauling a trailer packed with supplies for Sun Dance, and it was whipping back and forth behind us. As far as I could tell, we were constantly hydroplaning on the almost flooded highway.

By now I was petrified, but my experiences in the last two days had left me unsure when to say what and why. Finally I couldn't contain myself any longer, and I insisted that we check the truck again. I was relieved when Buster immediately agreed. We found an abandoned gas station with an overhang that we thought might afford some protection from the torrential downpour. Within moments we were both soaked and, despite the fact that we jiggled, poked, and prodded everything in sight, we still couldn't find a thing wrong.

At this point, Buster had had enough of my concern and told me that I was going to drive. I was a pretty good driver, so I thought this was a *great* idea. But that notion didn't last long. Once I had my hands on the wheel I realized we were not hydroplaning. I didn't know what was going on, but I couldn't keep the truck in the lane; it swung far into the right lane, then back to the left, then partway onto the shoulder, bearing no relation to where I was steering. Buster kept giving me steering directions, as if that would have made a difference. There was no way to control the truck, and I wasn't even going to try. At this point, I didn't care what Buster decided to do—I wasn't riding any further in this vehicle until it could go straight! As I attempted to pull off the highway, we swung completely beyond the shoulder onto the grass.

By now even Buster appeared to be seriously concerned. We looked up and saw a sign, which read: *Exit 74, to Tecumseh, Rt.108A.* "Looks like the right place to stop," Buster laughed, breaking the tension. I smiled, knowing exactly what he was alluding to: 74 is a sacred number to many Native Americans, symbolizing Spirit and Earth. Tecumseh was the name of an ancient elder of whom Thunder had spoken several times; she had once had a very strong vision of him. He was known for his efforts to bring unity to all the tribes. And 108 is a sacred number in some Eastern religions, and was significant because both Buster and I had studied yoga in the past. Somehow it seemed like a sign that we had pulled over exactly at the right time and place.

Since we had been unable to figure out what was wrong when we had stopped before, Buster asked me to stand outside the truck and keep an eye on the back axle while he pulled forward. I crouched in the grass, wondering what I should be looking for—no doubt something unusual. It came within seconds. He pulled forward about two inches and there was this horrible *clunk*—and the whole back of the truck dropped a half a foot! After that it wouldn't move at all. Once again we looked under the truck, but still couldn't see anything out of the ordinary.

Miraculously, we spotted a Texaco station nicely situated just across the median and down the road a piece. Suddenly the sun was out and the air was once again filled with the fresh, sweet smell of the country after a rain. As we walked over to the Texaco station, Buster—now jovial and friendly—said this was a lesson for him to listen to his female side, and to feminine intuition as well.

I thanked him for giving me credit. Perhaps this was a healing for Buster to help his gentle feminine side come out more. At the same time, I mused, when there are loud metallic scraping sounds and you can't steer the truck, it doesn't take intuition, but simple linear observation to tell you something is amiss! At any rate, we now took our experience as an adventure and jogged over to the station to get some help.

The mechanic who came to tow us saw right away what both Buster and I had missed: the lug nuts had not been tight on the truck tire and had all been sheared off, one by one. The little round holes the nuts go through were now gaping ovals, and the last lug nut had come off and fallen to the ground as Buster had pulled forward those final two inches! We stood and stared in silence. If I hadn't stopped *exactly* when I did...I shuddered to think what might have happened with a trailer in tow.

What had made me stop at that very moment? I had been frightened of asserting myself all day. By pushing myself to surrender and avoid conflict at all costs, I had experienced level upon level of mental and emotional stretching. Yet, when I suddenly became clear about my own boundaries, I'd probably saved both of our lives. This dichotomy was beyond logic. It could not be explained. Yesterday, inappropriate setting of boundaries had brought me a great awareness of my self-centeredness. Today, setting boundaries had taken us into the realm of boundlessness. We were surrounded by miracles.

I was reminded again of our human propensity—and my own pattern—of trying to control what is out of control. I thought, too, of the importance of paying attention to the signs that show us when things aren't controllable, and how difficult it often is to tell the difference. I felt truly humbled. The 12-step Serenity Prayer kept coming to mind:

God, grant me the serenity to accept the things I cannot change, the courage to change the things I can, and the wisdom to know the difference.

Yet I realized that sometimes I couldn't know the difference. What unknown part of me had made the choice to stop when I did? Only Grace could explain how I had been moved to pull over, with probably less than a second to spare, instead of being tossed into a rolling mess of metal between truck and trailer. I had no idea what part of this Mystery was my own intuition, and what had been Spirit's intervention. It left me wondering: How much does Spirit work moment to moment in our lives, without us ever really understanding the extent of the gifts we receive? And where was the edge between the influence of our intuition and that of Spirit—or was there an edge?

As Buster exchanged car-talk with the mechanic, I sat in the grass next to the filling station and pondered with gratitude what had just occurred. An exquisite sense of peace seemed to envelop me. I had been through so much in the last day and a half. Whatever my errors might have been, right now it felt as if a Beneficent Force was watching out for me. I thought about how much more trust and faith I could live with—if I could only remember to do so. A deep sense of humility set in as I reflected on this day.

By now dusk was falling and the mechanics could not get parts until morning. They were kind enough to give us a ride to the next town. We were taken to...the Thunderbird Lodge! The coincidences of the symbols were too great to ignore. Creator surely had a hand in what was unfolding—both in saving our lives and in the lessons that were being brought before us on this Sun Dance Road. I felt Thunder's presence in my life, marveling and wondering at how she worked with Spirit.

Early in the morning Buster and I went out to a field by the hotel and said some prayers of gratitude for our lives, for Thunder's help, for the lessons, and to get into alignment for

119

the remaining journey to Sun Dance. Buster then made a circle around us with tobacco, thus cutting the cords from whatever we needed to release so that we could go forward in a good way. We both felt an immediate shift in the energy with the cord-cutting; it was time to let go of the events of the last year and move on to the Dance. A new year was about to begin. Within moments, the man from the gas station was there to ferry us to our truck, and we were on our way to Sun Dance.

▲ ▲ ▲ ▲ ▲ ▲ ▲

120

Pondering where the edge of our own mind ends, and where the edge of Spirit begins, can give us great insight into the reality of the "Oneness," we have all heard about. When are *we* acting, and when is something the action of Spirit? And, can we ever know? Even so, it is worthwhile to keep contemplating the blend of our human and divine aspects.

1. As you consider the concept of setting boundaries versus stretching into boundlessness, list when each approach was of benefit to you. Then list the times when each approach was not beneficial to you.

2. Write about the times in your life when you narrowly escaped death. Did you stop to wonder at what occurred? What do you suppose the implications of that experience were for your evolution? How did that experience either stretch your boundlessness, or teach you to set better boundaries. How did it affect your feelings, attitudes, or beliefs about Spirit in your life?

3. Think about three or four times when you made an important decision or choice, and the outcome was completely different from what you expected. Write about what those experiences demonstrated to you about boundaries and boundlessness.

SUN DANCE

STEPPING INTO THE SPIRIT WORLD

The Sun Dance is not the name of a ceremony.
It is a Sun Dance.
It is not something to be looked at,
and it is not something "cool."
We are Sun Gaze Dancers, sacrificing things that are unhealthy
for our lives and for the lives of our relations.
To do this sacred ceremony, we go through purification.
Hell is not so hot.
We do this to realize the nature of Creation,
to be pure in our hearts, and also in our minds.

— Charles Chipps
Sun Dance Chief

There are many ways of entering into the Spirit world—into other dimensions, other realities, other realms where mind and heart join with Spirit in the act of creation. All religions have ways of transcending the physical world and entering into mystical union. They may be through prayer, chanting or singing, dance or movement, fasting, or different forms of sacrifice—giving up something of the physical world in order to facilitate that union. Some people discover this realm through intense spiritual practice; others stumble into it through sickness, through near-death experiences, or even by apparent accident.

Our Western, industrialized, and more materialistic lifestyles tend to be very grounded in physical reality. Most of the ancient forms of spiritual union are kept alive in scripture and stories of the saints and mystics of bygone days, but are lost in the busy-ness of the average person's daily life.

Communion with the higher realms—those of higher frequencies—is less unusual where the industrialized world has not gained a strong foothold. Spiritual interaction as a regular aspect of life is much more common to indigenous cultures around the world, and to people in "third world" nations where what we would call "poverty" yields a simpler way of life.

122

Stepping into the spiritual realm is stepping into the next level of evolution for each person as well as for humankind. The rules of life on higher dimensions are more creative, expansive, and loving. When we experience mystical union, it is a "spiritual" way of being that is simple, obvious, effortless. Once we have tasted that greater consciousness, we can never forget the potential we have experienced, and our life on Earth can never be the same again.

To enter into that spiritual realm involves releasing belief in, and attachment to, our three-dimensional world as our only reality. It also involves acknowledging and accessing a greater truth, a greater perspective, and a greater wisdom, which inevitably entails letting go of our own sense of superiority and "knowing how it should be." We can do this only when we become willing to move outside of our own comfortable sense of what is tangible and controllable.

To make this leap into the realm of the Great Mystery, also takes a certain amount of humility and surrender. Yet we often do not know what this means or how to achieve it. How easy it is to forget that God is running everything anyhow. Our task is but to get into alignment with the Greater Plan. For most of us, entering into the Spiritual realm can be somewhat like breathing: We take it in, then let it out. In other words, at times we touch that place where love is easy and peace is a constant, and then we lose it again, returning to all of the issues and hassles of normal life on the planet. We forget. We get caught up in other things—bills, other people's attitudes, career choices, family dynamics.

We forget. Then we remember. Then we forget again.

Yet we should not be discouraged, for this is the natural process of learning. Each time we touch the Spirit world, we gather experiences from the greater perspective of that realm which we can then ground, or apply, in our daily experience of Earth. Every gift of the Spirit becomes a step in the transformational process, not only for ourselves, but for those around us who see us gradually change and grow. Unseen from the three-dimensional perspective of reality, Spirit constantly serves us, helping us to fulfill our own prayers and dreams by magnifying the thoughts and visualizations that are our own creations.

While we may now and again lose track of that higher view and of the gifts we have received from the Creator, we can never completely forget. We are working towards a greater goal for this planet, and each time any one of us steps through to that higher reality, we bring back pieces for our daily lives, a greater vision for ourselves and others. Whenever any one of us attempts to integrate that greater vision into our three-dimensional reality, we close the gap a little more in the process of evolution towards our individual and collective magnificence. Each time we immerse ourselves in a spiritual practice that realigns us with the Source, it serves to bring us closer and closer to the reality on Earth as it is in Heaven.

▲ ▲ ▲ ▲

Of all my experiences of stepping through into the next dimension, I can think of no more profound way to see through the veils than stepping into the Sun Dance Arbor. The Sun Dance is undertaken in a spirit of sacrifice, surrender, and service. I have attended many Native American spiritual ceremonies

123

and, while I am no expert on these things, I can say that Sun Dance has always pulled at my heartstrings the strongest and touched me the most deeply.

I had attended and served at Sun Dance the four previous years and, at each one, I had received some gift of Spirit even though I hadn't danced. I hadn't even spent much time watching and supporting at the actual Dance Arbor, because it always seemed that I was babysitting, cooking for other supporters, or needed back in the kitchen area of our camp. People often asked if I had seen this or that in the Dance, but I really didn't have much of an idea of what went on in the Dance Arbor; mostly I was cooking and praying. Yet, each year that I attended, my life was moved in some beneficial way. Each Sun Dance brought vital changes and much insight.

Thunder had trained us carefully. She brought her white, Indian, and mixed-blood friends together to the Sun Dance grounds in a very mutually respectful way. She taught us to leave our New Age, feminine liberation, health food, white ideas behind, along with our sexual energy. We were on Indian land, and we were there to serve. We were not there to teach what we knew, but to be as unobtrusive as possible and to learn from these ancient ways.

Each time we prepared to go into the reservation, Thunder would say to all of us, "We are not here to create a clash of cultures or to learn what the Indians are doing and try to do it better than them. This is not a picnic and it's not a pow wow. It is the most sacred event of the year to the Lakota people. We are not here for anything but to be in service." She taught us this not only out of respect for the elders, but for all the people. I have always noticed that the rules and standards she set for us were made to benefit everyone, not just our camp, and not just the people we had come to support. She seemed to be constantly aware of the bigger picture.

Years before, Thunder had seen an old grandma cry because there was not enough food to feed all the hundreds of people

that had come to her family's Sun Dance. Thunder then made
a vow to herself that, as long as she was around, this would
never happen again. Every year, we all put our money and supplies together and raised enough to help feed the people and
help support the Sun Dance family. I am always amazed when
I see how Thunder gives away all that she has for the nurturing and benefit of all of the people and the Sun Dance ceremony. Each year, I would worry that I couldn't afford the
appropriate donations, the cost of the trip, and the month away
from work. Yet absolutely every time I was willing to give, Spirit
helped, miracles were evident, and somehow there was always
abundance.

The women in our camps always worked in the kitchen. We
quietly served all the Elders, men and women guests, and ourselves—in that order. To show cultural respect, we wore long
skirts and modest blouses, looked down at the ground most of
the time, and mostly spoke when spoken to. We put our good
energy and positive thoughts and prayers into the food, for this
was what sustained the dancers before the dance, and the
helpers during the dance. The men labored hard all day in tem-
peratures bordering on one hundred degrees, cutting pine
boughs to create shade for some of the Elder's camps and the
area surrounding the Sun Dance Arbor. When the men came
into camp, the women would offer drinks and food, and step
back into the shadows to listen while the Elders told stories and
talked with the men.

Several times I heard Elders—guests in our camp—say that
ours was probably more traditional than some of the Indian
camps at the Dance. This was a part of Thunder's wisdom—we
were in service, so the Elders felt comfortable coming to our
camp, sitting for a cup of coffee or a meal, and sharing some of
their wonderful stories and truths. Because of Thunder and the
respect that her Elders have for her, and because she taught us
to honor these old ways, we were rewarded with much laughter and many gifts of wisdom.

At Sun Dance, it is as if one is walking into a time/space warp; thoughts instantly manifest into reality instead of in the time-delayed manner of the "normal" reality of everyday life. The first time I noticed this phenomenon, I was washing some dishtowels in a little scrub basin, and I thought to myself, "Oh, I need a clothesline." I turned around and on the ground behind me lay a long, sturdy cotton rope. On either side of me, five feet away, were two trees, the perfect distance apart for stringing that rope. Instant manifestation!

Since then, I have experienced immediate creation through thoughts countless times during Sun Dance—and less often, at other times. There were times when someone's thoughts created needed chairs, or an item of clothing, or food for many to eat. Sometimes I saw something more dramatic occur on the physical level, such as the healing of cancer. I have also observed thoughts of fear or greed manifest just as quickly. The more I became aware of the power of thought, the more I started to monitor and carefully choose which thoughts I wanted to go forth into creation. I realized that this is why we offer tobacco to the Elders and ask their permission to Dance, for their experience and spiritual connectedness make them better equipped to say when someone is ready to enter into that arena where thoughts manifest themselves so powerfully. It is also why, I have been told, it is good to Vision Quest for at least four years prior to Dancing.

Whatever thoughts people hold in their minds are magnified in the energies of Sun Dance. Therefore, thoughts of clarity, cheerfulness, and love are necessary in order to support the prayers of the Dancers who are sacrificing and praying down in the Arbor. Service in thought and deed is why we are there.

Sun Dance has taught me a great deal about spirituality. After attending Sun Dance, I began to realize that the spiritual world is much more accessible to humans than I had ever thought. I was better able to comprehend the message of the life and words of Christ, as well as those of the saints of many religions. I understood with more clarity why people fast and pray. I began to see the idea of spiritual sacrifice in an entirely different context, one in which a person might joyfully give up a piece of earthly comfort for a greater benefit to the whole. It is an energy exchange, of sorts. Sun Dance is a place where one serves and sacrifices, but it is also a place where, because the veils between the physical and spiritual worlds are so thin, heartfelt prayers are always answered.

Thunder once sent me a description she had written of the Sun Dance:

The Sun Dance was the center of the Lakota way of life, a kind of communal Vision Quest. The center pole, the Tree of Life, was a cottonwood tree selected by a young girl. At the top, there were two cut-out rawhide figures: A man and a buffalo, representing fertility. Banners in the sacred colors—yellow for the sun, blue for the sky, green for Mother Earth, red for the red people, white for peace and purity, and black for night—hung from the branches of the tree, along with offerings of tobacco wrapped in cloth. The dancer's Pipes were placed at the head of the dance ground in front of a painted buffalo skull that was filled with sage.

For four days, from sunrise to sundown, the warriors danced to the great drums and the songs, blowing the high, piercing notes of their eagle-bone whistles, their heads, wrists, and ankles wrapped in sacred sage. For four days, the warriors neither ate nor drank, testing and demonstrating their fortitude and endurance, praying to Wakan Tanka, the Great Mystery, holding their vow in their hearts. On the third or fourth day, those who had vowed to do it demonstrated their bravery by piercing their flesh with eagle claws or wooden pegs attached to thongs hanging from the tree, or to buffalo skulls, which they dragged behind them as they danced; they thus demonstrated their generosity, gratitude, courage, and fortitude by offering their flesh—which is the only thing we may truly call our own—dancing until they pulled away and their flesh broke open in an offering and sacrifice, which might bring the wisdom of a vision.

127

*The dance ended with the dancers blessing all who had watched
the Sun Dance and a great feast was then celebrated by all.*

As I read over Thunder's words about Sun Dance, I recalled
how strange and foreign it had once seemed to me. Now I
couldn't imagine missing the opportunity to pray in that way.

The year before I danced, I was in the supporters' Sweat
Lodge the night before the Dance started. I prayed hard, "Great
Spirit, how can I better cleave to You?" As I prayed, I reached
my hands out, as if I was holding on tight to Spirit. At that
moment, I suddenly felt that I was holding on to the Tree of
Life—the Sun Dance tree in the middle of the Arbor—with my
head against the trunk wrapped in prayer ties. I didn't recognize it then, but that moment in the Sweat Lodge was my calling to the Dance.

They say one should have a vision to dance; it's certainly not
something one takes on lightly. The four days of dancing are
four days in the Spirit, but also four days of no food or water in
the hot sun. A pledge to Sun Dance is a pledge to sacrifice and
pray for the people.

At the end of the Dance that same year, the Sun Dance Chief
Charles Chipps asked who wanted to come into the Arbor and
pledge to dance for the next year. I stood, feeling pulled as if by
a magnet, yet scared to go. At the time, I was uncertain about
the meaning of the vision in the Sweat Lodge, or perhaps I was
just too afraid to admit that I did know what it meant. A friend
was standing next to me, and we both had talked about dancing some day. I could tell that she, too, was feeling the pull to
go forward and pledge. Then, suddenly, she took off and went
to the tree. Holding myself back was almost impossible, but my
fear of commitment kept me standing in place. Besides, I didn't
want to pledge to dance without Thunder's blessing. She was
considered by Charles to be an Elder, and asking her first was
the traditional and appropriate way. Yet, I thought to myself,
next year I'll be up there.

128

So "the next year" had now come, and although I had not prepared properly, I was about to dance. I was attending both Sun Dances this year. The first was on the land where Thunder has danced for many years, and where her family now dances. It is attended by mostly fullblood Indian people. Many of the dancers there had fought for Indian rights through years of oppression. Some ceremonies had been declared illegal by the United States government until only recently, and some still are "illegal," despite the supposed religious freedom in our country. This meant that those ceremonies had to go underground in order to be kept alive in the hearts of the people. Many of the Indian people there, including Thunder's Sun Dance Chief himself, had lost family members or gone to prison because of their attempts to hold on to the ancient ceremonies, traditions, and lands. Understandably, some of them were not well disposed towards whites. So we would try to serve with the utmost respect for the people and the traditions by being quiet, honoring, and being as unobtrusive as one can be when you're a different color.

The second Sun Dance, where I was to dance this year, was held at the ceremonial land of the Chipps family, whose ancestors were the teachers of Crazy Horse. The Chipps' dance is held in the same ancient and sacred tradition, although is attended by more white people, as well as other races. I think it must be a very great responsibility for a Sun Dance Chief to allow non-indigenous people to dance, for there is so much that is not understood about these ways by our Western culture.

Charles Chipps once explained to me: "This Spiritual Dance is based on the Red Nation, meaning the blood of the people. I allow people who are red, or indigenous in their hearts, to dance. We are translators of the *Tunkashilas*, or the Spirit, telling the basic truths of the Almighty and His Creation."

The time before the dance can be almost as significant a time of transformation as the Dance itself. This year I was part of the early group that went up to help prepare both camps for Sun

Dance. In the past, Thunder had always been in the middle of things, making sure the energy was flowing well, telling jokes, making people smile, keeping everyone busy and in service. But this year Thunder had to come in later, and it was time for some others to begin learning how to keep that equilibrium with an awareness towards the benefit of all involved. Horse, along with Thunder's sons, Rich and Johnny, headed up our camp, while Sparky, who had been Thunder's first woman "road crew," led the women's work.

We were all doing our best, but it was a real awakening to recognize how very much Thunder had always kept things in balance, and how much more difficult it was without her. In the magnified energies of Sun Dance, each person was discovering new ways to put the ego aside and merge with the greater good for all the people. I kept feeling paranoid, thinking that everyone knew about my argument with Thunder, and I needed to tell myself continuously to "surrender, give up control, just serve" over and over and over again. By the time I was in the Dance over at the Chipps', two weeks later, I was glad for the training.

In the context of Sun Dance, "woman's work" takes on a whole different meaning, for in joyful cooking and in keeping a consciously clean space, we could actually make a difference in people's attitudes and feelings, and hence in how the Sun Dance went. Thunder taught us that it is the quality of love, not only the quality of ingredients, that makes the food taste good and that nourishes the people.

That year I became the "fry-bread queen." Who would have guessed from undomestic me! The fry-bread brought many Indian people into our camp to eat, and that was good. Thoughts create reality, I kept reminding myself; I kept thinking about how nourishing and good this food would be for everyone.

Even the children seemed to intuitively understand the awesome transformative power of the Sun Dance. Joshie, Thunder's six-year-old grandson, was the greatest miracle of the dance. He'd been having a rough time of it that year, and he came to the Dance hell-bent on breaking every rule we made. He was in "time out" during most of the first week. If he wasn't doing exactly the opposite of what he was asked to do, he was bloodying someone's nose, stealing something, throwing food around, or building fires.

As the Dance got closer, and as Joshie watched the preparations of his "uncles," he seemed to think deeply about what he saw and heard. One time Jackie, a senior Sun Dancer in our camp, was massaging him. This was a feat in itself, since Joshie could hardly keep still. Lying pensively on the massage table, he pulled on his chest, looked up at Jackie, and asked, "If I was pierced, would I be good?" His question touched everyone deeply.

Then Joshie decided he wanted to go into the Dance. Each one of his "aunties" helped to make his Sun Dance skirt. Bonnie drew him a buffalo skull; I sewed it on; Jackie, Jude, and Debbie sewed hems while Gussy and Sandy appliqued a red border, just as Joshie described. He was so proud, not as a way of showing off, but because he was shouldering something very big. Quickly, some of his restlessness seemed to ebb away as he took on the seriousness of being out in the Arbor with his uncles. He seemed to take the Dance in stride in a very profound way, somehow sensing the deeper meaning of his participation in this ceremony. His little six-year-old mind seemed to grasp the transformational nature of Sun Dance. He intuitively understood that the days of purification and the days of dancing, sacrificing, and prayer were something that changed people, that brought blessings, that resulted in miracles.

Joshie has been very different since that time; though still childlike, he is more thoughtful, more centered, kinder, and more protective of his little sister. Before Sun Dance, it appeared as if he might never be capable of participating in

131

a classroom, but within the year after his participation, he was in an accelerated class at school. And Joshie is not the only one to experience miraculous changes after Sun Dancing. Adults and children alike, those who bring their prayers to the sacred circle, are greatly blessed in their lives. Changes do happen during the intense focus on the Creator during the days of the Dance.

Time is very different during the Sun Dance; in fact, the closer we get to the Dance, the more time takes on a different quality than normal reality. I could always feel the difference when I did a town run for supplies. Suddenly, errands would stack up into linear order and everything would seem to take forever. Trying to function in a supermarket was like trying to shop underwater. But when I returned to the Sun Dance grounds I was back in the circle again. Lists ceased to have meaning and Spirit would bring the order of the moment. Each day at the Sun Dance always brings an amazing, perfect package of interactions, service, lessons, stretches, enjoyment, and sharing.

My perfect package during the two weeks before first I danced seemed to bring me one test after another. My mind was still reeling with concerns about my relationship with Thunder and for the patterns within me that could create such havoc. While I labored to keep my mind clear and cheerful, still I suffered from the projection of my own "victim-consciousness"—expecting to be rejected, expecting to be left out, expecting to be overworked, expecting to be dishonored. And, as I expected, as my mind projected, so it was.

The woman running the kitchen had me get up most mornings at 5:00 to make breakfast, wanted the fry-bread made most days in the sweltering heat of the afternoon, and often put me on kitchen duty for the evening as well, which usually ran until midnight. When I tried to talk to her about this work imbalance, she kept quoting Thunder, saying "Don't think." At one point, I had important information for her about the Sun Dance supplies and budget, but she didn't want to hear about any of it and I watched helplessly as hundreds of dollars were spent buying supplies we already had in stock. When I tried to take a few minutes to complete my preparations to dance, she stopped me, and told me to be in service. So I worried about finding the time to get ready, but I felt too guilty to prepare during any free moments I had.

Then there was the problem of not having a place to sleep. The woman who had agreed to share her tent with me said she didn't want it to be damaged, so she wasn't putting it up. I stayed in the storage tent one night, in someone's truck another night; I kept having to move my stuff, and I couldn't find a safe place to put my gear while in the dance. I thought about how much we had supported and helped the dancers in the years before, but I felt no support at all. In little ways, my "inner victim" kept popping up to blame this person or that situation for things I did not take care of myself.

I didn't get into town for a shower for over two weeks. The night before we entered the dance, when I finally heated some water for a sponge bath, four pots of it were used up by someone else before I got a little luke-warm water—well after midnight. I stood in the dark under a big ash tree with the bucket of water at my feet, and sponged off. The water felt so good! I looked up at the bright starry night and sighed. This had not been easy! I had had to surrender control over and over and over again in the past two weeks. If Thunder had not pressed me the morning I left for the dance into a deep introspection, I never would have been even remotely prepared as I now was to enter the Mystery Circle. I determined that in the future I would take the responsibility for preparing myself better. Commitment was starting to look very attractive.

Then it started to rain. It was already late in the night, and it poured down hard as the dancers all huddled in a tent to finally finish getting ready to Sun Dance. Around 2:00 a.m. I had done about as much as I could do. What I couldn't do,

133

others helped to complete or shared what they had. Amazingly—despite all my concerns about getting ready—it was not quite the way I would have liked, but ready enough. How much I had worried about things! Where had my faith been? It was now time to meet my Maker.

Almost. I headed through the rain to the Sun Dance Arbor. They said once we went in, we couldn't come out. I slid under the rope that marked off the area for the Dancers, and stumbled towards the tent. I had imagined this would be a moment with heavenly hosts trumpeting and angels singing, but I was brain-dead exhausted; I wanted nothing more than to crash until they called us to the Dance. As I got closer to the tent for women dancers, I chuckled a little; it was the one my "roommate" had not wanted to use. I reminded myself that I wasn't the only one learning to surrender.

I had stashed my sleeping bag, Sun Dance dress, and sacred things in the tent earlier, before the rains had started. Now I dragged myself into the tent, exhausted, and ready to finally lie supine for a few hours. But no! My gear was floating in an inch and a half of water. I had stowed it in the lowest part of the tent that was now a lake. Fortunately, I had hung up the Sun Dance dress. At this point, I wasn't about to waste one microvolt of energy on disappointment. Shivering and aching from head to toe, I slid my suitcase to higher ground and found a place to hang my sleeping bag so the water could drip out, then waded over to the tipi next door, which was semi-dry, and huddled under a couple of towels until morning.

After all that went on before, the Dance itself seemed almost like a dream. In a way, maybe it was. It seemed as if I had endured countless humblings and hardships in the past two weeks. Had it really only been two weeks? It felt more like two months or two years. Maybe that's why people say that the "energies are speeded up" at Sun Dance. In that short time before the Dance, I'd had an incredible training in keeping my mind clear and learning not to react to other people's issues. Over and over again I had been called upon to surrender, to let go, to trust the Creator. Now I was going to need that ability. In the Sun Dance Arbor, there is nothing but your body, your mind, and God. If you surrender, then there is only God.

Thunder woke the women dancers at 5:00 am. She had been designated again this year as Mother of the Sun Dance, and here she was, enthusiastic, smiling, and ready to go. There was no hint of strain between us. "Bless her heart," I thought, "This woman is a saint."

She was there for the people. I had absolutely no doubt that, no matter what was still to be worked out between us, we both still loved each other very much. She was all smiles, with a joke here, something inspiring there, a gentle admonition over there—whatever was needed. She was love and compassion and nurturing. She called us out, encouraged us, and brought us to a state of prayerful readiness. We all loaded our Pipes together, then had a wonderful Sweat, emerging from the Sweat Lodge as the Sun rose. It was time!

But then we waited. And waited. First we waited for the men dancers, who woke up later. Next we waited for their Sweat Lodge, which was longer. Then we waited because there were no singers. They hadn't shown up yet and no one knew where they were. Finally we waited for the men from our camp to get ready to fill in for the singers since it was well past time for the Sun Dance to begin. I think we waited for some other things too. Thunder was out there, juggling the seen and the unseen, being unobtrusive in managing the unmanaged, and stepping back when another Elder decided this or that. She offered bright, twinkling, loving eyes of encouragement for each Dancer, as if it were no special stretch for her, though I know it was. But Thunder was in Spirit. It was her nineteenth Sun Dance that year, and she probably knew better than almost anyone the sacred space that we were about to enter.

At last the singers—our own beloved guys—at the drums,

135

doing their best and sounding pretty darn good...lots of heart
where some exact pronunciations might not have been perfect.
Thunder let me go in with my glasses, which is normally not
allowed—a great fear handled just like that. In fact, I marvelled
for a moment; I had completely forgotten how terrified I had
been of facing blindness in all the years before when I had con-
templated Sun Dancing. Without glasses or contacts, I can't see
more than an inch and a half in front of me. I wondered why
this very major concern had completely left my mind! I hadn't
thought about abstaining from food or water either. All I'd worried about was if my things would be ready. How strange.
What I had worried about turned out to be exactly what gave
me trouble; the things I didn't think about didn't turn out to be
a problem at all. "Yep, thoughts create reality," I pondered.
Well, none of it mattered now.

136

Finally, here we were, getting ready to go into the Arbor. The
men started blowing on the eagle-bone whistles, and one could
feel the electricity of the moment. As those first prayer-songs
filled the air, all else melted away. I remember lining up, each
of us with our Sacred Pipes held lovingly in arms, starting to
get the rhythm, the thrill of the opening song that always
chokes me up, and did so again.

Walking into the Arena, my heart leaping as I honor the Tree
with the Sacred Pipe—how beautiful that Tree always is,
wrapped in all the prayer ties, with all the colored banners flying!—honoring the four directions, stepping in time to the
drum and the song and the eagle-bone whistles. All that other
"stuff" is unreal. How could it have been so important? This is
all there is. All of life is here. I don't have to worry about what
to do—just follow Judy.

The Helpers get us to line up—"Keep those lines straight...the
Spirit is there watching...look good for the Creator." The phrase,
"Something Beautiful for God" keeps running through my
mind; it is the title of a book by Mother Teresa of Calcutta.

Something beautiful for God. As we get around to the East Gate, we look up, and it seems as if the parting in the clouds creates a huge beaming face with light streaming through. Truly, I think to myself, we are seeing the face of God.

Our lines get straighter. We start moving together as a unit. I can feel us moving as one—one body, one sound, one rhythm, one prayer. I can feel us synchronizing our steps and our hearts with each other. The male dancers blow their eagle-bone whistles in unison. If I lose a beat, I find it again in the eagle-bone whistles every time. Our feet all meet the Earth at the same time; we all turn simultaneously, facing each direction together. I think of Grandma Chipps, who had said to us the day before, "Make each direction a prayer," as she gave us a little talk about the four directions. In towards the Tree of Life in the center, spokes in a wheel, in a hoop, rays of the sun, pulsing energy in and out, shining, radiating, circling. Together.

137

We're facing the North, all in unison, and all of a sudden, mid-song, a tinny sound, different singers' voices, sounding disconnected, dissonant. The regular singers have arrived and taken over without waiting for the song in progress to finish. It's jolting, shattering. A smiling voice from behind us pulls us back together: "Shift in energy; go with the shift." Thunder's voice behind us mends the rift in the energy with one cheerful sentence. "God, she's amazing," I think to myself. The momentary irritation disappears; it is turned into prayer for union, and we are one with the new singers.

I see buffaloes in the sky, over and over again. Nurturing, taking care of the people. I pray very hard for help in making good relations with people. The message seems to be to nurture, nurture the people. I think of my spiritual family all out there doing what they can to help—Thunder keeping the balance; Horse, Mike, and Sparky are Helpers in the Dance; Rich, Johnny, and Jimmy have now joined the new singers. I feel a new sense of family sinking in. Lots of love. I start seeing relationships as a very personal thing—which probably should be obvious, but in my life it never was—having very personal concern for each individual.

Somewhere around the third round of the Dance, Thunder comes up to me. Just kind of dancing along, stepping sideways, she looks at me and says, with a big smile, "You've been busted for your glasses." I just laugh, take them off and hand them to her. I don't feel bad at all; I am finally ready to surrender. I am grateful I'd had a few rounds to see what was going on; it really helped me get through the rest. From that point on, all I can see is a blur that is Judy in front of me and another blur that is Connie behind me. Sometimes I go the wrong way, or the helpers motion something to me, and I can't see it, but I just keep praying and dancing. I really can't do anything else; with my vision reduced to almost nothing, it's now really only God and me. Later they say I looked like an angel; that's probably because all I can do is look up to the heavens. I am actually feeling very joyous. I feel like an infant, maybe, having to trust completely the Divine Order of things, because I have no other choice.

Day One over, we are happy and exhausted. Chris, the head woman dancer, watches over us like a mother, sitting in her chair, making sure everything's OK. We do a completion Sweat, then huddle for a bit in the tipi while Thunder tells some funny stories and a little bit of "You're doing great" for each person. She has such an ability to bring everyone together in a good way.

Day Two is hard. At least the tent had dried out. I have a hard time waking up. I feel as if I slept so deeply that I died and I am only halfway back. But I start being grateful for the little things. Each time we line up, I can barely stand. It feels as if I weigh 300 pounds. Then, as I step into the Arena, everything lights up the moment I raise my eyes to the Tree. The Tree of Life gives me strength. An antenna between heaven and earth, wrapped with thousands and thousands of colorful prayer ties, it is a physical and spiritual support.

But I start to feel all the little hills and valleys of the Arbor in my legs. I don't remember them being there yesterday. My lungs hurt and it is difficult to breathe between rounds, but somehow, when I'm dancing, my breathing is fine. One person snaps at me several times as we are resting. I just pray. This time as we dance, instead of buffaloes, I see weird cartoon characters—Sylvester the Cat and the Caterpillar from Alice in Wonderland—self-centered, malevolent characters. It's strange. I wonder if that energy is inside or outside of me. I pray harder. I pray for Thunder, for the elders, for my family, for the world. I ask for help in clearing that which keeps me separate from Creator. I remember the urgency I felt when I decided to dance, and that waiting another year would have felt like putting off prayers that needed to be made now. I pray for our world leaders to make choices that would benefit the people and this planet. When the day is done, I seem to be asleep before I even lie down.

139

I think Day Three will be almost impossible, since Day Two was so hard, but it is somehow much easier. I had really worried about my knees holding out, but they never give me a problem. I feel that I'm dancing strong, though I have a hard time thinking of specific prayers and I can't seem to remember what color is in which of the four directions. I have to settle for prayerfully feeling prayers, because my mind isn't working. With my heart, I offer the strength I'm experiencing this day for the other dancers; I can see that some seem to feel like I did yesterday.

Several important things happen this day. I am dancing, immersed in the light, the music, the motion, the prayerfulness. Suddenly I hear my name being called. At first I think it is Thunder's voice, and I look around. Then I hear it again from a different direction, then several directions. I hear my name being repeated over and over. In a moment it is coming from everywhere, calling me, calling me. I looked around, but of course I can see nothing. After a moment or two, the sound I am hearing becomes once again the eagle bone whistles and the song of the drummers. This happens again later. Each time, for some reason, I don't give it much thought, but looking back, it seems incredible. Only in retrospect do I see what a great gift of Spirit this was, calling me out, calling me into the purpose of my life, calling me to my spiritual heritage.

Somewhere around this time I also receive an insight about people's negativity—others' and my own. I understand better the message of the strange cartoon characters the day before, about the energy of selfishness. I recognize that negative energy is that which draws or takes, rather than gives and nourishes. This, then, was what Thunder referred to whenever she talked about people being needy or "sucking energy." I wonder how much of my time at the Ranch was spent in drawing or taking energy. On the other hand, I see that positive energy is that which gives or puts out. I realize that human interactions are the same as electrical currents in general, but with humans it is the emotions that regulate the direction of the current or energy flow.

Day Four is the hardest of all, at least in the beginning. Prayers are strong, but the body isn't. I'm nauseous much of the day and, at one point, as I am walking out of the Arbor, I'm not sure I can maintain consciousness. I will myself over to the post where I hang my feather and sage crown as the blackness starts to close in around my vision, and I lower myself to the blanket just in time to avoid passing out. I keep trying to dance strong, but slack off, then think about the other dancers; I try to dance for them and their prayers. I have to keep revving myself up, re-connecting myself to Creator to keep going. Someone says it is only going to be four rounds—then we hear it will be seven. I gaze at the Sun for longer periods the last day. Sometimes I feel nauseous afterwards, but it doesn't seem to matter; some kind of connection with Spirit happens as I gaze fully at the Sun, and the prayers are stronger than ever. Some sort of good changes are going on, I can tell. (Later I told my

140

eye doctor about it; she almost fainted: "You can't do that!" But she doesn't know the ceremonies of the Lakota.)

Then finally comes the healing round. I think I won't be able to stand for another moment, but as soon as we start praying for each of those human beings in the circle around the Arbor, the energy comes. Fatigue disappears; joy and celebration prevail. Each dancer touches and prays for each of the supporters in one last circling of the Sun Dance Arbor. I pray hard for each one. I can't see "the right way" to do the healing—or what the others are doing, so once again, I have to just open myself up and trust the Creator. The healing round is just amazing, just beautiful. Then, at last, we file out of the Arbor, shaking hands with drummers, now hoarse but glowing as much as we are, and with the supporters, whose dedicated work is now also done. It is time for the feast and celebration!

141

▲ ▲ ▲ ▲ ▲ ▲ ▲

Thunder always asked me to write about my experiences. In writing about them, I have integrated them as growth in my life. Every time I have reworked the manuscript of this book, I have understood more.

1. Write about some of your spiritual experiences and gifts of the Spirit. Write as much as you can in order to ground them into your awareness and to better understand the meaning of these experiences in your life.

9

THE SELF AS THE SOURCE

AWAKENING THE INTUITION

When life is running its normal, seemingly stable course, we tend to be somewhat reluctant to initiate growth. Yet, when we are experiencing upheaval, we have a powerful opportunity to burrow into our deepest sense of self and to discover the wisdom we hold within. Daily life sometimes keeps us too occupied with routine to discover our own inner resources. But when we are floundering directionless, we are in a unique position to re-evaluate, redefine, and redirect the course of our lives.

During these times of immense opportunity for reorganization, it is tempting to grasp for rules, structures, and habits from our old repertoire of behaviors. Yet that would be like using an old map in new territory—it simply does not apply. Relying on old thought processes and patterns does not produce new solutions; it only produces new ways of manipulating old variables to make things look new. But it doesn't last long, because we are still using the old map, the old tools, the old way of thinking. We need something completely new if we are going to have new results. We may not know what that something new might be, or how we will find it, but seeking a new way is the first step towards finding it.

In our culture, we call intuition our "sixth sense." Yet in some cultures, it is the first, most important sense, for it offers the greatest resource for survival. *Our intuition offers us the benefit of a choice based on a final outcome we may not see or know when we are making that choice.* Using our intuition involves the ability to bypass obvious logical solutions in favor of possibly illogical and seemingly incorrect "gut feelings." Cultivating our intuition requires taking the time to listen and feel within ourselves.

In order to develop intuition, we may need to make the conscious choice to do so, for our normal reality does not generally facilitate its application.

Set the intention of using intuition. Practice. Watch those who rely on intuition and notice how and when they apply it. Make games of your practice—guess when stoplights will change, or who's calling when the phone rings. Use your body as a barometer, paying particular attention to feelings of discomfort or joy when making choices. Then notice what follows. Stop. Pay attention. Feel. Notice the reaction of your physical body. Trust yourself.

The times when we are unsure of what to do and where to go are the ideal opportunities to apply our intuition. Ultimately, grounding, or integrating, that ability in our lives yields a new kind of freedom and mastery. As we practice following our intuition in the great and small things in our lives, from choosing a parking space to choosing a job, we gradually reinforce our ability to use this inherent skill. In doing so, we learn to stand firmly in our Self as an aspect of, and our greatest connection to, the Source. And this inevitably leads us to our greatest purpose and vision.

▲ ▲ ▲ ▲

My own intuition got immediate training after I returned from Sun Dance. They say Sun Dance isn't over when it's over. It is the beginning of a year when our Sun Dance prayers unfold gradually, when our prayers gradually integrate with our lives and in the lives of those for whom we have prayed. Little by little I began to recognize the magnitude of what I had taken on by choosing to Sun Dance.

143

I felt I had learned a great deal in a short time about being a Ranch crew member, about people, and about tolerance. In such a short time I had discovered what being responsible for myself and my thoughts meant, and what being more of a team player entails. I was looking forward to being back with everyone at the Ranch, to laughing and enjoying being together.

But when I returned, Thunder told me that my time was up at the Ranch, that first year Sun Dancers needed to learn to be responsible for their own energy—even though she desperately needed my expertise and help as her secretary. She knew what the unfoldings in the year after my first dance would be like, and I look back with great gratitude for her wisdom.

At the time, though, I was shocked. I had no thoughts of leaving the Ranch, although I'd actually heard her say this about first year dancers before. She also told me that our argument had frightened her too, and that she herself was afraid of repeating what had happened. She had even spoken to her Elders about how to atone for her part in what had happened. As much as she appreciated all I had given at the Ranch, she felt we needed time apart. We would probably both feel safer if we each had some space.

Somewhere in my consciousness I knew she was right. In fact, there had even been some part of me that had been ready to leave the Ranch before Sun Dance, but I did not have the courage to recognize or admit it at the time. Suddenly I realized how prophetic Thunder's earlier words to me had been back when I was moving to the Ranch: "Don't think badly of yourself if you don't get to complete the whole year." How often the words from Spirit would seem to tumble from Thunder's lips, and how often they went by unnoticed—or almost unnoticed. She must have known; she must have somehow foreseen what would happen.

During the next couple of days, I would have periods of great clarity about the miracle that was unfolding in my life, followed by periods of despair and confusion. At times, I experienced great feelings of peace and contentment, and an absolute assurance that everything was in perfect order. I would feel my heart bubble up with love, and feel an incredible sense of appreciation for Thunder and the people at the Ranch, my friends in Houston, my family—in fact, everyone I met. I kept feeling that I was finally gaining an understanding of the nature of community and, as such, felt suddenly closer than ever to my dream of the New Place.

At other times, I would fall into self-incrimination, become completely confused about my life, my work, even my purpose for being alive. If continuing to live at the Ranch wasn't next, what was?

I needed time to sort through all that had gone on, to integrate the massive amount of energy and information that had moved through my system in the past month, not to mention the past year at the Ranch. "I just don't know," was the answer to virtually every question I asked myself. I couldn't make any decisions. So much had happened so fast! I've heard it said that the energies of transformation are continuously speeding up; it certainly seemed that way. The only way I could function was by following what felt right in my heart at each and every moment. That's all I could do in the Dance when I couldn't see past my nose, and that's all I could do now when I couldn't see the future past this second.

I decided that I would hit the road instead of going back to the old patterns and solutions that would be inevitable if I simply returned to Houston. It was time for a new perspective, time for an adventure, time to do something I'd wanted to do for a long time—just drive wherever I felt like it at any time.

Suddenly I was excited. Suddenly I was relieved. Since I could not seem to put my recent past in perspective yet, perhaps I needed to focus on the present. What would happen if I did just what felt right at each and every moment? What would I choose if I decided to do something just for me? What if I were to live by right-brain intuition instead of by what my left-brain reasoning said was "supposed" to be?

It was time to find out. Time to follow my heart. Time to discover what the creative and intuitive parts of me would bring up if given the chance, unrestrained by superimposed disciplines of daily life and concepts of the "right way" to be "spiritual" and "a good person." I would turn this time of confusion into a blessing. It was time to awaken that intuitive aspect of myself that I had hidden away long ago.

On a Thursday morning, August 21st, just one month after taking off from the Ranch for South Dakota to Sun Dance, I was on the road again. How much had happened in such a short time! I was again reminded of the accelerating effect Sun Dance has on our growth. Who was I now? At this point I didn't have the slightest idea.

I made some tentative plans as a framework, not wanting to cut myself loose in the area of intuition too drastically. Images of my dream of the New Place started to surface again. I decided to head up to Arkansas to visit my best friend Melody, then maybe head over to North Carolina. These two areas seemed to be the most conducive to the establishment of a healing center that would offer a mix of healing disciplines in a mountain retreat environment. This seemed to be the time to check them out—maybe even the time to move.

I drove north out of Houston through the tail end of morning rush hour traffic. Normal people, leading normal lives, whizzed past me in the opposite direction, on their way into the city to do whatever normal people do. I wondered what that really was. I asked myself, "Why aren't I normal, like everyone else?" I felt scared and crazy. But another voice said, "Don't think about it right now...just enjoy the drive." I settled into the latter attitude. It just took too much energy to do anything else. I drove in silence, and as the city gave way to the green of the tall Piney Woods of East Texas, I began to allow myself to be absorbed into Mother Nature.

I pulled into Melody's drive early in the evening. It was still daylight, so we sat out in her yard for a while and talked. There was a little stream running through the property, and flowers everywhere—wisteria, hydrangea, roses, and a little herb garden surrounded by dahlias. It was the perfect place to unwind. Melody and I sat for hours as we always did, and talked of everything that was important to us, laughing and enjoying each other's company.

I really needed to talk, and to get some of the confusion and feelings about my recent changes out of my system. Usually Melody was very skilled and supportive in helping me see my lessons in a situation but, much to my surprise, this time she saw my recent experience as abuse, saying that Thunder just took my energy and my money and never showed any gratitude. She asked why I couldn't see that I was not meant to be working for someone else; that I had so much else going for me.

Part of me screamed that Melody was right and that Thunder was wrong, but the other part knew this was not true. I wanted to discover the good—the benefit—of my recent challenges, even if I wasn't seeing or feeling it yet. Some part of me knew that the Great Mystery had a greater plan and purpose in mind which simply had not been revealed to me yet. That's what I wanted to get to. If I were to immerse myself in how wrong Thunder was for getting angry at me before the Dance, or for telling me I had to leave the Ranch after the Dance, then I would miss the gift that was there for me, the blessing heretofore disguised. So I kept my thoughts for the most part to myself, pondering the fact that our best friends will often tell us what we want to hear, but not always what we need to hear.

The next morning we decided to head for Hot Springs. It was just what I needed. I sank into the healing mineral bath and let the warm bubbles swirl around my aching body. I surrendered to jet streams of healing waters, allowing them to play on my shoulders, which seemed to need to suffer and hold the burdens of the world; on my back, which seemed to be so bent over with the work that was never enough and never done; and on my stomach at my central core, which strained to contain and control and hold at bay all that was within and all that was without.

"Don't think. Don't think. Don't think." How many times had I heard Thunder say these words? Each time my mind started wandering through the past, I brought my awareness back to the waters and to the present. Gradually my awareness absorbed into the warmth and the gentle fluid movement of the water around me, as I felt the bubbles tickling and sliding over my body. The heat penetrated deep into my tissues, as if the water itself had a consciousness that was a part of the Great Mystery answering my prayers.

I moved to the large swimming pool and swam two laps. That was all I could do. I was so out of touch with my body; I had no idea how little physical exercise I could handle. But I noticed how grateful I was to be back in motion. I was feeling parts of my body that I'd forgotten were there. Backstroke, sidestroke, doggy paddle—the waters seemed to come up to meet me, to greet me: "Glad you're here. You've been gone too long, old friend!" I felt a sense of merging with Nature, or perhaps with the Spirits of Nature. It was as if the Divine Mother, the physical manifestation of the nurturing and loving mother that is our Earth, had heard my prayers and come to answer right away.

Melody and I emerged from the Hot Springs feeling vital and renewed. I realized that I would never again spend my customary weeks in depression and self-incrimination when things weren't going as I would like. It was time to synthesize the new information I had gained. It is said that integrating Sun Dance takes an entire year, and here it was less than two weeks after my first Dance. That was it! Time to be okay with being human. Time to look inside and see what new perspectives awaited my heartfelt desire to live a spiritual life and to be in alignment with God, Nature, my world, and myself. Time to start integrating and stop fretting about it.

That evening, feeling refreshed and energized, Melody and I sat together to meditate. Almost immediately, as was often the case when she and I meditated together, I began to open up to experiencing another level of awareness. These were usually times when I seemed to receive insights, visual impressions and answers to questions. As we both deepened our focused relaxation, I had the impression of an angel, or of a very bright and light being with a presence that seemed awesome, powerful, and wise. This being appeared somewhat distant and over to my right side, but at the same time, seemed to be present in our immediate space. Towards the center of my field of awareness, there were little bouncing, bubbling, cherub-like beings who seemed to be laughing and talking excitedly in tiny little giggles. This experience was not actually visual, but was rather, a series of impressions.

149

I realized that the bubble cherubs—I wasn't sure exactly what to call them—were spirits of the waters from the Hot Springs area, and that they were overjoyed to be perceived and recognized. I could tell; their effervescence was almost overwhelming. In fact, I even felt a momentary twinge of irritation at them because they were bouncing up and down and giggling so much. However, it was clear that they were completely in alignment with their bubbly nature, and that they were also very excited about having the opportunity to make contact. The other being, the one that seemed to be an angel, was neither male nor female; it had a very strong yet gentle energy. My impression was that this being was an overseer for the energies and beings who worked in the area surrounding Hot Springs where there are vast, underground crystal beds. Both Melody and I felt a much stronger vibrational force than we usually did when doing this kind of work together.

Then I began to hear an internal dialogue, which I consider to be a conversation with my Higher Self, but some might call it channeling. I have given this voice the name "Shanti," which means "Peace" in Sanskrit. As I heard the words in my mind, I shared them with Melody. Shanti asked us to notice how different we felt after the baths. We had both gone into the baths feeling tense and emotional. The experience had been soothing, refreshing, and very healing. She told us that the healing was the work of the water spirits. She said they had been working very hard since the waters in the Hot Springs were now capped and redirected through pipes to the different bath houses and thus were no longer connected to their natural surroundings. We were being invited to help with this situation, hence the great excitement of the little bubbly beings. They asked if we would be willing to return to Hot Springs and circle the city, doing prayers and ceremony to help this location return to its original purpose as an area of healing and light.

Hot Springs had once been a neutral area for Native American tribes from all over the country, a place where they could come and put down their arms, and join together in the sacred waters for healing. The water itself comes from rainwater that fell some 4000 years ago, and then travelled through many layers of rock, including the quartz crystal beds in the area. It returns to the surface at about 140 degrees Fahrenheit.

The area around Hot Springs has been greatly altered by the white man and, therefore, its energies are greatly reduced. One reason is simply the emotional overlay from human beings—much greed and fighting in the past two centuries around control of the mineral waters, which are now run by the National Park Service. Other reasons for the reduction of energies are the physical changes in the area—not only the capping of the Springs, but also the damming of Lakes Ouachita, Hamilton, and Catherine, and the extensive mining of the crystals, much of which is still being done with dynamite and machinery. All of this has been very disturbing to the sacred beings who work with the healing elements of the waters and the crystals.

Shanti indicated that there was the potential for some very

great service, if we so chose, in spending a day circling the city while making prayers to help heal the energy there. How involved we became was up to us—it was a mission, should we choose to undertake it.

We were excited. And maybe a little overwhelmed. It was surely not a coincidence that, as soon as we cleared some of our own "stuff" out of the way, our heartfelt desire to serve was immediately met with an opportunity to do something. It felt big, very big. Actually, at first I didn't like how big it was. I felt that, frankly, I had done enough "big" spiritual things recently.

But Melody pointed out to me, in her characteristically cheerful manner, "Hey, Shanti just asked us if we wanted to drive around the city and pray. We can do that!" She made it sound easy and fun. I was brought back to the Zen perspective of one foot in front of the other, or the basic twelve-step approach of one day at a time. Take it as it comes. This was quickly becoming the theme of my journey: Always "be here now." Each moment leads to the next. No reason to worry about down the road because, if you do, you aren't experiencing the present.

151

As the next day was Monday, we had to wait until the following weekend before Melody would be available for our "mission." This gave me time to drive around Northern Arkansas a little more. Originally I had intended to go on to North Carolina, thus exploring both sites for the New Place. But now it appeared as if I would be returning to Little Rock in five days to come back and join Melody in Little Rock before heading east. Okay. No problem. In fact, it felt as if it was the best option. I flowed easily with the change. I was amazed— that wasn't my nature. I started looking back at all the control issues that had been stirred up around Sun Dance. Something had been altered. Thunder always talked about "going with the flow." Not only were her words now starting to make sense, but practicing them was starting to get easier!

I drove up I-40 going west, then turned north up steep,

winding mountain roads, through dense and mysterious woods, towards Withrow Springs State Park. I drove the four or five hours in silence, reflecting on all that had gone on in the past month. I had been pressed to "let go and let God," over and over again. I thought again of how much I had learned from Thunder, realizing that there was something new inside me that was listening—listening within more carefully than ever before as I made each choice in each moment—to pull over and have a cup of coffee, to turn right at this road instead of left, or to take a moment and chat with this person. I felt as if my hand was being gently held and guided whenever I took a few minutes to listen. I had never before experienced the attunement within that was part of how I found myself functioning now.

I pulled in to the campground mid-afternoon and checked in at the Visitor's Center. It was a tiny park; most of the camp sites were very close to the road. Yet they were also situated by a lovely little stream, and surrounded by dogwood, oaks, and tall pines. I chose a fairly secluded spot which was still visible to the road, but was at least nestled near some trees across from a little footbridge.

No sooner had I picked my campsite when I noticed a couple of scruffy looking guys following me in a pickup. They were clearly eyeing me as I returned from the registration area and twice they drove by slowly as I pitched my tent. I started to feel really nervous. Suddenly, this whole idea was looking pretty stupid. What kind of fool woman would go out camping in the woods by herself? I had never done it before, and now I was frightened. What happened to that gentle-hand holding I had just been feeling? Then I remembered to listen within. I sat for a minute by the stream and tried to attune to my intuition as the guys cruised by for the third time. I just didn't feel comfortable there, as pretty as it was. I threw my gear back in the car and found a different spot, almost as nice, but hidden from the road.

I had just finished staking down my tent when an old pickup with a camper top pulled in next to me. An elderly gentleman stepped out and tentatively surveyed my spot, seeming to check either side of me. Finally, he said, "Hey, you're half in spot number four, and half in five." A little irritated, I looked for the invisible borders that he alone seemed to know about. I'd moved around enough for one day, and we were surrounded by plenty of empty campsites.

"Well, this is where I am." I meant it in a cheerful way, but I could hear the edge in my voice. I wondered when I would learn to set boundaries without having to bristle. Relaxed, clear, friendly boundary-setting—that's what I needed to practice. "There's plenty of room," I said, my voice more gentle.

153

"I always camp in five," he said, "except sometimes I camp in four."

"Well, do you think you'd be comfortable kind of in four and kind of in three? I've already moved once, and I'd rather not have to do it again, if possible," I asked. He thought about it for a minute, then a smile broke across his face. "Sure," he said, extending his hand. "I'm Ned." His eyes had a depth and a clarity about them, and I liked him right away. He went about setting up his camp, and disappeared in and out of the back of his camper carrying a little stove, a lantern, and all manner of makeshift camping gear as we talked. When he was all done, he came out one last time with an old Coleman fuel can filled with rocks.

"I'd like you to have these," he said. "I call them prayer rocks. They come from the desert in California near the Colorado River. That's where I camp in the winters." I smiled. A kindred soul. I kept looking at his face, thinking it looked so familiar. "Oh, I know," I thought, "he looks like Mr. McGoo!" I chuckled to myself. But no, there was something else. I felt very comfortable with him. Perhaps he was an angel, there to keep me company on my first venture out alone. The men in the pickup never showed up again, but their presence earlier had somehow sent me over to be with Ned, and we shared a lot in our two days together. I felt protected by Spirit, and also happy that my intuition, my "listening within," seemed to be kicking in somehow.

Ned talked about living on the road, and told many stories about how he had helped people spiritually. He was a Seventh Day Adventist, and talked several times about global changes that would come soon, and how it would therefore be wise to consolidate one's life. He'd look at me sideways when he spoke, to see my reaction, but I was interested. He talked about Revelations, and the signs of the time that we were now seeing, and the 144,000 that were to be helping with the transition.

These were not new concepts to me. I'd been hearing about pending "Earth Changes" since I'd read Edgar Cayce's books in the early 1970s. Some people thought Armageddon would be a cataclysmic rearrangement of the planet's surface; Mother Earth, fed up with abuse, would simply revolt by changing the planet's physical structure dramatically, and thus taking many people's lives in her process of cleansing.

Others described the changes as being more internal. They called it the dawning of the Age of Aquarius, or the New Age— a time of rapid expansion in human consciousness from one of materialism and self-centeredness to one of spiritual union and cooperation—cooperation with God, with fellow humans, and with the Earth herself.

I personally found all of these ideas fascinating. Without judging the accuracy of these predictions, I have used them to keep myself on the cutting edge of my spiritual growth.

So, I thought it was interesting that someone from a completely different spiritual tradition than I should enter my sphere and bring up these thoughts at a time when I was looking inside for my next step in life. Ned's words also reminded me of my global purpose for Sun Dancing; I resolved at that moment to use this time of attunement within toward that end.

Later that day, I took my first solo hike—it was remarkable

that I had never hiked alone before. I headed down the road towards a trail that Ned had told me about. I walked for a while—a long while—and never found the trail. An old knee injury had been acting up with all the driving I was doing, and walking on asphalt was not helping. My body certainly preferred walking directly on the earth, but I could find no trails. More old pick-ups went by and I started to feel vulnerable and alone again. I cut off on to a dirt road that I thought would bring me back to camp, but I ended up on another asphalt highway instead. I knew this one would get me back to camp; how soon, I had no idea. I walked for another hour. By now, I was limping pretty badly and starting to feel depressed. What happened to intuning with each turn of the road? Where did my intuition go? I'd really missed it this time.

155

Just then, I saw a butterfly on the road in front of me. "Better get out of here, little guy, or you'll get run over." I said aloud as I leaned over and offered my hand. As if he understood English perfectly, the butterfly climbed onto my hand and up my forearm. He was a dark, velvety black, with iridescent lavender on the lower wings, and little red spots on the top. I saw that one of his wings was torn and I imagined he would be grateful for a ride. We walked along together for a while. A large truck blew past, and my friend fluttered away. But, in a moment, he came back and landed on my arm.

My butterfly friend stayed perched on me the whole rest of the walk back, which was still a long way, and eventually he settled onto my shoulder. I felt glad to have him with me, and a happy smile crept across my face. Passing motorists started to wave and smile back. I realized that, besides looking for a potential home, I could spend my journeys sending out happiness and prayers for people as I passed through.

I thought about Thunder and how, when she was on the road, she'd stop at a convenience store and walk clockwise around the store, gently touching all the little things in the store. I knew she was leaving little prayers for the people who would come later and buy those things. Sometimes she would throw tobacco, or other things imbued with her prayers, out the windows as she drove down the road—little blessings for the motorists, and for the people and animals who lived along the way. I decided from that point I would send out little prayers wherever I went.

My little "butterfriend" and I arrived back at camp as dusk fell. I showed him to Ned, then set him down on the prayer rocks, and there he stayed until I left two days later. Periodically, I would go over and visit him. I wondered about the Spirit that runs through all things, about the fireflies back in North Carolina, and the bubble beings in Hot Springs. I thought of the appearance of Ned, and the butterfly, and the many things of Nature that seemed to participate in the miracles of Creator. How does it all work, I wondered? Then I remembered once again why we sometimes called God the Great Mystery, the Unknowable, the Infinite. Ned and I talked about it as we shared our dinners with each other by the light of a lantern he'd found at a pawn shop that day. Then I bundled into my tent for my first night of camping alone. I was beginning to like this adventure!

I spent the next day driving around northwestern Arkansas, both for fun and in search of the New Place. As I was returning to the campground late in the day, something inside of me said, "Drive up to Eureka Springs; this is your opportunity, and you'll be glad you did." Another voice objected, "Why? It's late and you're already tired. Stay and rest."

But the car seemed to turn left instead of right, and I headed north towards Eureka Springs. It was another hour's drive, and I soon lamented making the choice to go. But once there, I was glad I'd made the trip. Everywhere I looked, I saw townspeople working on their houses—painting, planting, reshingling, remodeling. It was remarkable. Here was a community intent on making everything as beautiful as they possibly could. The town was built on a hillside, and resembled a mountain mining town, but with row upon row of beautiful, cantilevered, Victorian houses along the ridges. Lush vines and bright flowers tumbled from balconies and rock ledges. Every single house and store was artistically painted and surrounded by flowers. I did not see one ramshackle home.

As I was wondering why my intuition had led me to Eureka Springs, I realized that what was so striking was the consciousness of beauty that permeated the town and its people. This kind of consistent charm could only be created by the unified thoughts and intentions of many people. If it was possible here, it could be achieved elsewhere. It's not that hard to create beauty—no, in fact, it's very enjoyable. This is something that we, as a community, as a people, as a world, could set as our intention to accomplish! I knew that when I found the New Place, this intention would be a very high priority.

157

I felt as if I were gathering pieces—pieces of what, I wasn't sure—puzzle pieces for the New Place perhaps, although the picture was not clear yet. I kept practicing to feel what to do next, to let Spirit guide me without worrying whether I'd chosen correctly, and to have faith that whatever choice I made was the right one. For whatever I chose, it would teach me something, even if nothing more than that I hadn't paid enough attention to my feelings at the last fork in the road. I was getting used to allowing that inner sense to guide me. I reflected back on my Sun Dance experience; how many times had Spirit—often through Thunder—presented a situation where I had to let go of control. Over and over again, I felt waves of gratitude to the Creator for leading me to such a wise teacher.

In the morning I said goodbye to Ned and my butterfly. As I headed east through northern Arkansas, I wondered again about the fireflies and the butterfly. Could they have been friendly spirits, or perhaps angels or protectors from the unseen worlds? I didn't feel lonely as I had always thought I would if I travelled alone. I felt safe and supported.

The drive was beautiful, inspiring, natural, and clean. The autumn leaves were at their peak of glory, and the weather was crisp and sunny. I continued to relax with Mother Nature, and to follow my heart at each turn. The journey seemed to be uncovering deeper and deeper levels of myself. But nothing reached out to say, "This is it. This is the New Place." By the end of the week when it was time to return to Melody's for our "Hot Springs mission," I was fairly certain that Arkansas was not my new home.

When I returned to Little Rock, Melody was excited and ready for our drive-and-pray expedition around Hot Springs. We packed a picnic lunch, and stopped to buy a few pouches of tobacco for praying. I thought back to my first reaction to praying with tobacco. Basically, it was "Ugh." But now I saw it as putting the energies of my positive thoughts into a physical form, and then casting those thoughts and prayers to the winds to land where they would remain as a prayer transformed into matter. I realized that my view of spirituality had been greatly enhanced and expanded by my study of other traditions. It made so much sense to me to release our prayers to the world through something that would actually hold those energies and keep the prayer "alive." This way to pray also made sense in terms of the whole Native American approach to the Great Mystery—bringing spirituality into the physical instead of seeing it as so separate. What we were going to do that day, then, was to distribute prayers all over Hot Springs. I liked it!

Now, Hot Springs is not exactly a place you can drive "around." The city is nestled in and between and around several mountains and lakes. There is nothing even approximating a "loop" to take you easily around the perimeter. So I sat with a map in one hand, and a bag of tobacco in the other, as we zig-zagged here and there, in and out, over and across, praying and laughing and casting tobacco from the car windows. From time to time, we stopped at key points to say special prayers for the areas that had once, long ago, been sacred to the Native People. Construction, gambling, tourism, and the economy had taken their tolls; Hot Springs had become somewhat seedy and run down. We prayed for the consciousness of the people and for the care of the land, the waters, and the massive crystal beds that had been recently so exploited. We prayed also for a return to the sacred purpose that this place once held. It felt so right; we were amazed at how energized and fulfilled we were by the end of the day. We were ecstatic.

I've visited Hot Springs several times since then, and there does seem to be a different energy in that town, a new pride. It is more like what I saw up in Eureka Springs—people painting the buildings in quaint Victorian style, new stores and art galleries, and more people interested in the baths. I don't know that our day of prayers changed it, but then, who really knows what moves things in this universe?

Melody and I completed our sojourn at the center of town for dinner. We stopped at the local New Age book store, and each wandered about on our own, browsing here and there. As we left, I pointed out a book in the window that had caught my eye as we walked in. "Hey, look!" I exclaimed, stopping to peer in through the window at the book cover. *Crystal Waters: A Guide to Hot Springs and the Ouachitas*, it read. Notes under the title indicated that the book included "vortex areas, fishing tips, attractions, hot baths, night life, accommodations, crystal mines, maps..."

Vortex areas? What was that?

I looked over at Melody, who stood with a great big grin on her face, fishing through her new purchases. In a moment she pulled that very same book out of her bag! "Well, I guess we're supposed to do something with this book!" I exclaimed. I wondered what it was.

That night, I bundled into bed with the *Crystal Waters* book—read the whole thing right through. Since we had just received information from Shanti about both the healing energies and healing the energies of this area, I thought that finding a book about local vortexes was an interesting coincidence.

The author identified seven energy centers, or vortex areas, of the Hot Springs and Ouachita Mountains area. They ran in a line a little east of Hot Springs, which was almost the center of the state, through the "Valley of the Vapors," or Hot Springs itself, and then through the lakes and mountains of the whole crystal-bearing area. The last vortex was at the summit of Queen Wilhelmina State Park on the edge of Oklahoma.

When I woke the next morning, I had a strong sense to travel the "vortex trail," and to continue the prayers for healing the land that we had started the previous day. I also sensed that this would be the completion of my trip, and that North Carolina would have to wait, since I was getting the feeling that my next turn in the road would be towards the south, back to Houston. There was something in Houston, my intuition said, that was not yet complete.

But now it was time for my trek through the vortexes of Arkansas. Of course, I didn't know if they were really vortexes. But the area had always seemed very powerful to me. Whether these energy centers existed or not, this trip provided an excellent focus and reason for doing prayers. If there were some kind of special vortexes, then all the better.

I had decided that I would do a Pipe Ceremony at each of the specified locations. I would offer prayers for the healing of the people of our planet, and the healing of the Earth herself in this area. It seemed appropriate to thus honor this land, central to the whole country, which once had been the peaceful gathering place of the Native people. It seemed appropriate, too, to take the blessings, the power, and the grace that had been gifted to me at the Sun Dance, and return them to the people, return them to the land. This was the purpose of the Sun Dance, and it felt like a fitting completion of the Dance before diving back into life in the city.

I said goodbye to Melody on Monday morning again, grateful

for the way we shared the growth and spirituality in our lives. As I started to journey through the vortexes, I discovered immediately that their exact locations were not actually specified. I had to feel them out, again taking the intuitive, "follow my heart" approach that had been the theme on this trip to a higher level. I needed to find out what felt right to me, but I also had to sense the land, to listen and feel very carefully for subtle shifts in energy. I kept dodging populated areas and exploring back roads until I found the place that felt appropriate for the Ceremony.

I was concerned when I started that not all of these seven "vortexes" were in isolated areas. Some were actually important tourist centers. I wanted to do the Pipe Ceremonies in a completely sacred and respectful way, which meant that interruptions by curious tourists would not be appropriate. Yet, even when I had to bring the Pipe out in a fairly open area, no one ever appeared while I was making my prayers. By the end of my five-day journey, I was comfortable with the process, and had reached a point where I was almost immediately drawn to a particular spot that felt just perfect for prayer.

As I got closer and closer to the end of this intuitive journey, I discovered that the more I trusted the little voice of guidance from within, the more I experienced a lack of separation between my Self as the Source, and the realm of the Great Mystery. More than anything, I was now exceedingly grateful to Spirit, and to Thunder, for all that I had experienced in the past months. Some of the blessings along the way had been well disguised, but they were rich, profound, and very great.

▲ ▲ ▲ ▲ ▲ ▲ ▲

It is time for us to understand that we have the power to create a whole new world—including new solutions to old problems—by acknowledging and using the intuitive and creative thought processes available to all of us. Training the intuitive mind is no different from training ourselves to play tennis, or to play the French horn—it takes practice. There are many books on the subject, but here are some specific exercises to strengthen your intuitive muscle:

1. Take a vacation by yourself. Don't plan, and don't decide anything until the moment you do it. Do stop, pay attention, feel, notice your body's reactions, and trust yourself.

2. Recall moments in your life when you've trusted your intuition and the outcome was beneficial. What were the benefits, or blessings, that resulted from paying attention to your own inner guidance?

3. Set aside a week during which you will make all choices by intuition alone. Notice the thoughts and fears that arise while you are going through the process.

4. Make a list of the social, ecological, and economic emergencies that faces human kind today: Now, letting your imagination run free, think about how our collective intuition might bring about solutions.

⬛➕10➕⬛

JOURNEY TO THE YUCATAN

THE COURAGE TO LISTEN AND LOOK

The cutting edge of self-empowerment is when we examine how and why we have created that which we do not want. By being willing to see and understand the power we have in creating that which we consider negative in our lives, we discover that this same power can create the fulfillment of our dreams. But to do this, we must be willing to see the dark and hidden within ourselves.

As we seek out a greater perspective in life, we walk from a belief in our own limitations to the beginnings of the ability to utilize the creative force within us. For each of us, this is "the hero's journey," because every time we face and seek to overcome our limitations, we evoke from ourselves heroic courage, effort, and the willingness to examine our own dark side. Each time we backslide, or fail at the same thing one more time, or discover a hidden darkness buried in our soul, it takes courage, effort, and willingness in order to stay on our path of evolution.

This courage, effort, and willingness are always needed if one is to strike forth in a new direction, or change old behavior and do things differently. Most adventure stories apply the principle of the hero's journey in the physical realm but, in fact, *it is in the realm of our own minds where the greatest acts of courage are required.*

It is an act of bravery for some of us to listen quietly and attentively, while for others, it takes courage to speak our truth, or to set our boundaries. For some, great determination is needed to finally get out of a destructive relationship, while for others it is the staying which requires strength. For some, to stand up in front of the public requires courage; for others, that effort may be the willingness to stand in the shadows, unrecognized.

To move forward—to face the obstacles in our own growth—does not mean we cease to fear the unknown, nor that we can find a way to make comfortable that which is difficult. Rather, it means we make the choice to take a stand for our dream, even when our knees are knocking, our teeth are chattering, and every fiber of our being wants to cut and run in the other direction. It means releasing our rigid perfectionism and just being a human being learning to fulfill our magnificence.

164

The ultimate test of the hero's journey is always facing the mirror created by the projections of our own minds. The proverbial dragon is always our own hidden dark side, the part we do not want to see about ourselves—the fears, the anxieties, the irritations, the judgements, and all of the other ways in which we limit ourselves. The dragon is nothing less, and nothing more. And, it is fully within our own power to face it and emerge victorious.

It is quite normal within human interaction to assign our dark side—that shadow part of ourselves which we do not see or do not like—to something or someone outside of us. It is easier to blame than to be introspective. Yet, when we receive evidence and information pointing to how we project and set up our own failures, how do we react? Do we want the feedback or do we push it away? Are we willing to hear and to consider the validity of others' criticisms? Can we find the courage to face truthful feedback? Can we listen? Will we do *more* than listen; can we be curious to know what lies within those parts of ourselves to which we have been blind? Do we actually *want* to go through facing our dark side so that we can emerge into the light?

Part of our armageddon process involves not only recognizing, but making peace with apparent failures and backsliding.

Forgiving ourselves (and others) and reckoning with our imperfections are integral aspects of any forward movement. Every path has downhills and uphills, as well as plateaus where it appears no progress is being made at all. To claim our victory, we must be willing to look in the mirrors, and hear the feedback, as well as to go through the apparent periods of back-sliding, the retrograde times of review, and still keep moving towards the dreams in our hearts. It is the courage of the heart to make this choice that moves us out of old patterns into a bright new present.

▲ ▲ ▲ ▲

I was called to draw upon such courage during a journey to the jungles of the Yucatan with Thunder later in the year after my first Sun Dance. This trip became symbolic of my willingness to journey into the hidden jungles of my own mind. That year, the "opportunities for growth" presented to me were countless! I had heard it said that Sun Dance would change my life, and I had thought, "Good, I want that." But I had no idea what I was asking for! I didn't realize what that change entailed. The upheaval did not abate during the entire year. The challenges were countless. And, I took them all on.

As I merged back into life in Houston, I was seeing many differences between how I used to be and how I was now. Control issues—the fear of lack and loss, the concern for what others thought of me, the struggling and striving—all seemed to be loosening their hold on me. I experienced an inner knowing that Spirit was holding me, guiding me, taking care of my needs. When things appeared to go wrong, however much I might struggle, underneath there was now a trust in the workings of Spirit, a belief that there was plenty, an awareness that there was a greater plan and purpose to all things.

I was experiencing a strange dichotomy. It was hard...and it was easy. On the one hand, I was still processing the growth brought on by my Sun Dance prayers; on the other hand, it seemed as if I was being gently carried through those changes. While the challenges appeared to be more difficult than ever, my ability to take them on was also much greater than it had ever been.

Thunder had planned the trip to the Yucatan for early November. I was still a little skittish about getting reinvolved in the Ranch activities since I hadn't finished clarifying for myself all that had gone on around Sun Dance. I had seen others at times step away from upsets at the Ranch, blame Thunder for the mirror she provided, and move on. But I knew that Thunder was a teacher who, regardless of people's reactions, would continue to hold that mirror for those who wanted to see more clearly. I knew if I kept looking, I would learn something important about myself—something I needed to know. Yet, at the time, that "something" was still so foggy.

Thunder had long hinted to me about the possibility of me joining the upcoming Yucatan expedition. I still did not yet fully understand or agree with her perspective on what had occurred just before Sun Dance, but I *did* know that whenever there were disagreements, time usually proved her greater wisdom. Understanding usually came with simply watching how events unfolded. So, while a part of me wasn't quite ready to join the group again, I took courage and made the choice to go to the Yucatan. I'm sure it was a stretch for Thunder as well to allow me to go, but Spirit had told her I should, and she always followed what Spirit said to her.

There was no doubt that something inside of me needed to be a part of this trip. During different periods of my life, I had spent much time touring the ruins of Peru, Guatemala, and Mexico. When I was a child of seven, my family had moved to Brazil, where we lived for almost four years. En route, we visited some of the ancient archeological sites in Peru. I remember standing at the top of a partially reconstructed stairway and feeling a great wave of sadness well up inside of me.

Experiencing a deep sense of loss, I burst into tears. "They're all ruined," I had cried. "Of course they're ruined," my father had laughed, somewhat taken aback by my emotionalism. "They're ruins!"

My father's response was logical, but he did not know that something deep inside of me had called from a distant past. It was as if there were a memory that lurked just below the surface, and I couldn't quite touch it. My seven-year-old mind did not try to make sense of my feelings; I merely stood there surveying the piles of rock and dirt, and sensing the loss of a magnificent culture that had once existed, that had once known how to live in harmony in a way that I had not seen in my young life.

167

The Yucatan expedition was, in fact, a journey into the past. Wherever we went, we attuned to the energies of past cultures still alive in the temples, the glyphs, and the land. Traveling with Thunder meant constantly keeping all senses finely tuned, and the awareness ever alert. "Did you hear that?" "What did you notice?" "What did that feel like to you?" At the end of each day we would all gather together in our hotel. Crammed around Thunder in her room, we would tell what we had seen, laugh at the mistakes that had been made along the way, and share what we had noticed and what energies we had picked up.

We caravanned from one pyramid to the next, having one spectacular spiritual adventure after another. As we went deeper and deeper into the jungle, it was as if we were symbolically peeling away layers of time and layers of our minds.

I felt as if we traveled in a time capsule, our two mini-vans transporting us in a bubble of radiant light through to another dimension, one where Spirit seemed more present and active than in daily life back in the city. Houston, now so far away, represented Earth, the practical world; this jungle became the realm of symbols and the archetypes.

I stood atop a tall pyramid and saw through ancient eyes the choice to sacrifice the physical body in order to soar to the realm of spirit as an Eagle. This choice was not negative or fearful as I might have imagined; it was ecstatic. I walked around ancient temples bearing glyphs which told of the connection to higher realms, mysteries that I knew could still be unraveled from the right state of mind. I journeyed through other ruins where the energies indicated a loss of connection to Spirit, a stubborn anger towards Spirit, and sacrifices made against people's will. We were seeing the rise and fall, not only of an ancient civilization, but of an advanced level of awareness that existed long ago. We stopped on a pristine beach, wandered among ocean-side wild flowers, and were renewed by the fresh salt air.

Thunder orchestrated our journey with the skill of a master conductor before the finest symphony. At the pyramids in Palenque, she held a Pipe Ceremony on November 11, one of the sacred windows in time and space for transformational energies known as 11:11.

Following her intuition, she led us through a series of amazing "coincidences" that enabled us to meet and share ceremonies with the leading Mayan priest, a magical, twinkly-eyed, 126-year-old man who stood about 4'11", wore the traditional white muslin dress of the men of the tribe, and had nary a grey hair on his head. A special ceremony was held, uniting these native people of the Mayan and Lakota traditions. A Sacred Pipe, carved for Thunder by a member of the Lakota Calf family, was gifted to the Mayan Elder; our interpreter told us that he said this was the first time in history that the Sacred Pipe was gifted to the Mayan people. Thunder was also told that she was the first woman ever to be invited into the temple there, and allowed to sit on a man's council chair and participate in ceremony. I watched as she and the old Mayan priest seemed to communicate independently of the translators by smiling and nodding at each other at times that otherwise didn't make sense. What a rich experience it was to see these two Spirit beings together!

The journey continued, and as we traveled through one section of the highway that felt dark and negative, Thunder told us the story of how, during another trip four years before, she had been moved by the Spirit to actually lift a woman out of the path of a runaway truck, withstanding the brunt of the impact herself. She had not even noticed her own injuries—two broken ribs and her left side bruised to a dark purple from head to toe—until hours later, after the other woman had received medical care hours later. We stopped briefly at the place where this accident had happened and, as the scene played in my mind's eye, tears welled up in me for this teacher of mine who always gave so much.

169

Later, we got lost in the jungle, but Thunder kept everyone's spirits high by leading us in the loud and somewhat boisterous singing of old spirituals. This was part of the magnificent way that she juggled energies; she kept us focused on light and laughter as we found our way out of the tangled Yucatan rain forest.

At Palenque, Thunder invited two other women and me to a little-known corner of the Pyramids known as the Queen's Bath, an enchanted series of quiet, hidden pools in the tumbling waters of a stream. Each pool was like a smooth bathtub, carved from rock over the eons of time. In these ancient waters, we helped Thunder cleanse and bless many of her sacred altar pieces: stones, gems, little carved animals, things which were special to her in different ways. The three of us, in turn, carried a few of these precious pieces down to the gently flowing waters and lovingly washed them. As we did so, once again it seemed we were in another time: I was a girl of eight, playfully drinking in the peace of this privileged, shared time with the Queen. I made little crystal dolphins swim and dive; walked a herd of miniature, carved elephants on an expedition across river rocks; and swirled in my hands sparkling amethysts and tourmalines through bubbling, light-speckled waters. Delighting in the day with the eyes of a child, I experienced only the moment—the sunshiny, magical, shared moment of women in their element of water.

Yet Thunder has often pointed out that, once we bathe ourselves in Spirit and receive divine nourishment, there is sometimes a part of us that wants to pull back into our old patterns, and to return to the familiar consciousness of separateness. Sometimes we bleed off the spiritual energy that we've built up by quickly returning to our normal earthly dramas. The darkness within us keeps wanting to return and balance the light; this is common to human beings at our stage of evolution. It is an aspect of the duality in which we still live on this planet.

And so it was, again. I discovered it was not the jungle that took courage for me to face, but the dark recesses of my own mind. At the time I thought once again that somebody else did it to me, but now I can look back and say, yes, I did it to myself. That's the way it usually is, though in the moment it is often difficult to see.

I had enjoyed a most magnificent journey as I sat in my little place in the middle of the second mini-van, hanging out in meditation and beaming out love. The rifts of the past summer appeared to have melted away. But there was an upset the day before we left the Yucatan. It was not major; a man who was on the trip with us was rude to me and a few other women. I certainly could have just overlooked it. Not recognizing Thunder's own vulnerability, and the need to be more of a warrior myself, I told her about what happened just as we were about to take off for the day. My timing was terrible, and once again it seemed as if I had caused an upset.

"How dare you treat these women this way?" she confronted him. She was at my side, defending me. Yet, as a child of a dysfunctional family, unaccustomed to receiving support and protection, my mind began to retreat into patterns of the past. Once again, I was involved in something that had caused an upset around Thunder, and this greatly disturbed me. I actually perceived Thunder to be angry at me, even though she was being extremely kind and loving, even watching out for me, smiling and joking a lot, and often acknowledging me. The little girl from long ago still living in my forty-something body, felt guilty and responsible, as children often do. I did not see at the time that Thunder was using this situation to help all of the women realign themselves from within, and take back their power from a man who had been abusive. I did not see until later how much Thunder cared about me; I simply did not know how to respond to that kind of support.

Carrying the past in my mind, I dove back into the perspective of the victim and, from that position, I began to push other people's buttons. I became fearful and felt way out of balance. My mind got stuck in "I can't do anything right," and I could not seem to shake it. During the remaining day and a half, I could never quite get back on course. I became very nervous and easily upset, snapping at several people as a result.

During our flight back to the States, I decided to walk to the back of the plane where Thunder, Horse, and five others were sitting. I thought I'd say hello, and maybe see if they were telling any good stories. More than that, I was probably looking for some reassurance, some way back to balance, though I did not recognize or say that. Feigning cheerfulness, I knelt on the seat in front of them, facing back towards the group, and asked what was going on. Thunder replied that several of the others there had been saying they were angry with me, and would I be willing to listen to them talk about it?

I was shocked and scared. Just petrified. I did not yet feel secure in my reconnection to my spiritual family, and now it seemed as if I had messed up again. But I also knew that my victim stance of the past couple of days had been an irritant—I had seen people react to it. What Thunder had been trying to tell me the morning I left for Sun Dance was still a great fog, and I knew that most of my imbalance over the past two days was because I still did not yet see or understand what had happened. Despite my fear, something told me that this was a unique opening in time to get clarity.

Sometimes I'm not sure whether I'm courageous or just stupid, but I am always instantly curious when someone says they want to clear something with me. I want whatever barriers that might arise to be aired so they can be healed. I knew I could say no to Thunder's offer, but in order to take responsibility for myself, and to learn about my "victim-consciousness" patterns, I would have to stop hiding behind my hurt inner child. I would have to be willing to hear the feedback the group wanted to give me.

I surveyed their faces. "Firm compassion" might sum their different expressions. I knew this was not about "dumping", but rather about clear, concise feedback, the kind we don't get very often because of our defenses, our come-backs, our "yes, buts". Although Thunder and I had talked some about our argument that summer, I still felt unresolved, unsure of exactly what had happened. I thought if I listened, I'd be better able to understand what had occurred between her and myself. But what I did not yet comprehend was that Thunder's feedback before Sun Dance was not about Thunder and myself, but about my relationship with the others. Thunder had simply been a reflection for me so I could see my patterns. Now she was taking this opportunity to help me directly face their feedback.

I was finally willing. From some place deep inside, I knew this was another blessing in disguise. Part of me wished I had just stayed in my seat up in the front. My knees shook, but I took a deep breath and said yes, I would listen.

Thunder started and, as she did, I felt my resistance leap to the forefront within seconds. She told me that they were all angry at me, and that she was going to ask each one to speak. God, I was sweating! Why had I said yes to this!? Whatever they had to say, I wanted to explain. I knew I had done my best, and I wanted them to see it the way I did. Whatever it was that they had to say, I was certain it was not totally justified, and I wanted assurance that I would get the opportunity to answer. But, at that moment, Horse told me, and kept reminding me, to just listen and not answer. I hadn't counted on that. And I didn't like it! But he was very gentle when he said it, as he looked me in the eye and reminded me to breathe, just breathe and listen, breathe and listen.

Some part of me understood at that moment that *when we insist upon on our own time to talk, we miss the feedback; we miss the gift.* We do not hear the answers to "why me?" and, "what did I do wrong?" and, "why isn't this working?"—questions which we sometimes ask when we are busy feeling sorry for ourselves instead of really wanting the answers. We keep the information out, and thus maintain our old patterns, while we continue to complain about how the other person "did it to me." I realized that this was exactly what I had done time and time again when offered insights at the Ranch. Somehow I needed to do things differently now. I kept breathing, kept trying to remember each word instead of shutting it out. It was hard. Very, very hard.

Thunder asked Gerrard, a spiritual teacher and counselor who was traveling with us, to be the first to speak. He shocked me by launching in with a very angry but contained voice, "Get your anger out of my space!" I was immediately taken aback. At first, I didn't know what he meant, and I didn't think he had seen me angry. But it seemed as if he was somehow modelling what he was saying to me by the way he expressed it. I realized for the first time that it was possible to express anger without verbally or energetically dumping it onto others. In other words, one could speak one's anger with clarity without projecting it onto another person or trying to make that person responsible for it.

Then Thunder told me she had felt hurt at my reaction to her story about being hit by the car. She said I had identified with the story so much I had been crying for myself instead of see-ing her pain. At first I thought she was wrong. But since my energies were not being expended in defensiveness, I consid-ered what she said. I realized there was truth in it, and even more so at other times. I certainly had been thinking only of myself during our big upset that summer, which had been one of Thunder's main points that day. It was a pattern I was to starting to see with increasing clarity. I thought of her as such a master, that I imagined she didn't need my concern. I realized that there were many other times I had become so caught up in my own needs that I had missed the needs of others.

Thunder also told me that I had a habit of making great con-tributions and doing marvelous, fantastic work, but then creat-ing bad endings. When I did that, no one could even say "thank you." Wow. I hadn't thought of all the endings in my life as having to do with me. But of course they did. I was the only common denominator! During my childhood and ever since, I had always "moved on." In doing so, I would sometimes create a big emotional separation, which would help me feel safe, and able to escape from accountability and commitment. It would provide me with an excuse to leave by blaming the separation on the "other," and feeling as if I was moving on to better things. I had heard this pattern referred to in 12-step programs as "the environmental fix," a device for extending denial a lit-tle further, for putting off responsibility a little longer. The only problem was, I had been using this device for a long, long time. I could no longer say that the other person always created those separations. It was me. I created them, and I needed to face my responsibility.

Because I had agreed not to speak, the mixture of hurt at the truth being spoken along with the pain of seeing what I had done became almost unbearable. We were towards the back of the plane, and I was perched on the center of three empty seats, facing back towards the seven of them. It was somewhat private, but not completely. I could feel the tears starting to well up, and I began to silently heave deep breaths, trying not to make any sound.

Still I listened. Jane spoke next. Her mother had died the previous week, and in spite of her grief, I'd snapped at her a couple of times. She said that now she didn't think she could trust me any more. At first I bristled, straining against answering back; it seemed as if she had been so irritable towards me. Then I thought about her loss. I hadn't given her any margin for her grieving!

Again, I had not been thoughtful about the extenuating circumstances of the other. I felt ashamed, and the tears rolling down my cheeks dropped silently on the seat-back.

Horse spoke next about how I had "provoked" Thunder before Sun Dance. Again I was shocked. *I* provoked *her?* My experience of it had been that she had provoked me! But since I was just listening, I took it in, and gave it a great deal of thought. Later I recognized that *defensiveness is indeed a provocation, for it assumes that the other has ill will.* Explaining something away, or even just waiting for someone to stop talking, were not the same as listening, as I was doing now. That defensiveness was often a way of invalidating the other; it is an expression of unwillingness to listen or to see another perspective, and often includes projecting negative energy toward the other person while seeing oneself as innocent. I'd never realized this before.

Donny spoke, too; he had been my client for a long time before I introduced him to Thunder; now he was one of her staff members. He reminded me of a time in the van when I had asked that a window be closed because I was getting a stiff neck. He talked about how irritable I had been. I just looked at him, feeling betrayed, but I didn't speak. This whole situation felt so shaming. Once, Donny had really looked up to me; now he was criticizing me. I felt utterly naked, with no protection, stripped of all dignity. Yet I stayed and listened. It took every bit of courage I could muster. It wasn't until much later that I

175

gave serious consideration to what Donny said, and realized that my irritability was also something Thunder had addressed before Sun Dance. This time, though, I had heard it. Some part of me had faith in this process and in about anything Thunder offered.

Blaze spoke next. She had been the one at Sun Dance who had scheduled me for almost constant kitchen duty. Remembering all the tension between us at Sun Dance, I didn't think I could listen for another moment. Yet, I was surprised, for although she, too, sometimes carried an irritable edge, at this moment she was soft-spoken, kind, and compassionate. I don't even remember her words; what stuck with me was the love in her face when I expected rejection, and how that helped me to keep sitting and go on listening.

Then came Trent—Trent who never seemed to lose his cool and who always seemed to know exactly what Thunder needed at every moment. Trent, who was never unkind, and was often very wise. He looked at me in his normal detached way and said that he didn't understand why I always told him what a good support person he was, even though he was a relatively new member of this group.

It was an odd thing to say in the midst of this difficult feedback, but somehow his words cut through all my remaining defenses to my very core. Suddenly, I was sobbing uncontrollably. I muffled the sound as much as I could, but I knew that other people were turning around to look. It didn't matter. At that moment I was six years old, comparing myself to my younger sister who was always cute and gentle and easy to get along with, and wondering what was wrong with me; no matter how I tried, I could never seem to please my parents. I realized I had spent an inordinate amount of energy trying to be "good enough" around Thunder. I never let go and just allowed myself to be myself. I laid my head on the chair back and just cried. The tears, though, were not of the present; they were releasing something from long, long ago. This journey with

176

Thunder through the jungles of my mind had surfaced a key to my childhood, and brought about a repatterning of my past.

Something very important broke at that time, and it was a lifetime of thinking I was not good enough, and that I had to control others by attempting to avoid their anger and by somehow keeping them happy.

It just wasn't possible.

It just wasn't possible.

I had tried so hard to be perfect at the Ranch—perfect like Trent (or my sister.) But I could never be perfect and I could never be either of them. I had struggled so hard for Thunder's love and approval without seeing that it was always there. In the process, I had once again abandoned myself, abandoned them, and abandoned my faith in the workings of Spirit.

As the tears fell, Thunder reached out and put her hand on my head. Some part of me knew that she had never stopped loving me or holding my highest interest in her heart but, at the time, I just wanted to hide, and I shook it off. Thunder told me she had not expected so much to come out, and she asked if there was anything I wanted to say. I shook my head. It made sense that the others were taking this opportunity to address their concerns with me after all the time I had shut out their feedback. I was finally listening.

Inside somewhere I knew that the people before me really loved me and that they were trying to give me some important information for my life. Yet I had just lived and breathed and listened through my greatest fear—being told I wasn't perfect. I was still alive, but my head was swimming. I could barely look anyone in the eye. Some truth had been spoken, maybe some truth that long needed to be said, and I felt ashamed. There was so much to assimilate. I needed to be alone. The plane landed, and I staggered like a zombie through customs. I was glad when I finally stepped out onto the muggy streets of Houston to head home.

It was some time before I could integrate all that had been

177

said. I would have liked to have been able to look at each one of my friends and say with a cheery smile, "Gee, that was great information; thanks!" It would have been nice if I could have said to Thunder, "Wow, you have such an uncanny ability to carry a person through a series of experiences, and then just at the most magnificent moment, pop them through a quantum leap into another level of growth; I am so grateful!"

But it took a while to integrate. I didn't experience that situation with the gratitude I do now. Becoming willing to hear has taken constant intent and work. Today I am much better at receiving feedback.

At first, I wanted to be angry with all of them, but gradually I came to accept that they had told me the truth. I started to settle back into that surrender that I had started to learn at the Sun Dance. I began to accept that I could not control others or their feelings. As for the latter, I could barely control my own! Gradually I found myself loosening my perfectionism and, as I did, I relaxed further into my own humanness and became more accepting of others and their imperfections. I began to discover a greater connection to and comfort in my feminine side—the receptive, the nurturing, the listening.

The rest of that year brought me countless opportunities to surrender. At times, I seemed to go forward; at other times it appeared more as if I were going backwards. But, somehow, that process had become more comfortable. I had prayed in the Sun Dance to be closer to Spirit, to become more able to surrender. Now it was if the Creator was sanding down my rough edges, using finer and finer sandpaper. I started to discern the *difference between vulnerability and being a victim.* I began to reckon with the *choice between the receptivity of grounded feminine energy and the addiction to the drama of being powerless.*

I had often heard Thunder say that what we need to know about our lives is sometimes hidden from us, and that it takes others around us to act as mirrors, thus showing us the truth. Many times she has said that when someone is upset or yelling

178

at her, she imagines the face of Jesus or Mother Mary on that person so she can truly hear what they have to say. Doing this, she says, helps to open the listening mechanism inside of us so that we can have the opportunity to become responsible for what we have done.

As time passed, when I found myself hurt, confused, or angry, I tended to find refuge in myself. But, at the same time, I had more courage to examine external feedback system. I allowed a safe place to be created inside of me where I didn't criticize or get angry with myself as much as I once did, yet I was able to hear better when others had information to help me improve my life. I would get into my heart and allow the pain to happen if it was there, allowing the tears to wash through whatever I experienced, if necessary, without ignoring any feedback that might be given. If there were choices to make, I tended to feel more for the answers instead of finding them through logic. In the past I often cringed at my mistakes; now I would sigh, say a little prayer for improvement, let them go, and keep doing my best.

I was finally learning that God was in charge after all, and that any time I thought I had a better answer, I was soon to discover otherwise. So I began to trust the Creator. I began to look more for the blessings, getting caught less and less in the disguise, the illusion. Each challenge I walked through seemed to sand down more of the rough edges, the resistance, another little piece of the ego. Because I had found an authentic teacher who was willing to both see her own issues and encourage a fair and open exchange in group dynamics, I finally began to experience myself as an integral part of this wonderful spiritual family in an authentic way. And because I had taken the courage to face my greatest fears about myself, I was beginning to find a new kind of peace in the midst of whatever unfolded in my daily life.

179

▲ ▲ ▲ ▲ ▲ ▲ ▲

We cannot change the thoughts that create our reality if we aren't aware of them because they lie so far below our consciousness that they are imperceptible to us. It is often the very hardest of times that helps us bring to the surface those very thoughts and beliefs that keep us from moving forward. Are we willing to look? Can we take the courage to be curious? Can we find the difference between perfectionism and simply being a human being with dreams and aspirations? Consider the following.

1. When has a friend or loved one told you the truth about some aspect of your behavior? How did it feel? Did you blame yourself or the loved one, or did you choose to listen deeply, take the feedback to heart, and look at what you might or might not want to do differently?

2. What feedback have you resisted that you know is true? Take the courage to look at it by writing it down. Then sit quietly for a while and open yourself to the idea of a healing taking place within you.

3. In what areas of your life have you been a perfectionist? In what ways have you been intolerant of yourself when you have not met your goals? What are your pictures about how a "good" or "spiritual" person acts? How do you criticize yourself when you don't "measure up?" Write a page of affirmations that allow for your humanness even while you are still working towards your goals and aspirations. Practice saying these affirmations five minutes a day for a month.

RETURN TO PALENQUE

UNCOVERING THE SEEDS OF MAGNIFICENCE

Sometimes, seeing our dark side takes courage, but ironically, seeing our light side often presents a challenge as well. Our dark side is an old friend, an identity we recognize easily. Whatever negative patterns we may carry, they have usually been there a long time—in our own lives and even in the lives of our ancestors. Our dark side carries with it all of our excuses and reasons for not growing.

Our light side, on the other hand, is expansive by nature. It often involves extending our limits and doing things in a new way. For that reason, our light side may also be a little frightening. It exists in the present, but also represents our future, our potential, our gestating seeds of magnificence. What would our lives be like if we embraced it more fully? What favorite parts of our dark side would we have to give up? What changes would we experience if we allowed ourselves to express more of the greatness within?

The perspectives which we use to define and interpret our world, and the resultant social patterns which have served us for centuries, apply less and less to our rapidly expanding global community. Finding new solutions for life on this planet requires entirely different systems of governing, doing business, educating, and otherwise supporting life. But more importantly, new solutions necessitate a completely new way of thinking, perceiving, and accessing ideas.

Our true mental and emotional abilities have been ignored in our culture since long before the time of the industrial revolution.

When it is said that we use only ten percent of our brain, *don't you wonder what life could be like if we used the other ninety percent?* We will soon know the answer. Fragments of these unusual abilities have been kept alive by the indigenous cultures of our planet, by those peoples whose survival still requires attunement to the self, to nature, and to the Spirit within, rather than attunement to the location of the nearest supermarket and the 6 o'clock news. The time will come when we will be enormously grateful to native and third world peoples who have held to their old ways, and thus carry a thread that can help us return to our natural connected state.

This is one reason, in the Native American tradition, that a person "Cries for a Vision" at Vision Quest, or why a dancer often receives a vision as a part of the Sun Dance. The dancers "pray for the people, that the people might live." In other words, they hold a picture in their minds of benefit for everyone; and they carry in their hearts the feeling of highest good for everyone. We can learn from this "win-win" principle as we focus on that which we choose to create.

If we are to bring forth our most heart-felt desires and dreams, if we are to express the Self that we were born to be, and if we are to allow the seeds of magnificence that lie dormant within each of us to blossom forth into manifestation, then we must hold those dreams in our minds and hearts, and walk towards it.

One of the easy ways to walk towards our own magnificence is to find or create pictures or models for the direction in which we want to move. Studies show that basketball players score substantially more points if they first visualize their move and the ball going through the basket. Whatever visual we hold in our minds about what lies ahead will be that picture into which we step.

In other words, if we can hold a image before us of our dreams, it becomes much easier to literally step into that picture. This picture can take any form: symbol, dream or vision, writing, music, movie, photograph, drawing, or painting. There are infinite ways to keep our dreams in our daily awareness. This book has become the picture I hold for my dream. Sometimes I will cut up magazines and make a collage of images that support a dream. Other times I will create a hypnosis tape to help me stay in touch with the picture of what I intend to create. It doesn't matter what touchstone we choose for remembering our greatest expression of Self. What matters is that we keep the possibility and the picture at the forefront of our consciousness, and that we do whatever is necessary to give energy and strength and focus to our dreams.

▲ ▲ ▲ ▲   183

While I tend to fill my home with all sorts of art, photography, and sculpture that help me visualize my dreams and keep them alive, I decided about three months after the Yucatan trip to use hypnosis toward that end. I was plum sick and tired of struggling with issues, and I wanted to try hypnotic regression as a way to bring back some positive pictures from the recesses of my mind. The year had been packed with "processing," and I was ready for a more gentle angle on the unfolding of my dream. I decided to head back up to Arkansas to visit Melody again.

I was wondering how the Yucatan journey and the events of recent months had played into the bigger picture of my life. The end of the trip had brought me some much needed and sobering feedback, but there were also many times during the journey that stirred vague, familiar feelings of a powerful and happy time long ago. I wanted to tap into that part of me buried within.

I had used past life regression in my work to help clients explore and release old traumas, but right now I wanted to bring to the surface of my awareness a time when life wasn't such a struggle—when there was wisdom, clarity, and sacredness, and when humankind's connection to the Creator was much greater. In my life and in my work, I was moving towards an increased emphasis on empowerment and acknowledge-ment. Now that a large chunk of my emotional baggage was getting cleared out, it was time to empower and acknowledge the mystical aspects of my spirituality and to start grounding that mysticism into my physical life.

Once again, Melody and I settled onto her sofa. I had taught her how to do regressions long before, and she was a natural at it. As soon as we started, it was clear that there would be a great deal of information forthcoming. It came to me like a memory; I think of it as a past life but, even if the experience was only a play of symbols from my subconscious, it still had as strong an impact as if it had actually occurred, for the impressions were vivid and real. My sense was that we were somehow being given a picture of what life on earth was like at a more balanced time, and what humans are capable of being and doing. I recognized that, while the regression did not actually provide a model for The New Place, it certainly provided a context.

The information just seemed to drop into my head. It was as if I were physically back in Palenque, where I had recently vis-ited with Thunder, but it was another time, long ago. The ruins were not "ruined;" rather they were structurally complete and painted a kind of luminous white. Colorful, bas-relief murals decorated many of the walls. The central city was surrounded by jungle, but I was aware of agricultural communities nearby. Memories of a time less complicated, less materialistic, and more attuned to Spirit came flooding forth. I knew that experi-encing these memories was reawakening some awarenesses that would, in some way, be useful in the New Place. As Melody asked questions, I replied, sharing my visual and men-tal impressions as I surveyed the green jungle scenery before me. What follows is a partial transcript of the adventure in my mind. Parentheses enclose visual impressions that were not spoken, or other realizations that I experienced relating to pre-sent time rather than the regression.

I am standing at the top of a temple surrounded by columns.

I'm holding my hands up, and there are rays coming out of my fingertips, like little lightning bolts. I can see the jaggedness of the light; it's a kind of electricity, and I can clearly see it coming from my hands. I'm sending light—blessings—out to the people in the villages around this sacred/royal compound. I do this as part of my morning prayers. Although this is very specialized work, I don't feel special because I do it. We are a very centered people; we do not need to get our self-esteem from having pride in our work.

In fact, struggles with self-esteem do not exist in this culture. Children are encouraged from a very young age to follow their own natural orientations, their own natural abilities. Thus, they never question whether they are "good enough." People are not concerned about "career choices," because their natural, innate talents are encouraged, and they are individually trained from childhood according to their interests and abilities. So the personal identity struggle that we see in today's world does not exist.

185

Families "trade" their children, in a sense. For example, if you work with stone, and your child likes to work with stone, then you work with your own child. But if your neighbor works with fabric, and your child wants to go work with fabric, then he or she simply starts working with your neighbor at whatever age that interest arises. Every adult has an automatic responsibility to teach any child who wants to learn. This form of education is an apprenticeship system which can begin at a very young age. For the most part, there are male and female roles, but anyone can choose a different role. If a boy wants to cook, or a girl wants to work with stone, they simply do it. Adult gender roles exist, but there is complete acceptance of variation.

I am remembering being with Thunder at the Queen's bath when she was Queen. (As I surveyed the scene in my mind, I realized that when Thunder brought the three of us to the Baths, during the Yucatan trip, what we did there together was an exact repetition of what we would do with her in ancient times.) It is such a beautiful place, with gentle waterfalls and rock pools that actually look like bathtubs. When I was a child, we would often go there and bathe and play. We would do something with cloth as well. (I paused for a moment as the image in my mind came into focus.)

I see yards and yards of wide cloth draped over limbs and stones. (The visual image was long swaths of fabric hanging across the trees around the Queen's Bath area—draped back and forth, zig-zagging around the area like a huge canopy. As I looked at them with the eyes of a child, I kept thinking of how much value there was in all that fabric, that is, how much weaving was involved.) We played at the Queen's Bath a lot. Not many people got to go there, but I did. We washed all of her sacred things there, and got to play with them. (Surveying the scene, I take a long, deep breath.) It is so good, so peaceful here.

I was allowed to go to the Queen's Bath because I could see the spirit beings. As a child, I would go there and play with them. They resembled fairies or little angels, and I would tell the queen about them. She would just ask me about them; she never let me know that she could see them, too. (As I said this, I recognized that Thunder taught in the same way in this life; she often asked questions to which she already knew answers in order to help bring out that knowledge in another person.)

As I got older, I couldn't see the spirits quite as much, but I could feel them and see their energy; I could see light and auras. The Queen gave me my early spiritual training, because I played with her children. She really liked me a lot. Jane and I were good friends. (Jane, an artist, had also been a part of the Yucatan trip with Thunder.) She and I always made things together—things out of stone, dyes, and painted cloths. We would stretch the cloths across the different tree limbs so we could paint them, and also for decoration. And we made little cups out of clay, too. Now that we are older, Jane has been chosen to decorate the temples. She creates many of the designs, and only she is allowed to paint them, because it is sacred work and it has to be done with the right energy. My own work is in the temple, and I also work some with the children.

I think there is a man in my life, but I don't see him; relationship does not seem to be an important focus for me. There isn't really a marriage system but, rather, a different approach to partnering that is thought of as a combining of energies, and is done very consciously. Because mating is thought of as very holistic, there is none of this romantic emotionalism that is common in the 20th century world. People follow their natural way of being and thus also are naturally inclined towards a given partner. In some ways, this approach to choosing a mate is less personal because it is so intentionally conscious; yet in other ways it is more personal, because we are carefully matching energies with another person. The family is involved in selecting the partner; the parents help. This organic process of finding your correct mate is somewhat detached, yet very intentional, and also very ceremonial. At the same time, it is not artificial; we end up with someone very natural for us.

187

Relationships usually last a lifetime but, for some people, old age might be a more private time. People here are so private anyhow, and so internal. Yet relationships are always satisfying; it's part of the culture. Couples, especially couples of the temple, practice working with energy together. We do a kind of yoga, but it's somehow more staccato, more angular. Apparently what is being represented in some of the drawings on the temple walls. We hold a focused awareness in our movement—forward, backward, left, right, around.

In fact, consciousness of movement is very central to our culture. At times, when we walk in the gardens or in the jungle for instance, we are constantly aware of our motion within and in relation to the air that surrounds us. There is such a constant awareness that we are part of the energy, particularly when we move through the jungle and go to the villages. I am not a part of the villages but rather, a part of the royalty, or you might say, staff of the sacred city. We of the temple periodically go to the nearby villages, bringing the energy to them, which we create from our central core. In other words, we carry energy that we generate to the people. We are what you might call a ministry, although we don't think of it in that way; we bring them the energy because this is our job. We are very privileged, and we are grateful for this opportunity to serve. We are very cognizant that, in residing at the core of the "battery," so to speak—in the central temple complex—it is our responsibility to share the energy with the people. As a woman, I usually don't go out very far. The men go out further. But, once in a while, there is what you might call an expedition or a larger journey.

We don't talk very much. Walking is our meditation. Our presence alone brings the energy into an area. Each area also has its own people trained in the temple. As we walk through the central core or royal village, we gather the energy; we also gather it from the forest, from the jungle. Then we teach the people from the villages how to do this. You might say we do "workshops." We teach people, but we also transmit the energy directly to them. Our work is something like the laying on of hands. The people are not sick very much; our sharing is more of a spiritual experience, and many people know how to share energy. We are a very energy-conscious people.

We have many visitors here. We are an incredible hub. (At first I had the impression of ships docking at a shore; then I was surprised to see people also arriving by "air.") I'm seeing that we also have visitors from another dimension, or perhaps from outer space. They are the ones who teach us about the energy, and they work telepathically. We are very conscious of them, and many of us can see them, especially those of us in the central core. In many ways, they are models for our culture, except that they are able to communicate with us entirely through telepathy.

These beings are *big*—very big—compared to us. They emit an enormous amount of electricity, like the hum you feel when near electric high-tension wires. In fact, because they carry so much energy, they sound like a generating station or like the OM of the Universe.

We learn from them how to radiate, which is actually what the Peace People did: We would go into mediation and absolutely become light bulbs. No, that is too small a picture; we were like generators—Z-Z-Z-Z-Z-Z—just opening up to receive the Universe as a Source, and then sending it out to the planet.

Yet, in this ancient lifetime, we don't have to go down into deep meditation. We just live that way. We don't experience this world pulling at us constantly, so we don't have to retreat into a space of harmony. Our culture lives in a space of harmony. We can go into meditation, but it isn't that far from our everyday experience. (As I perceived this, I realized that I am now so drawn to the dream of the New Place because within me are still the seeds—the memory—of living that way. And I know that it can be created again.)

We have a kind of Sun Dance, too. Our experience within the ceremony is not unlike the Sun Dance in South Dakota, but the external expression is quite different because of the personality of our people. We are very small, and very gentle. We aren't "warriors". The concept of being a warrior doesn't even exist in our culture. We are almost like spirits ourselves.

We have ceremonies throughout the year, and we often join together with the villagers for these ceremonies. They are choreographed dances which feel very much like that bungee cord dance they had at the opening ceremonies of the Olympic Games of 1992. (Two years later, a friend returned from a trip to the Yucatan with photos of a ceremony that involves with cords from a high tower, confirming the image I called the bungee cord dance.) The dances are very organic. Corn is an important part of the ceremonies too, as is bringing the Sun's energy down to the corn. We have wonderful rain dance celebrations too—dancing in the rain. They are very joyful. Our ceremonies are very much about celebration.

There are great feelings of gratitude in our culture. Our

189

prayer is not as focused on the asking as it is on celebrating the receiving. Since we are so oriented around energy, we are very aware of drawing the energy from the world around us, and also of giving it back to the universe. Like breathing. When we walk, our breathing is a very important part of bringing the energy in from the Universe and grounding it for our use in daily life—breathing in, and breathing out. That is our way of merging with the Universe. I now recognize that not expressing gratitude is like not breathing out. You have to breathe out in order to breathe in; so it is that you have to give gratitude in order to complete your receiving.

190

Thus walking and breathing are very important to us. Even today, if you watch Mexican Indian people walk, especially those from the Yucatan, it's such a conscious walking, so internal and present.

(Pause) I'm going now to meet one of the other-dimensional beings. We respectfully call them "fathers and mothers." They have so much energy compared to us, it's amazing. They just radiate.

I need a moment to switch levels...(deep breath)...and to be able to match vibration. (As I lay on Melody's sofa, time and space became confused. I was in a Palenque of long ago, but my body of today was responding to the magnificence of these beings. My breathing became much deeper, my speaking slower and more labored, and I felt very light and expanded as I experience myself communicating with a very tall, luminous being.) They are so...overwhelming isn't the right word...wondrous. To be in their presence is completely absorbing because they have so much light...even though we are in awe when we are with them, we know that they, too, are so small compared to the greater Source, to God. Yet their energy is so powerful that we can immediately absorb into it, which is such an ecstatic experience...it's beautiful. We don't think when in their presence; we just radiate. (Even for me to be able relate this experience, I had to jump back and forth between levels of consciousness. I continued to breathe deeply, feeling a powerful peaceful energy coursing through my body.)

In their presence, we become merged with them, although we have the choice whether to do so or not. We simply become...a part of their energy, and when they want to convey an idea to us, they think it and we receive it. As they share a thought with us, we simultaneously experience their wisdom and knowledge. This sharing is very loving, but it's not a love in the attached way that we might think. They simply impart their energy...which is luminous and peaceful. Being with them reminds me of when I was little and I played in the water...with the Queen...it was so happy...I was just so happy...it was so...it was just like heaven.

When the mothers and fathers come to visit, they go up to the top of the temple with us, and they show us how to radiate. And...WOW! They can put out so much energy! (I suddenly saw myself standing next to one of these beings. We were both sending energy from our hands, as I had at the beginning of the regression. The being is projecting what appears to be a steady bolt of lightning stretching far into the distance.)

191
〰〰
〰〰

When we are with them, we can somewhat experience what they are experiencing, which is how they teach. We are sending energy to the different villages where the farmers work. We are like a generating station here at the central core, and especially in this one temple, which is the sending place. It is a living place, too, for the priests and priestesses, that is, for those of us who work with the energies most of the time. As the mothers and fathers come, they show us how to do it. As they stand at the top of the temple, they can see a whole village five or ten miles away. I now see that when they send energy, they are consciously projecting it *into* the people. The rays that come out of their fingers are going into every individual. Although we can't do that, we can experience this ability through their "sharing," and we can then approximate it or visualize it when we do it. When we project energy by ourselves, we can only see about five inches of energy coming out of our own hands.

The mothers and fathers also share with us the images for

our ceremonies. (When I received this impression, I suddenly understood how we receive from Spirit. I realized that when we are willing and open, Spirit is able to simply put things in our minds, to share telepathically. This is often how we "hear" answers to prayer, but first we have to ask, because the spiritual law of free will—the "prime directive," you might say—otherwise prevents interference with human evolution.) Because we have the ability to actually see these beings and commune with them, we are more aware of how they communicate. We know we have chosen to merge with them, or actually, to allow them to merge us with them, and thus we are conscious of exactly when they are sharing with us. (In modern life, thoughts pop into our minds, but we don't have any image of Spirit or a picture of where these thoughts come from. These impressions are gifts we cannot see.)

192

When my visit with Melody was over, I drove the nine hours back to Houston in pensive silence. *"We have the power,"* I thought. How long had I believed and taught that our thoughts create our reality? And I had truly lived this philosophy over the past ten years, but perhaps not as much as I might! Even as I write this, I know I must remind myself regularly of how much power exists in our minds, if only we were to tap it! How much knowledge exists within us if only we were to access and use it! How much a greater connection to the Creator could be ours if we only could become quiet enough inside to hear! I wanted that deeper inner connection, not just while sitting in meditation, but in every moment of my life!

My experience in the past life regression made me aware that there was an enormous amount of wisdom within each of us. The narrow focus we exercise in daily life was but a minute portion of the reservoir of experience from which we could draw. I realized that I no longer needed to identify with the struggles of life as I had been seeing them. I had other options! Other realities! Other personalities within me! Mastery and clarity were mine, if I held that picture before me. Now that I had created that image for myself, I knew solidly that the power to create my own magnificence was at hand.

▲ ▲ ▲ ▲ ▲ ▲ ▲

The more we can bring our dreams into current daily consciousness, the more they become the thoughts which are creating our reality. There are so many ways to make our dreams and visions come alive each and every day. Choose a few, like:

1. Close your eyes, relax, and take about four to seven deep, deep breaths. Create in your mind the most beautiful place you can imagine. This will be your place of relaxation and rejuvenation. Spend at least five minutes looking around and enjoying your special place. Notice the colors, sounds, vegetation, water, and food. What do you do there to heal and nourish yourself? Visualize and create in your mind while you are relaxing in your special place.

2. Draw a picture or write about your vision or dream—or whatever you hold dear to your heart. Elaborate as much as possible, using all of your senses. If you prefer, cut out magazine pictures, photographs, and other visuals, and make a collage of that which you wish to create. Write or paste words from magazines onto your collage—words of affirmation about your intended creation.

3. If you created a picture for number 2, now write about it. If you wrote about it, now create a visual. Post them somewhere in your home and/or place of work (your desk, bathroom mirror, or refrigerator), so that they stay before your awareness.

4. If you so wish, find someone to help you experience a past life regression or future life progression to a wiser or more fulfilled time or dimension of your consciousness.

193

BAMBI LEMONADE

THE PRACTICE OF DISCOVERING THE BLESSINGS

Everything is a blessing! Can you imagine seeing life this way? It is certainly not a perspective that most of us learned growing up. Yet when we can see reality from this perspective, we are freed to live in a constant state of creativity and awe.

When we pre-judge an apparently negative situation, we instantly lose both the blessing and the ability to enjoy it. Yet when we see it with the eyes of a child, a whole world of possibility opens up to us. When we do not predetermine an outcome, we live in the moment, thus enabling ourselves to see opportunities, solutions, and doorways to which we could otherwise be blind.

We live in a constant co-creative process with the Creator/ our environment/the Universe. I have heard Thunder say many times, "Every thought is a prayer." Each thought is an action that has an equal reaction from the physical world. If we spend a lot of time thinking of our fears, we will also spend a lot of time living the very things we fear. If our thoughts are about love, or benefit, or health, or solutions, these will be our experience. The more we live in awareness of this truth, the less we experience separation from the Divine.

Christ said that if we had faith as a grain of mustard seed we could move mountains. Yet how many of us actually believe we could mentally shift large piles of dirt and rock, (or make other substantial physical adjustments), with our intention and our faith? In our day-to-day living, we would rarely even consider it possible, much less train ourselves to consistently think, that it would be entirely feasible. Yet Christ said this was so, and many other spiritual masters have demonstrated throughout recorded time that this is true. The question then looms before us: How can we come to make knowing this a part of our reality?

In truth, we are inseparable from the Creator. The more we accept responsibility for the creations of our thoughts, and the more we *practice creating consciously and beneficially*, the more we merge with the wonder of The Great Mystery.

▲ ▲ ▲ ▲

My journey through time to ancient Palenque seemed, some-how, to help me integrate much of the massive growth I'd been undergoing in the past months. Each week felt as if it had been a year of transformation! Now, back in Houston, I took on the goals I had set for myself with renewed vigor. Yes, I wanted the New Place to happen, and the Yucatan experiences made it feel so close, I could practically reach out and touch it. The dream was just beyond a few more obstacles, a couple more boxes in my diagram. I began conducting corporate seminars, brought more guest speakers into town, and built my Houston Center into a successful business. If I were going to create the New Place, I couldn't act like a spiritual bliss-ninny. I had to learn how to ground that spiritual dream into the planet, to take what I had seen on the etheric levels and bring it into physical reality. For me, learning to be successful was part of that grounding process

I had already gone through the spiritual stages of renounc-ing the world—and it had taught me a lot of detachment. Yet if I espoused a lifestyle of unconditional love and global trans-formation, it certainly wouldn't be appropriate if I ignored or could not deal with the existing financial, social, and political structures. No, I needed to gain more mastery in these areas as well. Instead of hiding from the problems our world was facing, I needed to be part of the cure. Manifesting my reality was partly about emotional growth, but it was also about everyday living; I could choose between barely meeting my needs, or enjoying a degree of prosperity and success. It was clear that learning to manifest was part of the preparation, part of the training that was necessary to move toward the New Place.

By the time Sun Dance time rolled around again, my life was finally running pretty smoothly. The rough part seemed to be past, and I headed for Sun Dance with the idea that this year would be easy. My plan was to fly to Denver and meet two friends, Ken and Ted, who were going to Sun Dance as supporters. They would probably do most of the driving up to South Dakota, and I was grateful for their help. I kept telling myself, "You've really paid your dues this year, Carolyn. You can skate now." But, of course, Spirit once again had a greater plan.

I got my first hint about the "change of plans" when no one was at the airport to greet me in Denver. Getting separated from someone in a big public place has always left me somewhat phobic. My old abandonment stuff creeps quickly to the surface. But, here I was, taking off for Sun Dance. Hey, heads up—it's *always* an adventure! How would the adventure unfold, I wondered? Taking courage, I checked with the paging service periodically, got myself a sandwich, and hung out by the passenger pick-up area for an hour and a half.

Finally, Ken wandered by, looking every which way but straight at me. I stuck my fingers between my teeth and whistled several times. Finally I caught his eye, and we laughed and hugged; we hadn't seen each other in a long time. Ken had a very special relationship with eagles, and worked as a volunteer in rehabilitating injured birds of prey. Although he, like myself, had no Indian blood, he had "walked the Red Road" for many years, and had been good friends with Lakota recording artist, Buddy Red Bow and some of the elders who frequented Denver. It had been three years since he had left

Houston. We were both looking forward to trading stories about what had transpired in our lives over the past few years. Ken grabbed some of my bags and we headed towards the parking lot. "Oh, by the way," Ken said cheerfully, "I had to put my car in the shop yesterday, and they couldn't get it done by today..." I stopped dead in my tracks and looked at him quizzically, thinking that this was sign number two that things weren't going according to plan—*my* plan, anyhow. "Oh, don't worry," he added. "I have this great friend who was kind enough to offer us his car. He volunteered to ride his motorcycle for the two weeks we're gone so we can have wheels to get to the Dance." Gee, I thought. Now *that* was really nice. It was amazing how people came forward to support the Sun Dance, even those who didn't even really know that much about it. It seemed to be a part of how Spirit worked.

197

Then, chuckling, he added as an aside, "And it's already broken down. That's why we were late. But I figure the breakdown energy is already handled, so we won't have to deal with it again."

I liked his explanation. At least, I wanted to like it. We laughed and talked excitedly as we headed up to the parking level where Ted was repacking the car. But as we rounded the corner, I stopped short for the second time. A little gasp issued forth as my jaw dropped and all I could do was stare. There, beneath many layers of dirt, was an old, one-time hot rod, with car parts and pieces of bondo missing from here and there. I couldn't tell if there was a back seat—yes, maybe a little one. Teddy's back was turned as he stacked bag after bag on the dirt-laden roof. Each time he threw a bag up, a cloud of dust would burst forth from the vehicle. The inside, too, looked completely full, and I wondered exactly where they thought my bags were going to go.

Teddy turned around. Seeing the expression on my face, they both stood there laughing deep belly-laughs. Then we hugged, said quick hellos, and set to work on finishing the packing. It was already early evening, and we intended to do the entire eight hour drive that night, if possible. We worked together quickly, packing in record time; it looked as if we were going to be a good team. We settled into the car and Ken tried to rev up the engine. It took several tries.

"Oh, it always does this," he said, thinking he was reassuring me. Once again I had misgivings about the vehicle. I suggested that we each "check inside" and see what our intuitions said about it—whether to take off now or rent a nice, clean, new car while we had the chance. We all got the same answer: The "bondo-mobile" might present some small complications, but the bottom line was that everything would turn out just fine.

So we hit the road, heading northeast out of Denver, and suddenly we were finally on our way to Sun Dance. One always knows that there will be some kind of transformation at the Dance. I had never come back the same person. There are challenges, struggles, pains, stretches, sharing, laughter, lots of prayers, and ultimately some personal and group triumphs to experience. I always left for Sun Dance filled with awe, mixed perhaps, with a little fear—the kind of anticipation that reminds me of the very last line in one of Carlos Castaneda's books, where he runs to the edge of a cliff and jumps off. The end. You are left sitting there with the book in your hand with nothing before you but the unknown, having no idea what was next.

And so it was. Ted was very quiet as we started out—at once introspective but also listening. As we left the city behind us, with the Rockies fading in the distance, Ken and I did some catching up. We had been heading northeast towards Ogallala, Nebraska, but after passing a turnoff that offered the option to head straight north, we unanimously decided to make a U-turn and drive up through Kimball and Scott's Bluff instead. Our intuitions were again aligned. Besides, the vast Nebraska countryside was empty, and since we were going to be traveling at night, it seemed like a good idea to choose a route that passed through a few more towns to break up the monotony of endless dark stretches of flatness. Then, too, there would be fuel and help if anything did happen with the car.

The sun was setting as we left Colorado. It was spectacular—brilliant red with some purple hues as dusk set in. Red for the blood of the people, and for the path of the Native American people. Purple for Spirit. We were driving through the heart of America, through endless "waves of grain." We were laughing and talking, and I was telling Ken and Ted about last year's trip, about losing a wheel off the truck, and my adventures with Buster. At that moment, a large coyote dashed across our path from east to west. He was running, but at the same time appeared to be moving very slowly and looking directly at us.

We were instantly sobered. It is said that the coyote is the trickster. In a way he symbolizes what the Hindus call the illusion of this plane of existence. He walks in the Direction of South, the place of relationships and of purity. But I had always thought of the coyote as being a bit sinister. We instantly became more watchful and more alert—Teddy and I in particular, because of the training we had had from Thunder. The coyote had clearly seemed like a message or maybe a warning—but of what?

At around 11:00 pm, we pulled off the highway to gas up in Kimball. We lingered for a bit over the snacks and knickknacks for sale, just to stretch our legs. But when we piled back into the car, it wouldn't start. While the guys looked under to hood, I went shopping. Might as well turn a disadvantage into a benefit, I thought. And, it also seemed like a good idea to leave a few bucks with the station owner, since we were tying up his pumps.

I found a couple of toys for the kids at Sun Dance; then my eye was caught by this beautiful little snow scene, the kind that you shake up and snow falls over the little figurines. At the center was an angel reaching out to feed a little deer. I loved it; I wanted it. But I decided I would buy it for Thunder. She always liked angels.

199

I paid for my gifts, chatting with the owner and his son as I did. Peering out of the door, I saw the guys were still under the hood. As I wandered out, so did the store owner and his son, and soon there was a bevy of analysts and experts gathered around our vehicle. One told us we could jump-start an automatic transmission if we could get it going fast enough. I was skeptical about whether it would work, and also quite unenthusiastic about the downhill direction in which they wanted to push us, which was into town and away from the highway and the hotel.

But push us they did. At 45 miles per hour, the engine still hadn't turned over, and we were now tearing into the little downtown, directly towards the one and only traffic light, which was red. We had no choice but to brake. Ted steered the car over to the side of the road as it slowly rolled to a halt. And there we stopped.

We all clambered out and just stood there for a few minutes. Now what?

The streets were pretty deserted, except for an occasional Saturday night celebrator wandering home from the bar. Our friend who had pushed us had to leave—but said he'd try to find a policeman to help us. Great.

We stood on the sidewalk in the chilly Nebraska night, our hands in our pockets, each surveying our surroundings with the silent numbness of lost waifs in a strange town. We were in the middle of *nowhere!* What were we going to do? What were our options?

Determined not to let discouragement set in, I declared this an adventure. This was going to be *fun!* The guys did not reflect my enthusiasm, but neither did they allow themselves to be dejected. We started to look at what the possibilities might be, given that I was supposed to be in South Dakota to start the purification process in preparation for Sun Dance the next day. We were still about four or five hours away. We might as well have been a hundred hours away!

I immediately suggested that I go on ahead by hitch-hiking, leaving the men to handle the car. Just as immediately, Ken and Ted both nixed the idea—we had too much gear. Besides, Ted said that there was no way he was going to let me hitch alone. I wasn't about to argue about it. My feminist issues flew momentarily to the surface, then I decided to take the perspective that he was being protective—maybe wisely so.

I looked around. Suddenly I noticed that we were standing next to the T. Boynton Insurance Agency. That was Trent's name—T. Boynton! He and Thunder were up in Cincinnati, also on the road to the Dance, so I took this as a sign to call Thunder. Then I realized that in the alley right behind us, five steps away, there was a pay phone. What amazing luck! It was 12:47 am. There was that mystical 47 again. "So many positive signs," I thought, and we placed the call, hoping they were still awake. They were, and I talked with Trent for a while, laughing as I told him all that had happened. Thunder and he were no doubt having just as wild a time as we were; it seemed the trip to Sun Dance was always that way. He chuckled at what we were experiencing, offered a few ideas along mechanical lines, and conveyed our story to Thunder. I could hear her cheery voice in the background. That in itself gave me confidence that all would turn out well. She told us to keep praying, that they would, too, and that we all would see each other soon.

The call didn't solve our immediate situation, but it brought us back to the truth—that we were on a spiritual adventure. It was time to apply that mix of surrendering and creating. We grabbed the phone book and scoured the pages for car rentals in Scotts Bluff, the next town over (and the only one within hundreds of miles.) It was about two hours away, but surely we could get a ride that far, I thought.

Before we could launch on a phone quest, two policemen pulled up. They surveyed the car and listened to a few more of our attempts to start the engine. The men talked car-talk as we all stood around with our hands in our pockets, but neither of

201

the policemen had any ideas of what to do. We were clearly the best entertainment on the late night beat in a long time. They told us that the chances of renting a car were pretty minimal, since the folks at the rental agencies didn't usually listen to their answering machines on Sunday—but we could try.

I kept affirming aloud and to myself that everything would work out, and that something really good was going to come of this adventure. On one level I actually did believe this, but on the other hand, I needed to keep convincing myself. It felt important for our little threesome as well, to keep affirming a positive outcome.

The policemen mulled over the situation for a bit longer— which we eventually came to realize was a major past-time in this town. Solving the problems seemed to be much less important than the social interaction involved in discussing them. But then, one of them thought perhaps Jacob would help. Yes, Jacob would be the one. He always kept his tools in his van. He just lived around the corner, and he'd probably be willing to come take a look at it. At one o'clock in the morning, I asked? Oh, sure, Jacob wouldn't mind. They took off in the patrol car to find Jacob.

I came to really wonder, I mean *really* wonder, later, if perhaps Jacob wasn't actually an angel. Within moments the policemen returned, followed by a VW bus. Out stepped Jacob, a slender man with a kind face and gentle demeanor. His van was clearly a mobile shop, and he acted as though checking on people's car in the middle of the night was a normal part of his workday. He slid under the car as Ken periodically tried to start the engine. The rest of us returned to our hands-in-the-pockets stance, talking a little about the town and about our trip so far. As Jacob continued to jiggle wires and juggle wrenches, the police decided we were in good hands, gave us special permission to pitch our tent in the city park a block away, and then headed out into the night as we waved a grateful goodbye.

Jacob said maybe he'd be able to jerry-rig the car, but it was a long shot, and if he got it going, we couldn't stop until we got where we were going. That sounded okay to me—the tank was full! He rummaged around in his van for a bit, pulled out some nondescript part, and replaced something. We all had high hopes, and when Ken jumped in to start it again, we all visualized a quick and easy start-up and getaway. Instead, something clanked and sizzled and sparked. Death to the borrowed car was instant. Jacob said he'd done his best, but at this point it would be at least three days before he could get the needed part from Denver to get the car running again. Denver—that was ironic; were we really only four hours away? It now seemed like days.

Again, we were silent for a few moments. Now what? Time to start thinking about camping in the park. Time to start thinking about those unlikely car rentals.

But I was not to be discouraged.

"I know!" I said excitedly, "Maybe we can *buy* a car! How about a van? I've been looking for a van."

The guys looked at me like I was nuts—it was that amused and tolerant look I've seen on men's faces when they think they're dealing with a woman who is obviously stupid. But I didn't doubt that they secretly appreciated this Pollyanna approach. We needed to keep looking at the positive side, keep looking for the doorway, keep reminding ourselves that Creator already had the solutions. We needed only to silence our minds and attune to the gifts of Spirit. But what were they?

I turned to Jacob and asked if there were any car dealers nearby. He actually offered to drive us around to the three dealerships in town and show us what was on the lots—at 2:15 in the morning. All right!

We left Ken at the city park with his tent so he could set up our home for the night. In the meantime, Ted and I took the tour through town with Jacob. Within a half hour, we had hit all three lots. One place, Bryson Auto Sales, had three vans that actually had potential—depending on price. I'd been looking for a van

203

in Houston, but what I wanted was out of my price range. Maybe a little country dealership would have one I could afford. Bryson's was within walking distance of the park, so that was certainly in our favor. We could check it out in the morning.

Jacob drove us back to the park, gave us his phone number, and made sure we knew where he lived. He told us he'd come by and see how we were doing early the next morning, and also would arrange to tow the car over to his house. We thanked him again and again; he had gone way beyond the call of duty. With a mixture of gratitude, exhaustion, and concern, we crammed into Ken's tent, head to toe and toe to head, and fell asleep.

Moments later, it seemed, our little alarm clock was calling us back into action. It was 6:00 am, and it had been a very short night. But we leapt up, ready to go again. I had to be at the Sun Dance grounds before evening. Somehow I would be there—somehow.

We climbed out of our cramped quarters to greet a bright, sunny morning. I decided to greet the day with enthusiasm and determination. We rolled up our sleeping bags and started to break camp just as Jacob pulled up in his VW camper—just to see how we were doing, and to let us know he was about to tow the car back to his place.

Teddy stayed to break down the tent, and to help Jacob tow the car. Ken and I headed for the Minute-Mart; it was time to hit the phones and/or to find out if anyone there could help us. It was still early and relatively deserted when we arrived; I left messages at all of the car rental places, and Ken called his lady, Nancy, in Denver. She was our back-up plan; we would ask her to drive up only if it was necessary. It was starting to look necessary. It meant a hard sixteen hour round-trip drive for her, and we didn't want to ask her to do that unless there was no other way we could get to Sun Dance. We told her we'd call her back in a couple of hours if nothing jelled. In the meantime, the local men started congregating for coffee. We told our story again and again. Each guy was very interested and concerned, but the main help offered was always referring us to someone else who, incidently, was about to show up. Within an hour it was clear that our reputation was proceeding us—folks were actually showing up to find out if we'd found a solution yet. One was another car dealer, who drove me over to his lot to see a car that didn't start. But by 9:30 that morning, we had made zero progress.

Teddy finally joined us at the Minute-Mart, and we left Ken to call Nancy and make arrangements for her to come up. In the meantime, Ted and I hiked down to Bryson Auto Sales. It was a long shot, since it was Sunday, but as it turned out, Bryson was out in front painting the building, and he was happy to show us the three vans we'd seen the night before. First, he showed us the two I liked the best—both a real pretty metallic blue—my favorite car color. But the prices were out of the realm of possibility.

We moved on to the last one. It was big, really big—one of those long conversion vans with a little table and convertible sofa in the back, and four captain's chairs in the front. I'd never driven anything that huge. It was also tan—and *not* my color. But it was kind of nice, actually—very clean, even though it was a little old. It had 74,000 miles on it, and the dealer tag read #4701. There were those numbers again: seven symbolizing Spirit and four representing the Earth. I started to feel a little excited.

"What do you think, Teddy? What do you think?" I kept asking him. He was very non-committal and cautious, not wanting to be responsible in any way for a decision that was both major and mine. But I watched him survey the vehicle closely. He seemed to be impressed. We started it up and it turned over immediately, humming happily. Bryson had wandered back to his painting, so we walked over, trying to act kind of casual, and asked him the price. I cringed at his answer, dickered with him a little, then asked with finality:

205

"What is your lowest, lowest, bottom lowest price?"

Miraculously, he answered, "$2650." I had put a royalty check in the bank two days before that would just cover that amount! Instantly, the joke about buying a van moved into the realm of possibility. So Teddy and I took off in the van for a spin around town.

We gathered up Ken at the Minute-Mart. He just laughed when he saw us drive up, and half the store emptied out, amazed to see how we were coping with our now-famous transportation situation. Ken seemed as excited as I was; Teddy continued to be the rational thinker in the group, but I could tell that the idea was starting to catch hold of him, too. We drove over to Jacob's to get his appraisal. Gentle, quiet, and methodical, Jacob dropped what he was doing and looked over the van, checked the engine, climbed underneath, and shook a few things. He gave it a clean bill of health—for the asking price, we probably couldn't go wrong.

Once again, we dropped Ken at the Minute-Mart where he was to meet Nancy. I was a little concerned about what we'd say to her if I bought the van; but on the other hand, since it would save her at least eight hours of driving, maybe she'd be relieved.

I was excited. The van felt so right! But when we settled into Bryson's office to complete the deal, it became evident that paying for the van presented another entire set of obstacles. Bryson had thought I could somehow get a cash advance from my credit card at the bank. He'd already called the banker, who said he could help us out, even though it was Sunday. But my credit card had a two thousand dollar limit. So I called my bank in Houston which, amazingly, was open on Sunday, and asked them to transfer $2650 up to the bank here. I had assumed there would be no problem with that. "I'm sorry, Ms. Ball, but you need to come into the office and sign the papers for any transfer to be made."

"But, you don't understand! I'm stuck in the middle of

Nebraska and need to buy a car so I can leave! There must be
some way you can transfer the funds!" "I'm sorry Ms. Ball, but
we need you to come in and sign the papers first." It was a little absurd. But the signs had been so clear; my intuition had
been so strong! I put Bryson on the phone to talk with her. He
verified my credit and the amount in my account. It seemed as
if he were making progress with her. But in a moment he
handed the phone back to me, and I heard once again, "I'm so
sorry, Ms. Ball, but we really need you to come in and sign
some papers before we can transfer your funds."

I thanked her and hung up. My shoulders drooping, I stared
at the floor for a few moments. How could we have come this
far just to have it all fall through? Suddenly I looked up at
Bryson, stared him straight in the eyes and said, "Will you take
a check?"

"A check for two thousand, six hundred and fifty dollars?!" he
cried, obviously taken aback that anyone would even suggest
such a thing. But then, he seemed to think about it for a
moment. He'd now spent a good part of his Sunday on this
sale, and the office was still waiting to be painted. "How do I
know I can trust you?"

I continued to look straight at him. "How many times have
people driven out of here with a car wondering exactly the
same thing about you?"

I paused. This was definitely a dramatic moment. Then I
added, "You don't really know if you can trust me. I can tell
you that you can trust me, but there's no way for you to know
for sure until my check clears later this week. You're just going
to have to base that decision on your intuition."

He just looked at me for a moment. I could tell he was sweating a little.

Then he broke into a smile. "OK, we'll do it."

I was so excited, I could hardly contain myself. Teddy, until
that moment reserved and silently supportive, now jumped in
with enthusiasm, reassuring poor Mr. Bryson that my word

207

was good, and that he knew me well, and whatever else might put the man at ease. We did the paperwork in record time, and were all somewhat awed by the fact that a stranger was writing a check for that amount and just buying a car that way. Teddy and I looked at each other and, with unspoken words, acknowledged that Spirit was surely at work in all that had gone on in the past day. No, it hadn't even been a whole day!

Then Bryson walked outside and affixed a temporary transport plate to the window. It was the final act of making the van mine. As he stood back and I looked up at the plate in the window, it was transport plate number 747!

We were just thanking Mr. Bryson, standing for a few moments in awe of the van and in awe of all that had transpired when, with the perfect timing of a grade B movie, Ken and Nancy pulled up. Unfazed by her extra day of driving, Nancy was as thrilled about my purchase as we were; we jumped in and out of the van, excitedly showing it off like kids in a fun house. Her two dogs bounded out of her car, leaping and dancing around us, picking up and expressing the excitement of the humans. How could something that seemed so bad turn out so good? This was the classic Blessing in Disguise. And I knew that our attitude—keeping our spirits high, being willing to look for the good in all that transpired, and applying positive creative thoughts to the situation—had a lot to do with how this blessing transpired.

We had just loaded the dogs back into Nancy's car, and packed the "new" van for the road to Sun Dance, when, with immaculate timing, Jacob happened by again in his little VW camper. He leaned out of the window and said he was just stopping by to see if we bought the van. I looked over at him, then walked up to him, kind of tilted my head sideways, and asked, "Are you an angel?" Oddly, he didn't seem to react to the question. He just kind of smiled, then asked if we would like, before leaving town, to join him for lunch over at the restaurant where his daughter worked. We were delighted with the idea, and asked if we could buy him lunch. Within ten minutes we were all gathered around a little cafeteria table.

Jacob's daughter came out and waited on us. She was very beautiful, and had a grace about her that was as remarkable as her father's. She took our order and, as soon as she left, Jacob told us a story that was at once extraordinary, and completely in keeping with the events that had unfolded this day.

When Jacob's daughter was eleven, it was discovered that she had a brain abscess. It was actually the first time in United States medical history that such an abscess had been discovered while the patient was still alive, and it drew medical attention from around the country. However, the doctors doubted she would live; but if she did, they said she would never walk again. The family gathered together around her and prayed unceasingly. They did not give up. But what moved and touched Jacob's family, was the strength and faith of his daughter. After she came out of the coma, it took almost a year for her to learn to walk again—but she did! Her quiet determination and faith never wavered. It had changed everyone around her. The Holy Spirit had healed not only her, but the whole family.

And not only them, I thought, but through Jacob's kindness, us as well. The power of faith...what a gift we had received....

We hugged goodbye to our friend in Spirit, to his beautiful daughter, and to Nancy. It was now early afternoon. How could so much have happened in so little time? It looked as if we still could make it to the Sun Dance grounds in time for the first purification Sweat Lodge.

As we headed North into the vast yellow expanse of the Nebraska grain fields, I marveled over all that had unfolded in the last eighteen hours. How incredible it was, after looking for months for a van in Houston, that as I was now on my way to do my spiritual work, the perfect vehicle had practically been gifted to me. The van would enable me to move on to the next step in getting the New Place. Now I'd be able to camp and

209

move around more easily, and thus make that connection with Nature which was such an important part of my dream.

I was *so* pleased. I liked the van so much I wanted to give it a name. Teddy was driving and I was sitting in the front passenger seat, surveying the details of the vehicle and thinking how nice it was, even though tan wasn't really my color. I looked up at the roof and noticed little white spots—it looked as if someone had shaken up a milk bottle or a soda and it had somehow splattered on the ceiling.

Suddenly Teddy was stepping on the brakes, and I quickly looked out of the window to see why. Racing down the shoulder to our right were a mother deer and her little spotted fawn, looking for a way through the fence into the corn field beyond. Teddy stopped the car so we wouldn't frighten them any more than we already had. The doe jumped the fence, but the baby ran back and forth for a while, looking for a way through. We sat quietly, saying little prayers for the fawn, but enjoying this unique opportunity to watch a wild fawn running so close by. What grace, what beauty! In a few moments, the little deer found a way through, and disappeared into the corn field—just as we had found a way through our obstacles this past day. Teddy pulled back onto the road, and I heaved a deep sigh. What blessings we had received! I looked up at the ceiling of the car and, once again, my eye landed on the white spots. White spots on the tan ceiling, like the spots on the back of the baby fawn.

That was it! I would name my van Bambi. Bambi Lemonade. Bambi for the deer that looked like the van, and the purity that the fawn represented. Lemonade because that's what you might as well make when life gives you lemons. Bambi Lemonade was not only my key to finding the New Place, she also represented the perfect practice of discovering blessings in disguise.

At that moment my eye fell on the little snow scene that I'd bought for Thunder, which had been sitting all this time on the dashboard before me. Very slowly I reached out and shook it

◀ BAMBI LEMONADE ▶

up and watched in wonder and gratitude as the snow fell on the angel and the deer in that little blue world. This could not be a coincidence. How awesome was the working of Spirit when we are willing to assume that all things are blessings!

▲ ▲ ▲ ▲ ▲ ▲ ▲

Transformation is a gradual procedure. Our passage through the "armageddon process" may initially appear to be in the physical realm, but the challenge is ultimately how we manage our thoughts and how much we are willing to see Spirit as blessing us in our process of growth and change. As we discover this to be primarily an internal process which is necessary and beneficial, we begin to allow the higher consciousness concepts to become a waking part of our daily lives. But it is essential to practice by constantly seeking to see with eyes that look for blessings. Here are a few ways:

211
〜〜
〜〜

1. Write about a time when you were able to keep a higher perspective about something that was difficult for you and/or others. How were you able to maintain that perspective? What were the results?

2. What did you learn from writing about the experience in question #1?

3. Where in your life would you like to practice maintaining a positive picture or belief about an outcome? (Consider the different areas of your life, such as career, relationship, family, income, health, etc.) Decide what the picture is that you would like to hold for any given situation and for how long you will practice it (eg., 1 week, 1 month, 3 days). If something beneficial occurs that is beyond your expectations, be sure to express gratitude, which will help you integrate your receiving of the blessing.

SWEET ILLUSION

UNVEILING THE DISGUISE

An astrologer I once knew described life as a process of constantly cycling around the chart, or around a series of abilities and challenges. When we are undeveloped, the forces on the outside of the chart pull hard at us, like centrifugal force, and it feels as if we don't have much effect on our own lives. As we grow, we cycle through the same challenges, over and over again. The same forces pull on us. But our growth is like an upward spiral, so that we take on the challenges in a new way each time, with the benefit of all of our past growth to help us. As such, we slowly move toward the center of that spiral, and the "centrifugal force" of the external events gradually ceases to pull at us as hard, because we become more and more "centered."

Sometimes we get caught in the anguish of "oh, no, not AGAIN!" When we've worked so hard, and we don't seem to be getting anywhere, or when we've tried and failed again, we can sometimes get discouraged and even angry with ourselves. At other times, we may blame another, or feel that someone has let us down.

This discouragement and anger tend to be rooted in the belief that we might not succeed. If, however, we notice that each time we pass through a purifying fire, we are further along our path, then we can see every "mistake" or "failure" as an important and necessary step in the process. In fact, it is often the very worst mistake, or the most difficult of circumstances that can catapult us to an entirely new level in our ability to create. Thus, it is often *the very worst situations* that can be the most beneficial because they force us to re-evaluate, to adapt, to stretch, to draw new abilities and solutions from within. Even death, divorce, and illness, not to mention financial, career, health, and family problems, can *all* be blessings—unless we *assume* they are not, which is, of course the normal human reaction. We can become so caught in our assumed view or interpretation of a situation, that we may not even look for the benefit. Yet often, it is when we are the *most* steeped in our illusion, that we can finally see the illusion for what it is.

Each time we cycle through the opportunities for growth and expansion in our lives, we further hone our evolution. Gradually, we discover a balance, a balance between the creative and the receptive forces within us—our external and our internal, our action and our quiet, our masculine and our feminine, our yang and our yin.

213

At some point, when we've experienced the same error time and time again, we reach a point where we suddenly see the dynamics of our creation and discover a way out of our old patterns into a new creation. As painful as that breakthrough experience might be, it brings the ultimate unveiling of the disguise of the blessing, revealing that at the core is the Self, finally willing to undertake its Divine expression.

▲ ▲ ▲ ▲

Apparently, in order for me to really grasp the concept of "blessings in disguise" in my life, I needed to somehow immerse myself in the illusion, in the disguise aspect of the blessing. Sun Dance that year brought me face to face with my issues about relationships and the masculine and feminine balance. I looked back at my diagram of ten boxes—the ten steps to get to the Vision of the New Place. It seemed as if all the boxes were either complete or well in progress. All but Boxes Number Nine and Number Ten.

Box Number Nine represented the partnership, the relationship, the man with whom I would carry out the dream—but I'd about given up on him. We all have some area of weakness, some area where we have to work harder and longer than other areas of our lives. Finding that partner was mine. When I'd gotten divorced from a "perfectly good husband," as my mother had put it, some eight years before, I thought I'd be married to my ideal mate within a year, or two at the most. I had no idea that relationships would be my constant honing stone, my ever-present sand-paper, always bringing me back to my growth, always back to the feet of the Creator. I'd loved and lost so many times, it was becoming increasingly difficult to trust my choices in men. I had worked on it so much; I seemed to be an extremely effective counselor in the area of relationships but, for me, Box Number Nine was still off in the foggy future. So, at this point, I wasn't even looking.

However, I woke up one morning with the clear memory of a dream, which in itself was unusual—I almost never remember dreams. As I awakened, it seemed that the dream was still going on, and I had an overwhelming sense of happiness and of joy.

In the dream, I was shopping for a man. I went from store to store, trying on different men, so to speak, like you'd try on overcoats. You know how things are in dreams—more or less half reality and half symbol. Each man I "tried on" seemed to fit in some ways, but was disastrously mismatched in other ways. One had legs where the arms should be; one was too tight; another hung heavily on me and weighed me down; still another had bright, disharmonious colors into which I completely disappeared.

As I wandered through my dream mall, I could find no one who fit, and I was starting to get discouraged and tired. I decided to rest, maybe find a little coffee shop and nurture myself with a little something good to eat. Just then I discovered what seemed like a little New York style hole-in-the-wall deli, with lots of delicacies and the smell of fresh-baked bread. I sat down at a corner table, relaxing deeply, taking long slow breaths, and settling into my spot. I put the shopping out of my mind and just focused within. The waiter brought me a sandwich and a cup of coffee, and I gave him a big smile, grateful to be served and nurtured. I let my mind wander lazily, like a butterfly fluttering from thought to thought, alighting here and there with no particular agenda or direction.

Gradually I became aware of a man at a nearby table; I don't know if he had been there all along, or if he had come in while I was lost in my reverie, but he struck up a conversation with me. Talking with him was immediately natural and effortless. As the conversation meandered through subject after subject, I noticed that, at some point, he had moved over to my table; apparently, the conversation had never missed a beat. I was talking with a kindred soul.

I suddenly realized that I was awake but, somehow the conversation was still going on. We were just chatting, talking about nothing special and, at the same time, about world-altering ideas. I was filled with an incredible sense of joy. "Yes!" I thought, "there are men out there who I can talk to, men I can share dreams with, men who fit right, just right!" I had been feeling so hopeless about it, but no, if there was such a man in my dream—and so clearly—then there were such men on earth. I knew it. I just knew it in the very marrow of my bones. Something had changed inside of me. The hopelessness I had lived with for so long was gone. The inner knowing that there was one who could match me in my life was absolutely solid. And I knew from my studies about how we create our reality that, if I knew it on this level, it would be so.

It was nearing autumn, and I had made plans to go to North Carolina—up to the mountains west of Asheville. I'd had those plans for almost a year, since the trip to Arkansas the previous fall. I was beginning to recognize that trying to fulfill Box

Number Nine from Houston was probably not going to work. Whoever shared this vision would most likely already be living in the place where the vision was, wherever that was. I was feeling that it was time to go to North Carolina to see if I wanted to move there. I'd now been in Houston an unthinkable twelve years. It had never felt like home. Now I wanted roots, and all I longed for was fresh mountain streams and thick green forests.

So it was time to go check it out. I had found a job opening in Hendersonville, just south of Asheville; I thought I'd stop in for a visit, scope out the area, and get some "R and R" at the same time. I made plans for late August.

It was around that time that a friend introduced me to Peter. We had an instant connection. When I told him of my plans, we spent an amazing phone conversation comparing notes, each with our own battered Rand McNally maps before us. It turned out that he regularly vacationed way up in the western mountains of North Carolina each fall, in the same corner of North Carolina where I was headed. He spoke of it with the same love and longing that was familiar to my heart. He spoke of the tall pines; the rich black soil teeming with life; the clean, clear, cool streams rushing over mossy river rocks; and the sweet pungent air filled with the smells of living growing things. We both talked of hikes through virgin forests, brook-wading and rock-hopping, and playing naked in the sun because there was no one within fifty miles to know about it or care.

Amazing, I thought, that our dreams and experiences matched so well. I was thrilled to find a man in Houston who even thought of these things. Houston is basically an indoor community of people whose idea of getting out and exercising is to make a daily run down to the local fitness club. How exciting to find someone who spoke my language!

One night as we sat in a little Italian restaurant, long after dinner was over, nestled over one more cup of decaf, I looked around the room and realized that this famous Houston late night spot was now completely deserted. Our waiter and the owner were waiting patiently in a corner. We had been talking excitedly about everything that interested us both—our dreams and visions, and the mountains, and all the ways we might work together in our missions and in healing the planet. We had been so immersed in what we shared, that time and space had disappeared. Suddenly I had the feeling of *déjà vu*. This was just like my dream! This was the man who had fit so well!

Peter and I began to spend more and more time together. He was a "New Age" musician of the highest order, a composer and pianist who had trained with the best in the classical tradition. Yet his work transcended traditional classical music; it even transcended the third dimension. He had designed a special room for listening to his compositions, and his music so moved the consciousness about in that room and within the mind, that it took you to other dimensions, other times, other levels of awareness. In this room, the mind expanded beyond all imagined limits and the heart soared beyond any imagined heights.

217

I don't think Peter was really from Earth, actually. He didn't dream about people and relationships and past issues like everyone else I knew; he dreamed of other planes of consciousness, of lands of light and sound, of sacred geometry and organic architecture that would create the means for transcendence to higher and higher levels of existence.

I resonated with everything that Peter was about. I felt as if all of the spiritual parts of me gathered together as in a joyful homecoming each time we were together. He had always been shy about sharing his secret spiritual world; people had long ago called him crazy so he had always kept his wondrous world of sound to himself. But with me he opened up; my resonance to his being gave him the knowing that there was a world waiting for what he had to offer, and that there could be safety in sharing it. During my own sessions in his music room, I experienced some of the same visions that he did. As I pored over his journals, which seemed to be visual and sound dictations from angelic realms, something inside recognized his world; it felt like home.

We began to work more and more closely together. I set up a workshop for him at my Center in Houston, and we started planning for a major concert toward the beginning of the year. I began doing guided meditations to his music, and the effect was unsurpassed in creating transformation and growth. There was no doubt in my mind that what we could create in terms of the New Place would be awesome beyond words.

As my North Carolina trip grew closer and closer, so did Peter and I. It felt as if Box Number Nine were falling into place. When we compared our schedules, it seemed that the Universe had set them up for us to be in the mountains of North Carolina at the same time. There was an overlap of about five days. Those five days seemed to take place in a magical kingdom far away from life on Planet Earth.

I flew into North Carolina in a small prop plane that skimmed over the tops of the mountains. The day was absolutely clear and I kept my eyes glued to the window, surveying the emerald majesty below me. I could see Knoxville. I could see the Smokey Mountains in the distance, their valleys characteristically filled with the fluffy clouds that gave them their the name. I could see the Pisgah National Forest, and maybe even make out the Blue Ridge Parkway. I wasn't sure. I was descending into a land of enchantment.

The plane landed late, and Peter was waiting. He had been alone in the mountains for almost a week now, and he was bursting with excitement at seeing me. There was so much to share! He looked like Indiana Jones. When we saw each other, we held each other for a long, long time.

It was about a three hour drive to his friend's land where we were to stay; the last half hour was a challenge even for a four-

218

wheel drive. We forded a couple of streams, pitching and lurching over boulders and giant pot-holes along the steep and winding dirt road. As we drove, Peter told me with great elation about what had transpired the week before.

Since childhood, Peter had heard celestial sounds; he heard them inside his head where no one else could hear them. There was certain music, in particular, that he could hear, a sound of purity and light. It was music which had the ability to transform. During his time in these ancient mountains, Peter had heard these sounds almost constantly—he heard them in the waters, heard them in the trees, heard them reverberate through the hills. He was bursting with excitement about it. As we climbed higher and higher up the mountain, I wondered if I, too, could hear this music coming out of these ancient forests.

219

We arrived at sunset. There was just enough time to walk about the land before darkness fell. It was spellbinding. This was ancient, ancient, untouched land. No tree had ever been cut; no bulldozer or chain saw had ever ravaged these towering forests. Undisturbed, the stillness was thick in the atmosphere. I kept breathing huge gulps of the sweet, oxygen-rich air.

Nestled against the hill was the start of a giant A-frame house made with huge beams, a sturdy roof and loft, fully open to nature. In front, there were two rocking chairs and a fire-pit. Ten steps beyond was a bubbling, rushing, rocky mountain stream, pristine in its purity, and refreshingly icy cold. A thick timber lay across the stream, and up the trail on the other side was the finest home-made hot tub one could imagine. It was set into the top of the hill in a clearing just big enough so that when you leaned back in the tub, you could gaze upon the heavens that were, it seemed, closer than any other place on Earth.

By day, we wandered the mountains and explored the woods; by night, we sat by the fire overlooking the stream and talked—talked until daybreak was just around the corner. He had always believed that he did not have a good voice; I taught him to trust his voice, and we danced as he sang. As he sang, I heard not only his voice, but the whole orchestra, the whole composition he was hearing inside. Together we sang to the hills, and then, in the silence, heard the music come back to us. Unseen voices, so faint they were almost inaudible, returned the song, returned the harmonies. We both heard it.

Peter taught me to hear the music he heard in the forests around us. At first, I thought the sounds might be coming from the brook. I became acutely aware of the babbling, notes and tones that gushed forth as the waters played upon the rocks. Sometimes it seemed as if whole conversations were going on. But the sound of the music coming from these hills was something different. Peter would sing the notes he was hearing, and then I would listen—listen intently. Initially, there was only one note I could consistently pick out. It was a deep, guttural AAWWW sound, and I called it the Tibetan's chant. (Later I was to discover that this was actually identical to some forms of Tibetan chanting.) I didn't hear it all the time as Peter did, but whenever I sat still, I could hear it as long as I attuned to it.

It was harder for me to hear the higher notes, so we took my guitar up on the hill one day and he tuned it to the exact notes he was hearing. I practiced with each string, listening for that particular note. As we came down from the hill that day, I strummed the guitar at different intervals, and noticed that certain notes were easier to hear in different locations.

Then, as we were walking toward the house, we passed an oak rain barrel. By chance, I strummed the guitar as we walked by, and we stopped in amazement; the sound echoed and reverberated for minutes. There was something about that particular location and, no doubt, the water in the barrel, that not only seemed to pick up the sound, but also kept the strings of the guitar vibrating—not just one or two of them, but an entire chord! I stood there, strumming over and over again, clearly hearing each note reverberating through the hills long after the guitar was silent. Each note had its own quality, like the singers in a choir. Each seemed to have a different vibration or feel to it, as if it had a different message to convey. Later that evening, Peter sat with the guitar against his heart, strumming the tune until tears ran down his cheeks. I looked at him, both loving and envying his deep, inner life, not knowing what a struggle his solitude had been for him. He looked at me and said softly, "Now I know I'm not crazy. Now I know what I hear is really there."

For me, there had never been any question about the reality of Peter's experience. I longed for the depth of connection to the higher dimensions that was a part of his world. I watched as he stood naked in the rushing waters, performing silent ablutions: He filled his cupped hands with water, offered it up to the heavens, then emptied it over his own head—a personal baptism that felt reverent and holy. Later, he emersed himself in the icy river; overcoming the urge to burst back to the warm air, he contained himself there, disciplining his mind and body to be silent and receptive within.

Gradually, tentatively at first, he shared his journals with me, opening up more and more as he saw that I did not judge, but rather, resonated with the images before me. He had drawn spirals of energy; and designed sound rooms of geodesic domes. Long ago, I had spent many hours chanting in a geodesic dome. I knew how the sound moved, how it could come from everywhere at once. I had learned of the spiraling energies from Thunder. He showed me a diagram of many people lying in concentric circles, vibrating sounds that could affect whole dimensions of consciousness. I had seen this vision, too, and had trained several meditation groups to work in a similar way. Yes, our visions matched so incredibly well; what a positive influence we could have on this planet working together!

Late one lazy, sunny afternoon, Peter and I were sitting in the rocking chairs by the stream. We were ambling through his journals, talking about what was in them and what could be

221

created from them. From time to time we looked up to watch as early yellow autumn leaves floated down and butterflies fluttered between our thoughts. Suddenly, from behind a rock slithered a snake with a diamond pattern on its back, just five feet in front of us. At first I was alarmed, but we sat very still and watched as it disappeared amongst the plants and leaves, sliding over the twigs and rocks as it went. Then, in a moment, it reappeared, very slowly at first—so slowly I leaned forward to see what was happening. It had caught a part of its skin on a stick and, as we sat watching in awe, it slithered, centimeter by centimeter, out of its old skin. It emerged slick and bright at the other end, as it slowly deposited that which it no longer needed directly at our feet.

How absolutely stunning! The molting snake before us seemed to offer a multitude of spiritual symbols, messages for Peter and me: Transmutation of the negative, the power of creation, the transformation from the mundane to the spiritual, the balancing of the male and female energies. I saw it as a metaphor for Peter's and my own merging, coming out of our past and being renewed in our shared commitment to help in the days of change on this planet.

Awesome, beautiful, transformational experiences like that were common when we were together. The next day we walked high up the mountain, and discovered a rocky overlook that hung above layers and layers of ledges teeming with verdant life, and bright with hints of coming autumn. As we perched atop our little Shangri-la, I taught Peter some of the yogic breathing techniques I had learned long ago. We absorbed into each other's eyes as we breathed together, inhaling and exhaling until there was no separation between us. As if intoxicated by the sweet air and the depth of our communion, I began to experience a change in his face and a change in the scenery around us. Suddenly we were in a temple some place long, long ago, or maybe in a different plane of existence. We were communicating our commitment to each other and to the work that lay before us. We were at once very light and at the same time very intent on our mission, our purpose, and our resolve to be of service in these days. I experienced my body expanding—expanding way beyond its physical bounds—and my heart filled to overflowing with the ecstacy of the radiant love I knew we were to ground in the Earth. It was some time before I experienced myself fully back in my body and able to walk back down the mountain.

Later in the week, we walked deep into the woods in search of a walking staff for me. Peter had a staff he called Eagle, and it had been a part of one of his own spiritual experiences during his last visit to this land. He encouraged me to get my own staff, and so we wandered into the woods, looking for a sapling that would become my own walking stick, my own antenna to the spirit world.

From the beginning it felt like a magical, mystical excursion. We walked through a hemlock and pine forest rich with the pungent, tangy smells of the woods. Sprite, Peter's dog, seemed to anticipate that something was at hand; she darted back and forth, yipping at the air, then burying her nose in the musky wet leaves on the ground. She appeared to be responding to the thick spirit energy that seemed to be around us. Speckles of sunlight sprinkled through the trees, spotting the dark woods with pockets of light. As we walked further into the forest, we moved from what felt like a lyrical, moss-and-fern-filled anteroom into the tall, stately stillness of the sacred inner chambers of this ancient forest.

We were both looking for the right sapling that would be my staff. All ears and eyes, we were steeped in awareness as we walked. From time to time Peter would find a nice-looking tree, and ask, "How about this one?" But now the time for intuitive connection was mine. It was my staff; I would know the right one—I would know it absolutely. I turned to him, gently letting him know that this was my process. "I'll know for certain when I see it."

223

As I turned back around, I stopped short in my tracks. I could hear Peter stop two steps later, for he saw it almost as quickly as I did. Directly in front of us, a brilliant ray of light descended through the forest, surrounding and backlighting one tiny tree. Every leaf was a radiant medallion of gold. Strung from what seemed to be every point on the tree to every other point were thousands of tiny spider webs, all lit up by the encompassing shower of light. It appeared as if infinite glistening rainbows radiated from the center of the tree in every direction around it. I wasn't sure, but I thought perhaps there were choirs of angels singing hallelujahs from the source of light high above the forest floor. We just stood there, transfixed, unable to speak or to move. This was Tree, the one we had been seeking.

It was a unique moment in time and space and light. At first I didn't want to cut Tree down; I thought maybe I would wait a day, and perhaps return later to bring it back to the house. Then I realized that it would never be the same; the light would change, the leaves would fall. Never again would there be that wondrous moment. I had asked to be shown the right tree for my staff, and that request had been answered: This small tree had presented itself. Reverently I went to the foot of Tree—now my friend and ally—and gave thanks.

I had no tobacco with which to pray and offer gratitude for the gift of Tree's life, but I had read that the Cherokee Elder Rolling Thunder once offered a few pennies when taking an herb because he had no tobacco with him. Peter had a candy bar in his pocket, so I prayed with the candy bar in hand, and then spread little pieces around Tree's base. I knew Creator was much less concerned with form than with intent. I was so thankful. Peter handed me the ax he had been carrying, and I made the first few chops at Tree's base. It reminded me of the sacred ceremony of bringing in the Sun Dance tree. Peter finished separating Tree from her base as I sang, sang the honoring songs I had learned in my time with Thunder. Then I carried Tree myself back to the house, not letting her drag on the ground, and lovingly placed her in the stream to loosen her bark. Later I would spend many hours stripping off exactly the right amount of layers to bring out her natural sheen, and prepare her to be the staff she had offered herself to be.

After what seemed in some ways to be many years, but in other ways, only moments, our time together in the mountains of North Carolina was over. I took Peter down to the airport, then rented a car and headed back up into the mountains alone. The job in Hendersonville, as it turned out, did not exist. I camped by another river for three more days. But it rained the whole time, and it wasn't the same without Peter. I was glad when I was finally back in Houston; in his ever joyful face and his enthusiasm over our ventures, our magic picked up where it had left off.

225

One Sunday morning towards the end of September, we were sitting on the doorstep of his townhome, looking out at the woods that bordered the property, sipping coffee, and eating my home-made apple muffins. It promised to be a beautiful day: The sun streamed through the leaves, brilliantly backlighting them as shafts of light snuck through the spaces between and gently lit up little patches on the lawn. Sprite lounged in the grass nearby. We both breathed deeply the fresh, clean Sunday morning air. It was going to be a good day.

Suddenly above us, swooping from the north towards the rooftop directly over our heads, appeared a white hawk. A white hawk! I had been nestled between Peter's legs, with my head against his chest. In one motion we both leapt out of the doorway, and landed on the sidewalk just in time to see the great bird make a sharp turn to the right, veering off to the east and disappearing into the trees.

We stood in amazement. I thought I remembered Thunder telling me that a white bird was a spirit bird or a messenger from Spirit—and the message of the hawk is one of responsibility, of seeing things from a higher perspective. We stood in wonder.

What was the message? Was it meant for Peter, for me, or for both of us? I wondered. Perhaps it was a blessing for the work we were doing, and the work we were going to do, since that is what we had been discussing when the hawk appeared. I was beginning to realize that the job at hand was very large. I felt as if we had just been given a very great gift.

It was time to head down to visit Peter's friend Terry and his wife Corina. We drove down to their house out in the country south of Houston. There were kids playing out in the road, horses in the back yard, and a small menagerie of dogs and cats lounging on porches and under cars. The land is very flat there—Texas style—but with large sprawling shade trees, fences for climbing, and an atmosphere of deep relaxation.

After dinner, Peter and Terry were throwing a frisbee back and forth over in the adjacent yard. Corina and I sat under a shade tree and shared stories. I started to tell her about seeing the white hawk that morning. I was in mid-sentence, pointing up, inscribing an invisible semi-circle to demonstrate the hawk's flight pattern when I was interrupted by a cry from Peter.

"HEY!"

I looked over and he, too, was pointing up the sky. I rolled onto my back and scanned the vast blueness. I didn't see a thing. "It was an eagle," Peter called out; "a white eagle!"

"Yeah, we see them down here sometimes," I could hear Terry saying in the distance. But for the second time that day I was in awe. At the precise moment I was describing the circling of the hawk, an eagle—a spirit eagle—had appeared, again apparently magnifying the work Peter and I were doing together. I sat in silence for a while, trying to fathom what had just occurred, but the best I could come up with was that we were up to something very big.

Several weeks later we were at my house, visiting with

226

Lawson, a friend and psychic who I had sponsored to come to Houston. He was doing a joint reading for Peter and me. Suddenly, outside, we heard a high-pitched sound. We all stopped talking and listened; something was very different about this sound. It was hard to tell exactly where it had come from, but it felt as if something had changed inside the room the moment we heard it. Peter and I both spontaneously entered into some kind of altered state of consciousness—still conscious, but filled with great amounts of energy. It felt very much like the deep meditation work I had done with the Peace People, but without the hours of sitting to still the mind. This energy was radiant, loving, and wondrous, and so expansive I found it difficult to keep grounded in my body. Lawson wrapped up the reading, saying that this energy was being given so that we could experience working together with it.

Peter and I laid down, meditating, breathing deeply, and fully conscious in this half-in-the-body, half-out-of-the-body state. This extraordinary experience lasted the entire night. While I had felt this kind of radiating with the Peace People, and had always believed that the energies were given from higher realms for service to the planet, I had never experienced them starting so abruptly. Peter, for all of his own spiritual adventures, did not seem to be familiar with this kind of energy either. We could not move or talk. We were consumed in a very blissful and powerful energy that seemed to be magnified by being together, yet I knew it was somehow moving through us for the benefit of the Earth. Here, I thought, was yet another sign, and other gift of Spirit, showing us that we had important work to do, and encouraging us on our path.

Yet things are not always what they seem. As immersed in love as I was, and enthralled with our shared mission, I was blind to the fact that Peter was not accustomed to sharing on such a deep level; he had lived too private a life for too long. That separation from others, in fact, had been what created his deep spiritual connection. He was not yet ready to expose

227

himself and his music to the world. Although it was his dream, like mine, to be a part of the healing process in this world, he was not ready for the magnitude that our partnership would have involved. He even told me that, but I somehow believed that there had been so many signs from Spirit about our work together that he would change his mind. I was so certain! Yet slowly he began to pull away, at first saying he wasn't ready for that deep a commitment. Later, though we continued to work together, he found little ways to create separation, gradually shutting me out more and more.

In past relationships, when I experienced rejection, I would cut and run. This time was different. I stayed with my feelings through the hurt, through the tears, holding my heart and breathing deeply. I prayed a lot, and began to find new ways of loving Peter, respecting his need for distance without losing myself in the process.

At the time, I was doing some work with Thunder that involved calling her every day. The bond between us grew deeper and deeper during those months, and she offered me immeasurable kindness and compassion in my loss. She kept encouraging me to keep my heart open. Keep my heart open, and don't have expectations.

However, I did have expectations. I tried my best to wait out Peter's need to separate, hoping he would change his mind. He still wanted my company from time to time, and appreciated my enthusiasm for his work, but I gradually became aware that he seemed to have no interest in my work or my dreams. It hurt, and I kept hoping for change. But I was in a honing process, unaware that Spirit was working on me in other ways.

Then one day I walked into his house and found another woman's picture where mine had always been. The shock lasted for weeks, and reverberated through my system for years, but it was not long at all before I finally I saw that I had been fooling myself. My idea about our future together had been an illusion; it had been in my mind, not in Peter's. I had thought that Peter would be that male counterpart to my vision, but now I realized that I had wanted to fit into his dream but he had no thoughts of fitting into mine. My time with Peter had never been about doing the work together, but was about discovering my own masculine energy within—that strong, assertive, powerful, and protective aspect of myself that would help take me forward into my destiny.

I had seen Peter as the source of all of the amazing spiritual experiences we had shared. But no, they had also been my experiences. They were a reflection of my consciousness! The destiny which was before me was to take complete responsibility for my dream.

I had assumed that Peter was Box Number Nine, and that he would be a lifelong partner. Although this relationship was not Box Number Nine, it was perhaps an even more important, more basic step—that of *creating the most essential partnership of all, one with myself and Spirit.* I realized that what Peter and I had shared was a gift from my Self to myself. He had been the mirror of my own consciousness unfolding. The disguise to the blessing had been the illusion of the perfect partner outside of myself. Finally the disguise had been lifted, and I was ready to move forward, claiming that creative, active, masculine side of myself that would finally take responsibility for my creation. Like the phoenix bursting forth from the flames, I was finally freeing myself to go forward into my dream.

▲ ▲ ▲ ▲ ▲ ▲ ▲

What a surprise it is when an illusion in which we are involved suddenly reveals its truth to us. The illusion will dissolve before our eyes over and over again, until we are finally ready to see the truth. The greatest awakening often occurs when we have abandoned ourselves to a powerful illusion and its breakdown sends us tumbling in chaos, and thus seeking the truth. That is to say, it is often the blessing which is most disguised that tears down the strongest illusion. Thus, this blessing can be the greatest of all, for it leads us back to our relationship with Self and with Spirit, and to the blossoming of the seeds of magnificence within.

1. Who are some of the people with whom you have shared ideas, dreams, or visions? How did you feel and what did you think when another person's version of the vision did not match your own?

2. What dreams do you now hold in the hope that someone else will take responsibility in some way to fulfill them? How can you take back that responsibility for fulfilling them yourself?

3. Think of several times when someone else canceled plans and you ended up doing something alone—and you were glad. What was better about being alone each time?

4. What illusions in your life have been broken—only to reveal a better way or alternative?

THE BLESSING REVEALED

THE WISDOM AND POWER
OF VULNERABILITY

It is in times of chaos and crisis that we have the greatest opportunity for transformation, for making alterations in old patterns, and for stepping back from our daily routine and seeing the greater picture.

But how can we best utilize these times of growth? What can we do to maximize these opportunities, and to allow the blessings to be revealed in the present? How can we take these challenges and convert their energy, not only for our own benefit, but for a greater global purpose?

Ironically, vulnerability is our greatest tool for transformation. For the most part, we have learned the opposite: Be strong, keep a stiff upper lip, don't show your feelings.

Being vulnerable is actually very simple. It involves giving up our obsession with control and letting ourselves and others experience who we really are. It involves allowing the humanness of ourselves and others to exist. It means being open—childlike—and allowing things to be as they are anyhow, without the barriers and walls that would protect us from the truth. Our vulnerability is like water: Despite the fact that water is soft and fluid, it has the power to completely alter land, which appears more solid and unyielding. In choosing to be vulnerable, we give up attempts to control and manipulate, simply allowing ourselves and others to be who and how we each are. We allow our true Self to show, making no apologies, no excuses. In our willingness to feel hurt, anger, or fear, as well as joy, enthusiasm, and caring, we begin to understand unconditional love. We begin to understand the meaning of acceptance, both of ourselves and of others.

In order for the Self within us to be heard, perceived, and understood, we must listen to our feelings. We must allow the discomfort to be there, love ourselves in the midst of our discomfort, and embrace the child within who still knows how to feel. When we allow all the feelings to speak to us, when we honor them, the mind soon clears to receive the message from the pain we are experiencing. Feeling our feelings allows us to receive the information that the discomfort is trying to offer us.

I believe we are coming into a time when each person's thoughts are "known by their fruits," where we will understand fully the direct relationship between what we think and what we experience in our lives. All people will proudly claim their potential, yet humbly (and without shame) acknowledge their incomplete growth. There will be no need for secrets; we will openly acknowledge our interconnectedness and the telepathic ability we've had all along. We will stand as naked before man and God in all our glory and with all of our baggage, knowing what we now pretend we don't know—that everyone can see everything about us anyhow. When we become willing to acknowledge and live according to this truth, we will be free in both our humanity and in our divinity.

Vulnerability allows the higher self to come through and give answers—answers of truth born of a willingness to hear; answers that give solutions to whatever causes the pain; answers of the Spirit.

Vulnerability is not victim-consciousness. Victim-consciousness attracts pain and assigns responsibility to an external person or situation. Vulnerability, on the other hand, involves being open and fully responsible. When we habitually listen to and feel the truth within, whether we experience it as positive or negative, we cannot help but know that we are the creator of our own perceived universe. We begin to grasp how the Great

Mystery moves through us and all of creation and, as such, we see how our own life is our own special creation.

What springs from this vulnerability is our power: True power, spiritual power, and the power for creating benefit for self and others. *When we are not afraid to feel our hurt, we become willing to take the risks involved in moving toward our dream, for those who are truly guided from the Spirit within cannot be stopped.* When one is backed by Spirit, many doors open. It is a power that cannot be abused. It is the power of Good. It is the power of Truth.

Choosing our vulnerability merely involves a few moments and the decision to allow it. Feel. Fully experience the vulnerability. Let your awareness dive into your body's experience of whatever emotion is there. Notice where in the body you experience your emotions. Is it in your chest? Your stomach? Your throat or your jaw? Put your hand over whatever part of your body houses those feelings and allow your awareness to be present with what you feel five or ten minutes, or maybe much longer. Feel the hurt, the happiness, whatever is there. If you need to, yell into a pillow or jump up and down to release stored negative energy. *Deep breath* and let the *feelings* be *felt*.

We can avoid years of stuffing feelings (or eating, drinking, or working them away). When we *focus inwardly; feel and listen to the internal messages,* we are vulnerable, we surrender to the Higher Power within us and, we open our connection to Spirit. In doing this, we let go of our automatic walls and make wiser choices for ourselves. The good news is that, when we can feel our pain, we can also feel our joy. *If we can recognize that we create our own misery, then we can also see, finally, how we can make our dreams come true.* We thus enter into alignment with the Greater Picture. We give God permission to do what God is going to do anyhow. We go with the flow.

Our hearts open...

We radiate love...

And we fulfill that which we came to fulfill.

233

The result is spiritual strength. Humility. Self-esteem. Love.

▲ ▲ ▲ ▲

During those days of waiting and hoping for Peter to come back, Thunder taught me the wisdom and the power of vulnerability. During those many months, she kept saying to me, "Keep your heart open, love yourself, and love others." And so I refused to shut my heart, and in keeping my heart open, I learned the vulnerability that became the door to my Self and to all of my dreams.

Ironically, after wondering for so long what Thunder "did" to effect change, I finally realized that her vulnerability is the key—an openness to the world of Spirit and to the world of humanity. Her own hurt and anger, as well as her love and compassion, are all a part of one package, which she does not hide. She allows her humanness to show and thus teaches this principle by her example; it is how she lives. She taught me to love, even when someone was doing something that felt hurtful or that I didn't like. "Hold your heart and breathe!" she would say. Being vulnerable was not about making choices that were hurtful to myself, nor was it about being a martyr or not setting boundaries. It was about being open, receptive, and willing to be myself and let others do the same.

This was the period of time when I was going to the little chapel in east Houston where Mother Mary and the angels were appearing. I went there often to pray, to sort out the changes in my life, and to ask for clarity. Kneeling in the little chapel, I would feel a great peace descend over me, and within minutes my prayers would invariably turn from my own personal hurts and healing to prayers for global healing. It was during this time that I received the vision in the pink light of the peaceful dimension where people took personal responsibility for their lives. In my openness and vulnerability came not only personal healing, but visions for global healing.

During another visit to the chapel, my friend Gloria shared

with me that she finally understood why Jesus is sometimes portrayed pointing to the Sacred Heart. He is opening his chest, revealing a heart surrounded by thorns. "What he was teaching," she said, "was that in order to love, we must allow ourselves to hurt."Allow ourselves to hurt?

I pondered this a great deal. How often I would resist feeling pain: I would try not to feel it, stuff it, tighten up against it, do something addictive to avoid it, be too busy to feel it, or just pitch a fit. Anything but just feel the hurt and allow it to be.

Yet did this mean one had to be a victim or that one should choose hurt? Not at all. I started to realize that if I would simply *feel* the hurt when it was there, and honor what was inside—listen to the message that the pain (or the joy) brought—then I could *never* be a victim, because in allowing myself to feel what was inside of *me*, and to *make choices accordingly*, I was taking *full* responsibility for my life. It seemed that each time I thought I had grasped this concept, then I would discover still more layers and ways in which I needed to integrate it. I recognized on a deeper level that, when things happen which we don't like, if we look at how we are responsible for creating them, then we begin to be able to *change* the creation. We *own* it as *our* creation, hence the responsibility and the power. When we are applying our energies and power towards something we *can* change (ourselves) instead of something we *can't* change (like someone else), then we can truly effect massive improvements in our world.

How would the world be if every person, every nation, did this?

The intense introspection that accompanied the great vulnerability I was now experiencing led me to realize the subtle way in which I had *not* owned my own dream of the New Place. I had been making the "other" responsible for *my* dream! I had wanted Peter to be the inspiration and the energy to fulfill my desires, while I supported what he did. It sounded

235

a lot like codependency, and I suddenly realized the magnitude of codependency in our culture. I began to recognize that since I was the common denominator in all of the amazing spiritual experiences I'd had over the years, there had to be something greater was at hand, though maybe something I could not yet see. It had to be so! These dreams of a new kind of spiritual community would not be alive in me for so many years if they were not meant for fulfillment.

If this were so, then it meant it was time for me to face those things that I was waiting for someone else to handle before my dream could come true!

That was it! As long as I made others responsible for my own dream, it could not come true! I had to own it! I had to do it, no matter how frightening it might be!!!

As I saw it, there were four things necessary for me to move toward the New Place. The first was to know where it was, and I still had no idea. The second was to own and acknowledge my own spiritual connection. That meant I needed to recognize within me what I had looked for in Peter. It was time to see how that magnificence was already mine. Third, I needed the willingness and courage to go forward with the dream even if no one else was there to share it.

Fourth, it was time for me to trust that my greatest ally and support was Spirit. Spirit would help me go in the right direction, and if I got off course, Spirit would help me get back on track (probably through one of those blessings in disguise!)

In my vulnerability, my new willingness to stand alone, I suddenly knew what I had to do: I had to face the next question. Was I was willing to take full responsibility for Box Number Ten—the New Place?

It was scary. It felt so big. As I asked myself this question, over and over in the next couple of weeks, I walked about in a daze. Take full responsibility for myself and my vision? Do it by myself? Or maybe not do it by myself, but be *willing* to do it by myself if necessary?

Gradually it became clear that at this point, the only spiritually responsible position was that I needed to make the choice to go out on a limb by myself. As each day passed, I remained receptive and open, allowing myself to mull over the idea of leaving Houston and heading out alone to parts unknown. I stayed vulnerable: I faced the fear and felt it, hung out with it, and let myself become familiar with it. Soon I could feel that there was movement afoot. I put forth a little prayer: "Lord, I don't really want to go alone, and I'm scared and have no idea how to do it, but if it be Your will that I go now to the New Place, please let me know where it is."

Then one morning, I awoke from a very deep sleep and heard a very loud voice in my ear—yet there was no sound:

"ASHEVILLE"

"Asheville?" I asked silently to the empty space around me.

"ASHEVILLE," I heard again.

Asheville, North Carolina? I didn't even know what the place looked like! Several years before, when Susie, Bart, Lucy Morningstar, and I were on our way to Cherokee, we had stopped at a funny little motel called the Mountaineer Inn on the outskirts of Asheville, but I no idea what the town was like. The area around the hotel was filled with little strip shopping centers. I had not thought of it as particularly appealing. Yet the mountains of western North Carolina were filled with a magical majesty. And, of course, I'd only seen a very small part of the city of Asheville. I decided to wait a few days and see if this idea stuck, or if it would faded away as so many dreams do after a little time.

By the next morning, the idea was, in fact, even stronger. Asheville was growing on me very quickly. By the third morning, I was feeling fairly certain that the time had finally come. I was amazed. After years of dreaming, years of training, years of looking, I wake up one morning and just hear a name, the name of a place about which I had almost no information. Yet it *felt* right. More than that, I *knew* it was right.

237

I went out to the Thunder-Horse Ranch that weekend for the Saturday evening Sweat Lodge. I wanted to pray about this idea. And I wanted to ask Thunder if she had any input on it. I offered her tobacco and asked her what she thought. I was hoping for a whole big discussion on it, but Thunder never wastes time or words. She just smiled that wonderful cherubic smile of hers, so full of love and brightness, and said, "That would be good. It seems you have a mission there." It was reassuring to hear her words, but I also kept thinking that if I had told her I was moving to Japan or Istanbul, she would have said the same thing. She seemed to know this choice was internally inspired, which was the whole point of her teachings.

I decided to take a month to wrap things up in Houston, but also to cut any escape route that might allow me to return if I lost courage heading out to unknown territory by myself. My friends would look at me somewhat askance, shake their heads, and mumble something like, "Well, you sure are brave." But I had no doubt that "Asheville" was the message I'd been awaiting for years.

On Easter—the time of resurrection and renewal—Thunder threw a goodbye party for me. I remembered that Easter of long ago when, following that green van, lost in thought and wondering about my purpose in life, I had almost ended it. I had cut free that day from a spiritual system that no longer rang true for me, and that ultimately led me to meet Mary Thunder. Now it was Easter again. So much had happened in those years. I was once again cutting loose, but this time it felt as if I were graduating, that I was somehow taking wings and flying. The purpose had been found and was unfolding magnificently before me.

At the Easter goodbye party, Thunder had created a little book with photos, images, and quotes from all of our time together, and everyone signed it like a yearbook. Leaving my spiritual family at the Ranch was the hardest part of my new adventure.

Friends from all over Houston started stopping by, asking me

238

out for lunch, and helping me pack. Calls, cards, acknowledge-
ments came in from everywhere, statements of gratitude for the
difference I had made in people's lives. I was floored. Over and
over again came the information that I had touched people in
ways that I had never imagined. Part of me wanted to stay; I
had no idea how much I had bonded with the people in
Houston. Yet, another part knew it was time to fulfill that which
called from within. In the days to come, those acknowledge-
ments and thank-yous would give me the strength to carry on.

On a bright spring morning in late April, with Bambi
Lemonade packed to overflowing, I headed North. I had with
me my most precious possessions—my music things, my altar,
and my plants, which created a little jungle in the back of my
van with a tiny spot for my sleeping bag. The rest of my possessions were already in transit with the moving company;
I had ten days to get to Asheville and find a place for them to
unload my furniture. The time had finally come. I was bursting
with excitement. I was on my way to the New Place!

239

▲ ▲ ▲ ▲ ▲ ▲ ▲

We are culturally conditioned to avoid vulnerability; therefore, mastering it takes a conscious choice to learn about it and
to make it an important part of our repertoire. The gentle listening without judgement which constitutes vulnerability ultimately allows us to hear the life-altering answers that transform
our lives. Listen closely to your own answers to these questions.

1. Think of several times when the experience of vulnerability
brought about a breakthrough in communication or in a difficult situation in your life.

2. What have been the turning points for you in choosing to
make important changes in your life? How did vulnerability
play a role in helping you make those choices.

THE NEW PLACE

THE END AND THE BEGINNING

When you set out for Ithaka
pray that your road's a long one,
full of adventure, full of discovery.
Laistrygonians, Cyclops,
any Poseidon—don't be scared of them:
you won't find things like that on your way
as long as your thoughts are exalted,
as long as a rare excitement
stirs your spirit and your body.
Laistrygonians, Cyclops,
wild Poseidon—you won't encounter them
unless you bring them along inside you,
unless your soul raises them up in front of you.

Pray that your road's a long one.
May there be many a summer morning when—
full of gratitude, full of joy—
you come into harbors seen for the first time;
may you stop at Phoenician trading centers
and buy fine things,
mother of pearl and coral, amber and ebony,
sensual perfumes of every kind,
as many sensual perfumes as you can;
may you visit numerous Egyptian cities
to fill yourself with learning from the wise.

Keep Ithaka always in mind.
Arriving there is what you're destined for.
But don't hurry the journey at all.
Better if it goes on for years
so you're old by the time you reach the island,
wealthy with all you've gained on the way,
not expecting Ithaka to make you rich.

Ithaka gave you the marvelous journey.
Without her you wouldn't have set out.
She hasn't anything else to give.

241

And if you find her poor, Ithaka won't have fooled you.
Wise as you'll have become, and so experienced,
you'll have understood by then what an Ithaka means.
        —*"Journey to Ithaka," by C.P. Cavafy*

As we sail our ship toward the horizon, that infinitely fine line that divides heaven and earth recedes ever before us, yet never ceases to sit at the center of our vision. Sometimes, on vast empty seas, it may not seem we are going anywhere. But then one day we see before us the shoreline we have sought for so long. At that moment, we can finally look back and say, "Ah, the journey has been worth it, well worth it."

When we first experience the dream in our heart, it is foggy, vague, undefined. It is often more a feeling or a sense than a clear picture. The journey to the fulfillment of our dream is beyond our imagination for, if we were already aware of the change in consciousness that the journey would bring, it would not be a dream and we would not need to make the journey.

Does it matter if we ever fulfill our dreams? Maybe yes, maybe no. What do we see when we get to the mountaintop? Another mountain. At each and every moment, we can add all that we have learned on the way to our dream, and then evaluate whether that dream is still our goal or whether it has been altered in some way by the journey. We get to choose whether we settle on that mountaintop, or whether we want to explore further. It is *always* our creation!

What does matter is that we feel, acknowledge, and fully receive the blessings along the way, for they will help us either refine or reach our dream.

We are coming into a time when we will constantly, yet comfortably, live with the awareness that our thoughts create our reality. Consciousness will not be as it is now: We have to keep reminding ourselves, pointing out the evidence to ourselves, and trying to figure why such-and-such happened, because we have forgotten that we are our own creative force. In the future, each of us will know every other person's thoughts by what that person manifests. Respect, acceptance, and cooperation will be the natural byproducts.

As we enter into the coming consciousness, more and more of us will be moved by the dreams in our hearts. We will draw from the inner space that is the connection between our own personal Self and the greater wholeness and connectedness that is the Great Mystery. We will experience a workable world, for each person's dream is one piece of the puzzle, one part of the whole. When it is completed and revealed, it is more magnificent than any one of us could have imagined.

But first, we must go for the dream.

▲ ▲ ▲ ▲

The drive to Asheville was a complete delight to the senses. Spring was bursting forth from every corner and bend in the road. I stayed in Hot Springs, Arkansas my first night on the road, taking the time to bathe in my favorite nurturing spot. Before I left I drove around the town a little. Had it only been a year and a half since Melody and I threw handfuls of tobacco with loving prayers all around this city, and since I had travelled

the trail of vortexes with my Sacred Pipe? The energy here was
so different now, so much cleaner. The town seemed to have a
new kind of pride in itself. I was reminded of something I had
read by Betty Eadie, in her book *Embraced by the Light*. She'd
had a near-death experience after an operation and, while she
was in the Spirit realm, she had been shown many things. One
image in particular touched me deeply:

*The heavens scrolled back again, and I saw the sphere of earth
rotating in space. I saw many lights shooting up from the earth
like beacons. Some were very broad and charged into heaven like
broad laser beams. Others resembled the illumination of small
pen lights, and some were mere sparks. I was surprised as I was
told that these beams of power were the prayers of people on earth.*

*I saw angels rushing to answer the prayers. They were orga-
nized to give as much help as possible. As they worked within this
organization, they literally flew from person to person, from
prayer to prayer, and were filled with love and joy by their work.
They delighted to help us and were especially joyful when somebody prayed with enough intensity and faith to be answered
immediately. They always responded to the brighter, larger
prayers first, then each prayer in turn, until all of them were
answered...When we have great need, or when we are praying
for other people, the beams project straight from us and are immediately visible...We all have the ability...to reach God with
our prayers.*

(Betty Eadie, *Embraced by the Light*, Gold Leaf Press, 1992)

I felt happy thinking that, in some way, the prayers we had
offered for this little town had done some good for the people,
the land, and for the waters there.

The next day I drove across Tennessee. The countryside was
stunning. Interstate 40 was lined with thousands of redbuds
and pink dogwoods, and they were all in bloom that day.
Never had I seen such an exquisite panorama of springtime
celebration. It felt as if all the nature devas had planned a

243

welcome in my journey to my new home. At the edge of the Smokey Mountains and western North Carolina, I began my climb into the mountains, then the descent down into Asheville. I thrilled at each turn in the highway, as it revealed one breathtaking view after another—rushing waterfalls, blazing orange wild azaleas, and countless early spring flowers all abloom. This was to be my new home; I had been guided to such an awesome place!

Within three days I found the perfect little house to call home while getting my bearings in my new town. The front yard was filled with tulips, azaleas, and flowering dogwoods; the inside was a quaint, little granny-type place. I loved it. Finding this home was another gift from Spirit; the owner accidentally left her phone off the hook right after we spoke, and then left town for two days. She discovered her mistake only moments before I drove into her driveway—which I did because I kept getting a busy signal when I tried to call her. No one else had even had the opportunity to talk to her about it or leave a message. But we hit it off right away. It was as if Creator was keeping this house just for me. It was a place to feel at home, to write, and to start the next phase of my work—a place from which to launch Box Number Ten.

So here I was, finally in Asheville. How long had I dreamed of the New Place, the healing center, the place where people would come and touch the core of their being, the place where there would be no separation of the body, mind, heart, and Spirit.

My plan was to write my book, while getting myself established as a therapist, speaker, and trainer in the community. Soon I would begin looking for an ideal building that would be a center for an Asheville-based group of practitioners and a location for workshops. While I made connections and networked, I would eventually be led to this location and to the people with whom the larger picture—the retreat, the community—would unfold.

My intuition had told me that Asheville was the place. But after I'd been here several months, much to my surprise, something didn't quite feel right. I would wake up in the morning with a very sense of discomfort, something I couldn't quite put my finger on. This feeling wasn't quite foreboding and it was not disappointment. Try as I might, I could not identify the source of these uncomfortable feelings.

There was something about Asheville when I first moved here that held a strange dichotomy for me. Oh, there was no doubt that I loved the mountains, the streams, the fresh mountain air, the hundreds of birds that chirped and sang all day, the endless variety of fragrant flowers, the crisp nights, and the warm days. I thought about the beauty as I sat on my little picture postcard front porch, swinging on my picture perfect porch swing. A robin hopped around the garden just three feet in front of me, tugging at tassels and stalks and dried stems, gathering nesting materials, continuously adding to the collection in its beak without dropping one straw.

245

This seemed like heaven—as long as I was enjoying my solitude and my connection to nature. But what about the people? It seemed to be very hard to make connections here. People seemed to be extremely friendly upon introduction—and then they would disappear completely. There seemed to be obstacles everywhere.

Over and over again people told me it was too hard to make a living here in Asheville. "There are already too many therapists here," they would tell me, or "It's almost impossible to make a living unless you go out of town to earn money." Everywhere I turned I heard "I can't afford it," whether it had to do with a class or the cost of bread. There seemed to be a survival-mode consciousness in those days. People tended to present themselves as if they were just getting by. Yet I looked around me and saw plenty of affluence. The words and the picture weren't matching.

I began to wonder if I had been rash in my decision about

coming here. Maybe Asheville wasn't the New Place after all. Perhaps I had made a mistake. Oh well, if that was so, it would only be one of thousands. I was getting to the point in my self-esteem where mistakes didn't bother me as they once did. They simply meant to "try something different or start again."

But I didn't want to give up! I noticed many people moved to Asheville and, after struggling financially for some time, they would leave. I resolved not to allow the negative experiences get to me! If I was the creator of my reality, I didn't need to buy into a cultural belief in scarcity. I could believe in God's abundance and in my own ability to hold a vision and create it. Rather than let go of my dream here, I became more determined to hold the vision even stronger. I decided I would not only hold this dream for myself, but I would model it for others. I would speak out for dreams, and creation, and abundance, and holding the vision, and being responsible for our reality. I would watch my own mind, not allow the negative thoughts in, and support others in this!

After all, why had I come here? If I were a Vision Holder for a new level of consciousness, then I had to face whatever obstacles there were in making the leap to that new level. I had to stand firm in my own vision despite any negative input that might come my way. I had to practice it; I had to do it myself. This is what Vision Holders do for the people. I had to inspire myself and, in doing so, offer that inspiration to others.

I thought of a quote I had once written in my journal from St. Therese of Liseaux from her biography, *Story of a Soul*:

"Instead of getting discouraged, I said to myself, God wouldn't inspire in me desires which can't be fulfilled, so in spite of my littleness, I shall aspire to holiness." (*Story of a Soul, The Autobiography of St. Therese of Lisieux*, translated by John Clarke)

Yes, I was charging myself with walking my own talk, as Thunder would say. "Go for it, Carolyn! You can do it."

I began to practice looking at everything as a blessing. The more I didn't like it, the more I would look for the gift in it. The more implausible or uncomfortable a situation, the more I would declare it wonderful. I got so I could find the blessing in anything. No longer would I let my fears run my life. Finally, I knew I had the capability to beat the fear and the negative feedback, and to create the Center that was to be the core of my New Place.

Then something happened that helped me to realize that, even though I'd needed to be willing to do it alone, others had the same dream, or dreams that interfaced with mine. And there were people who wanted to support and help the dream come true.

A business trip back to Houston took me to a conference focused on healing the healthcare profession. It was comprised of doctors, nurses, and therapists whose intention was to broaden healthcare to encompass a more holistic body/mind/spirit approach. Yet this group of professionals were reticent about sharing their deepest concerns, and the seminar leader was not encouraging them to do this. So the day was going very slowly; the conference was dry and intellectual.

As a seasoned seminar leader and therapist, I knew that the best way to keep things so safe that no change occurs, is to allow people to talk intellectually about theories or other people instead of about themselves and their experiences. It is a way for people to avoid their feelings and thus never get in touch with themselves or with what is deeply important to them. Creating a safe place where people can be vulnerable and fully express themselves is a necessary part of bringing about healing.

I knew that if the energy in this room did not shift soon, this seminar would be dead in the waters—and its purpose would not be realized. People had to start speaking their own truths. I also recognized that if my work was about showing people how to allow themselves to be fully who they are, I had to model my own vulnerability.

I gulped, realizing that I held an important piece of the context

247

of the day's work. If healthcare workers couldn't be honest about who they were, they certainly weren't in a position to facilitate any truly significant level of healing in others. Perhaps that fear of vulnerability was the very reason health-care professionals had shied away from the emotional, mental, and spiritual aspects of good health for all these years. Yet the history of religion, the grass roots rise in holistic approaches to healing, and abundant 20th century research all pointed clearly in that direction.

I stood up to speak, vaguely aware that my voice was a little shaky and that I had a death grip on the microphone. "Hi, I'm Carolyn Ball. Although, in my everyday life, I function as a psychotherapist and speaker and seminar facilitator, it's not easy to stand up before you and say this, to put myself on the line before other professionals. But, I believe that if we are to heal healthcare, we have to bring God into the hospital and we have to admit that we are human. We can't pretend our per-sonal lives are irrelevant in work. Nor can we heal people while ignoring our own or patients' spiritual and human needs. I'm not even sure how to do it, but I know that I must let my spiri-tual side show in my work, and that I must be true to myself and what I believe."

I didn't know what kind of reaction I'd get, but what I saw before me were clear eyes, focused interest, and heads nodding in agreement. I went on. I told them about the dream I'd had for all these years. I told them about its spiritual core, about its people living in community, about its healing and learning cen-ter, and that it would exist in a nurturing, healing place I had been seeking for many years. I even revealed to them that I had awakened one morning several months before, and heard, "Asheville!" After all these years I had finally found the place and moved there—and at this point, I was *really* scared because it meant that now was the time to make the dream come true. Just like the dream of healing the healthcare industry, my dream was no longer "out there", something in the future I wanted, but rather here and now. It was time for me to buckle down and create it. And I didn't even know how. However, I did know that holding and sharing the Vision was essential for any of it to happen.

I sat down, feeling as if I had been so vulnerable, and had gone so far out on a limb with these professional medical people, that I was a little numb. I hadn't really planned what I would say, and I certainly had no idea what the results would be, if any. At the same time, I knew I had spoken the truth—*my* truth for this moment. I looked around the room. Heads were still nodding and there were big smiles everywhere. A nurse and two doctors spoke next. They each shared from their heart what had brought them to this conference. They shared their fears, their failures, and their realizations. The energy in the room had shifted! What had been a bunch a strangers, each aware of being philosophically on the fringe of healthcare, was becoming a community of human beings sharing in the vision of bringing the fringe to the center.

Throughout the day—on breaks, at lunch, in the hall, in the ladies room—professionals from the conference approached me with enthusiasm and excitement about what I had shared. They thanked me, they gave me business cards, they gave me contacts in Asheville, and they asked if they could come visit me. The response was so overwhelming that I was reeling. I could no longer look at the situation in Asheville and think I couldn't fulfill my intention. If there was support here in Houston's conservative medical community, it certainly would exist in Asheville. The message was clear: As long as I held firmly to the vision, it would come together.

With my dream at the forefront of my awareness, I began living my days completely by intuition. I found that I could plan almost nothing, but rather, that I needed to be moved by Spirit within at each and every moment. It reminded me of how I had wandered about in Arkansas after my first year of Sun Dancing. I couldn't think about what to do, for my brain was

too full of options and possibilities. I had to move from within.
Now I was using those intuitive abilities in my life and, once
again, I thought gratefully of Thunder and her experiential way
of training. By now, I was fairly comfortable with following my
heart and trusting my gut. It was the only way to work here. I
would write for a while, see a few clients, make some contacts
in town, then head up into the mountains for a day or two to
write some more—each move, each decision stirred from
within and in the moment.

I gradually came to understand that, because so many people came and left from Asheville, folks in the mountains were
slow to let you in. It took a while to gain people's confidence.
The culture was one of self-reliance, and of keeping your problems to yourself. Yet there was also a warmth and kindness
which allowed for tourists to come and go from this beautiful
land and, if you could carve a little niche for yourself that did
not upset the beauty of this place, you were welcome to stay. In
a way you had to prove yourself. When I first arrived, this attitude hadn't made sense; I now saw it as a way to preserve this
sacred part of the country.

I also observed that I was meeting one person after another
who, when asked why they moved here, would say, "I don't
know, it just felt right," or, "Something just told me this was
where I needed to be."

There was an astounding number of people with very similar visions gathering here. Yet, at the same time, they felt very
scattered, not connected. What was this all about? Why were
people drawn here with such a sense of purpose, just to discover themselves floundering for direction? And what did it
have to do with me? What was my piece in this puzzle? The
answers very slowly started to fall into place.

I began to understand that the New Place was not just a
building where people worked together, though I felt sure that
would come in time. No, it was a New Place in the mind and in
the heart. It was a sense of community where each person lived

250

responsibly and in awareness of his or her creation. It was another level of human expression where, when people allowed themselves to be human, with their own strengths and weaknesses, they would be drawn naturally into magnificent expressions of their strengths and into healing situations for their weaknesses. It was simply awesome. And it was starting to happen.

Almost a year had passed since my arrival in Asheville. I was teaching a workshop up at a mountain retreat called the Light Center. It had been a glorious weekend—the edge of Spring—and we'd done a little hiking, some yoga, and some breathing exercises, so everyone was extremely relaxed. As one of the last exercises, I led a guided visualization about fulfilling our dreams. I had each person see, feel, taste, smell, spend time, and walk around in that which they wanted to create. As I allowed moments of silence to pass for them to visualize, I filled in my own pictures with my dream, the beginning of the Center I wanted to create: A nice house on Chestnut Street with two or three stories...painted a cheery yellow or peach...a nice big porch with a swing...surrounded by countless colorful flowers, with happy people coming in and out.

As I left the workshop that afternoon, I decided to drive down Chestnut Street just to see if there was any house such as the one I had visualized during the meditation. I didn't really expect to find anything but, at the same time, I felt compelled to go look. Much to my surprise, there was a new "For Sale" sign out in front of one yard—which was unheard of, since most of the houses in that area sold through word-of-mouth and never made it to the market. But there it was! Only it was grey. Ugh.

I started to drive away when something made me back up, look again, then take down the phone number. By the time I got home, something inside of me was buzzing, "Move on it *now!*"

"But it's Sunday and the house is grey," my mind countered. Nonetheless, I called, and within an hour I was touring the

251
〰

house. It was surrounded by pink and white dogwoods, yellow forsythia in bloom, with a giant, fragrant lilac tree in the back yard. The interior had been partially renovated and the floor plan was exactly what I had envisioned. My excitement was building. It felt right. The clincher came as we were walking out the door, and the agent said, "Oh, by the way, the current owners are going to paint the house; but they want to let the buyer choose the color."

Wow. I put down a deposit on the house the next day.

But then I had to find financing. It had never occurred to me that this would be a problem. Lenders kept saying, "Oh, sure, we can get you a great rate," but inevitably, the bottom line would be that since I was self-employed and in the city for less than a year, they couldn't help me. I think I spoke with every lender in town. I finally got to a point where I wasn't going to push it any more. Late one evening I surrendered to the flow, praying, "Lord, I thought from all the little miracles that this was Your will, but right now I've done all I could to get financing, and I don't know what else to do. If this is meant to be, Lord, I'll need Your help to get the money. And not only that, since there have been so many obstacles to the financing, I'll need a pretty clear sign, because this place is for Your work, and I don't want to do anything that is not in alignment with Your will."

I went to sleep that night with a sense of freedom. Buying a house at this point was quite a stretch, and the building still needed quite a bit of work. It would be just fine to spend my spring in the woods instead of cleaning and painting an old Victorian house.

However, the next morning I received a call from my bank. The loan officer had already told me I was not eligible for a loan, but she decided she'd call anyway and see how I was doing. That's unusual, I thought to myself. We talked for a while, and she decided she liked me, and besides that, she said, the woman who had referred me always sent her good people.

And there on the spot, somehow, she approved me for the loan over the phone in a matter of ten minutes. Not only that, but for an excellent rate!

"Okay, God, that was pretty clear," I thought. Pretty clear and pretty amazing. I wondered how many times Spirit had to prove Itself before we really understood how inexorably our lives are bound up in the realm of the Great Mystery.

But now it was time to get to work—moving, cleaning, re-finishing the floors, carpentry, painting—there was a lot to do. Out of the woodwork (so to speak) came people to help. Daily, hourly, I was amazed at how everything that was needed would come to pass. People resonated to the dream, and they kept popping in at just the right time to handle different pieces of the picture. Sometimes there were whole crews buzzing around the house. "I need two big guys to walk in the door right now to move all of these carpets I've just cleaned," I thought to myself at one point. Within five minutes, two friends arrived with just a few minutes to spare—did I need anything? And the carpets were moved. As I was painting late one night, and wishing for snacks and company, the phone rang, and a friend wanted to know if he could bring over some refreshments and visit for a while—maybe even paint some. Well, sure!

Whatever I thought of that was needed, it would be given almost immediately. People gave of their talents, and received back in the feeling of community and purpose and sharing. The process of creating this new Center was already a living exam-ple of what it was being created to teach. I kept holding in my heart the three concentric circles: Spirit, the People who serve, and the Community. I kept holding in my mind the picture of a giant column of light connecting the Center with all the beings of heaven, while the building itself radiated brilliant light in every direction. This was my service: To keep holding, holding, holding that vision so that it would come to pass, and so that others would know how to hold their dreams as well.

Thunder was, of course, the first to visit, as she had been in my center in Houston. It took about three weeks from the closing date to refinish the floors and paint the house; she arrived the very next weekend, traveling in a van with ten people. Her lecture was the first one sponsored by The Center. How fitting; how very perfect. Thunder had been my teacher, my model, the one who had shown me how to brave the dark recesses of my own mind and boldly break forth into my deepest, heart-held desire, the dream that was the unfolding of my purpose and the expression of my greatest sense of self. I sat next to her on the floor like a little girl after the lecture that night. As usual, her words had touched the hearts of everyone in the room in entirely personal and different ways. She spoke of how proud she was of me and of my work, and I felt nurtured and loved. I didn't want her to leave. But then, I knew I carried her always in my heart, in the way I now taught, and in the person I had become.

Within a short time, there were other practitioners sharing in the vision and working out of the new place, and two meditation groups meeting there as well. The vision in the pink light that I had received long ago, after my visit to Mother Mary, stayed clearly in my mind as I found the people whose dreams were a compliment to mine. Our creation was another level of reality, and it was being grounded here at last. People would walk into The Center, take a deep breath, and let out a long sigh. "What a beautiful house," they would say, not fully comprehending the love and light that was creating that sensation. The Center was already becoming a place where the heart could feel at home, the body could mend, the mind could find peace, and the spirit could soar.

Well, the story is not over, but then, neither is my life. An author has to choose an ending for each book, and I am near the end of this one—not the end of the story, but rather the end of the book, because that's the way life is.

As I complete what I wanted to share with you here, I would like to acknowledge that life is an ongoing process—our growth is never done. Writing this book has kept me constantly aware of the journey that we must travel in order to arrive at the expression of the dreams that we each hold deep within us. It has kept me ever cognizant of the hero that lives within me—that courageous part of self that will walk through my fears, allowing me to stumble, fall, pick myself up and walk forward, then stumble, fall, pick myself up again, and walk still further forward. I can look back now, and say the wasn't easy, but I'm happy with my New Place.

No doubt there are other New Places yet to come—other Ithakas—other dreams and visions. I can see more buildings, larger groups, even communities dedicated to a common purpose. I can see us all living life on Earth in that pink luminosity, fully owning our responsibilities, our selves, and our dreams. We are just at the beginning of an entirely new way of living together. But that creation is probably another whole book, and both you and I will be further along in our journeys and our dreams when it's ready to be revealed.

Until that time, I challenge you to walk your own journey into your magnificence. I challenge you to allow your own dreams to come to the surface—don't fight them but, rather, listen to your heart and your intuition. Keep walking towards those dreams, no matter how long it takes, no matter how many times you fall. And more than anything, look for the blessings in disguise, the silver lining in the clouds, the Bambi Lemonade in the lemons. For it is the very struggle that strengthens us, the willingness to walk through fears that creates the hero, and the ever questing towards the goal that makes dreams come true.

255

▲ ▲ ▲ ▲ ▲ ▲ ▲

1. DO IT! Start now by stepping into Box Number Two.

FOR MORE INFORMATION

Carolyn Ball is available for lectures and seminars on the shifting paradigms in creative thinking in our culture and on self-esteem. She also facilitates individual and group healing retreats in the Blue Ridge Mountains of North Carolina.

In addition, you may wish to order her audio cassette tapes: *Claiming Your Self*, a guided meditation for self-empowerment, and three audio tapes from lectures and radio interviews, *Healing Our Feelings, One Foot in the 4th Dimension*, and *Blessings in Disguise*. For each tape, please enclose $13.00 plus $2.00 for shipping and handling.

For more information on lectures and seminars, or to order cassette tapes, write Carolyn Ball, c/o Celestial Arts, P.O. Box 7123, Berkeley, CA 94707.

Please send me _____

_____

I am enclosing _____

Name _____

Address_____

_____ Zip _____

Phone_____